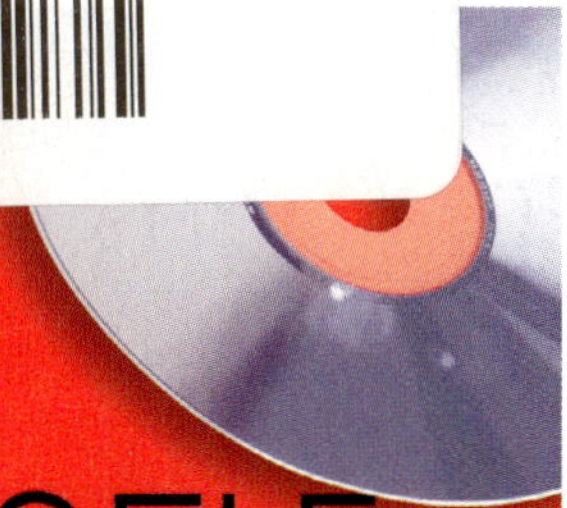

Includes a DVD featuring multiple ghost investigations and interviews with experts

PICTURE YOURSELF Capturing Ghosts on Film

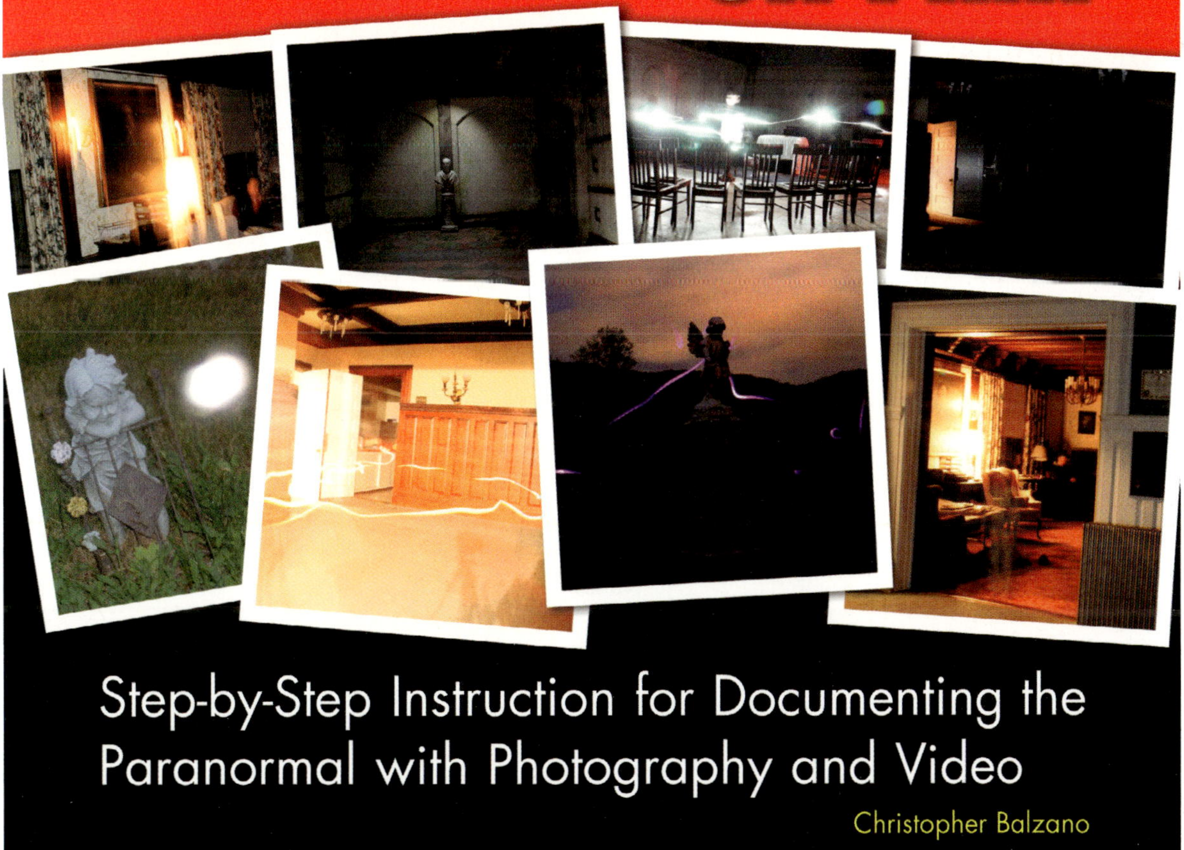

Step-by-Step Instruction for Documenting the Paranormal with Photography and Video

Christopher Balzano

COURSE TECHNOLOGY
CENGAGE Learning™

Picture Yourself Capturing Ghosts on Film: Step-by-Step Instruction for Documenting the Paranormal with Photography and Video

Christopher Balzano

Publisher and General Manager, Course Technology PTR:
Stacy L. Hiquet

Associate Director of Marketing:
Sarah Panella

Manager of Editorial Services:
Heather Talbot

Marketing Manager:
Jordan Casey

Acquisitions Editor:
Megan Belanger

Developmental/Technical Editor:
Jeff Belanger

Project Editor:
Jenny Davidson

PTR Editorial Services Coordinator:
Jen Blaney

Interior Layout:
Shawn Morningstar

Cover Designer:
Mike Tanamachi

DVD-ROM Producer:
Andrew Lake/Brandon Penticuff

Indexer:
Sharon Shock

Printed in the United States of America
1 2 3 4 5 6 7 11 10 09

Library of Congress Control Number: 2009933293

ISBN-13: 978-1-4354-5483-5

ISBN-10: 1-4354-5483-9

Course Technology, a part of Cengage Learning
20 Channel Center Street
Boston, MA 02210
USA

Cengage Learning is a leading provider of customized learning solutions with office locations around the globe, including Singapore, the United Kingdom, Australia, Mexico, Brazil, and Japan. Locate your local office at: **international.cengage.com/region**

Cengage Learning products are represented in Canada by Nelson Education, Ltd.

For your lifelong learning solutions, visit **courseptr.com**
Visit our corporate website at **cengage.com**

To my little girl Ella.

You may have been born at the same time,

but you will always mean more to me than my work.

Acknowledgments

THE BEST PART OF writing any "how-to" book is that you eventually learn that you don't know everything. There have been teachers for me throughout this book, and I owe them a thanks. I would especially like to thank Josh Mantello of the Berkshire Paranormal Group whose work and ideas inspired much of this book. I would also like to thank Gene Lafferty and Buckeye State Paranormal and Haunting Investigators for giving me a perspective on ghost photography I would never have seen.

I also extend my deepest gratitude to Andrew Lake of Greenville Paranormal for his great work on the DVD that comes with this book. Under great stress and time constraints you pulled through again. Thank you to the Fearing Tavern, the Lizzie Borden Bed and Breakfast, and the students of Notre Dame High School for their help on the DVD and the book.

Many investigators and paranormal photographers contributed their opinions and pictures to the book. I'd like to acknowledge Ron Kolek of the New England Ghost Project, Matt Moniz and Tim Weisberg of Spooky Southcoast, Sabina Besic, Jackie Masar, Allen Dunski of Wisconsin Paranormal Investigators, Pat Martin, Jessica Stone, Robyne Marie of the Lights Out Radio Show and Paranormal Investigating Group, Michael Markowicz, Clarissa Vazquez of Colorado Coalition of Paranormal Investigators, and Ericka and Rick Benson of Blue Spirits Paranormal Investigators, Spryng Benjamin, Jason Lorfice of the Paranormal Investigators of New England, Rob Conover of Conover Paranormal Investigators, Gary Manley of Night Fall Paranormal, Tom Elliott of Boston Paranormal Investigators, Luann Joly of Whaling City Ghosts, and Sheryl Vartanian. Special thanks to Jenna McFarland-Lord for helping to start it all and giving me a great picture of Elvis.

None of this would have been possible without the help of Megan Belanger and Jenny Davidson from Cengage Learning. They both were there to make suggestions and guide me through those dark days of June and July. Of course, my third editor and the little voice inside my head, Jeff Belanger, was vital in the development of the book and continues to provide me with support and ideas.

My thanks also go out to Mel and Louise Slater for opening up their house and their pool to my family so they could leave me alone in the house to write. I would also like to acknowledge the help and support of my family. Thank you to Devin and Ella for keeping me grounded and offering me the best distractions in the world.

Lastly, I would like to thank my wife, Jill, for her patience and help while writing this book. Her sacrifice and level-headedness pushed me on when I began to hit the wall.

About the Author

CHRISTOPHER BALZANO is the founder and director of Massachusetts Paranormal Crossroads, an online collection of legends and ghost stories from Massachusetts and the surrounding states. He has been investigating the paranormal for more than fifteen years and has been writing about those experiences for the past ten. He has been a contributor to Jeff Belanger's *Encyclopedia of Haunted Places* and *Weird Massachusetts* and was one of the writers behind *Weird Hauntings*. His writing has been featured in *Haunted Times* and *Mystery Magazine* and has been covered by the *Boston Globe*, the *Boston Herald*, the *Standard Times*, and *Worcester Magazine*.

Christopher is the author of several books about regional hauntings, including *Dark Woods: Cults, Crime, and Paranormal in the Freetown State Forest* and *Ghosts of the Bridgewater Triangle*, as well as the collection of true ghost stories, *Ghostly Adventures*, and the how-to paranormal book *Picture Yourself Ghost Hunting*. He has appeared on radio stations in Massachusetts and throughout the Internet, as well as being called upon by television shows to comment on ghosts and urban legends. He now runs the paranormal news from Ghostvillage, one of the oldest and largest websites dedicated to the paranormal.

Christopher is also the director of ParaRelations, a public relations company servicing people in the paranormal community.

Table of Contents

Picture Yourself Not Alone

I HAD MANAGED TO MAKE IT down the stairs without being heard, not an easy feat because I had to pass my parents' bedroom at the top, and they never shut their door. But I had gotten two books out of the library, one on weird and unusual stories and one on being a spy. I had already read both books cover to cover a month earlier, but I made a part-time job out of keeping both of them out of other people's hands. I made my way to the den where the television was and turned it on. It was about five in the morning, at least an hour and a half before people started to get up in my house back then. I was eight.

The show was just ending. It was a documentary on Bigfoot that ended with a showing of the famous Patterson film. The last shot was a close-up of the beast, and I specifically remember taking the covers I had draped over me and pushing them down to prove, at least there in the comfort of the den, that I was not afraid. The next show began with a crying couple talking about ghosts that were haunting their house. I already knew the word. Between my books and television shows like Scooby-Doo and Casper I was well acquainted with the occult, but this was different. They showed reenactments of a murder that had happened in the old Victorian house somewhere in New England and then a ghostly actor making his way down the hallway. The covers had just about made their way back to my eyes when they showed a real picture of the house.

It began with a shot of the entire house and a voice-over of the woman of the house talking about how she never felt alone. Then the narrator took over and he talked in an eerie voice about something I do not remember. The picture was starting to zoom in on a window on the second floor. Everything else faded away from that room except for the slow-moving camera. There in the window was the figure of a man. He had his hands pressed up against the window, a bit of blood dripping down from his forehead, and a silent scream.

By the time the rest of the family was up, a new show was on, but I was still staring at the television. Maybe I was thinking someone would come on and tell me it was not real, or the narrator would break into the next show to tell me the picture had also been a reenactment. Instead I was yelled at for having come downstairs in the middle of the night to watch television. The man in the window lingered the entire day, and even though I cannot remember the show anymore, I can still close my eyes and see the pain in his eyes.

I was hooked.

Years later, I would give in to that feel in my stomach and start talking to people about their paranormal experiences. I became a release for people and a way for them to let the world know what had happened to them. The more stories I heard, the more I would try to find anything I could to back up their stories. It began in the library, trying to find a newspaper article on the fire they claimed killed the little boy they saw, but eventually I went out into the field to try to get some proof that ghosts do share this world with us.

More than 25 years later I am still chasing the man in the window, and in that time I have realized that it is the photographic evidence that can mean the difference between believing and making the paranormal a punchline. There have been advances in the technology ghost hunters use, but some things remain the same. When you hit the field, the first thing you pack is a camera. Reading a meter can tell you if something might be present, and temperature dips or odd smells make the moment real for you, but the impact of those fade when the moment is done. You remember that it happened, but it starts to be like a dream you know you had but can't think of what it meant or recall if you have added details that weren't there.

There are very few people who do not have a camera or access to one. My son has his own digital with a cartoon character on it, and he is four. Of all the equipment you may eventually buy as you move through the paranormal landscape, it is the one tool you already have and already know how to work. Chances are you even have one on the cell phone you carry around with you. You have used a camera of one kind or another to record the moments of your life and lock them, as they were without editing, to open up when the time is all but forgotten and you want to think back on what was.

There are many things in the paranormal world I do not agree with, but two things still make my ears perk up and the hair on my arms raise: little children on EVPs and an unexplained ghost picture. There is a video out there shot by Matt Moniz of Spooky Southcoast at Waverly Hills. In it he is walking down the hall being filmed by a military grade nightglow camera. He is reenacting a moment from the television show *Ghost Hunters* and a dark figure looks out from behind a wall, sees them, and darts back behind the wall.

It is the kind of evidence that people see and assume was faked, but I know it is not. I see it, even now four years later, and I am instantly that little eight-year-old gripping the covers. I am filled with that odd feeling that is half fear and half exhilaration. Now it makes me grip my camera instead of my covers.

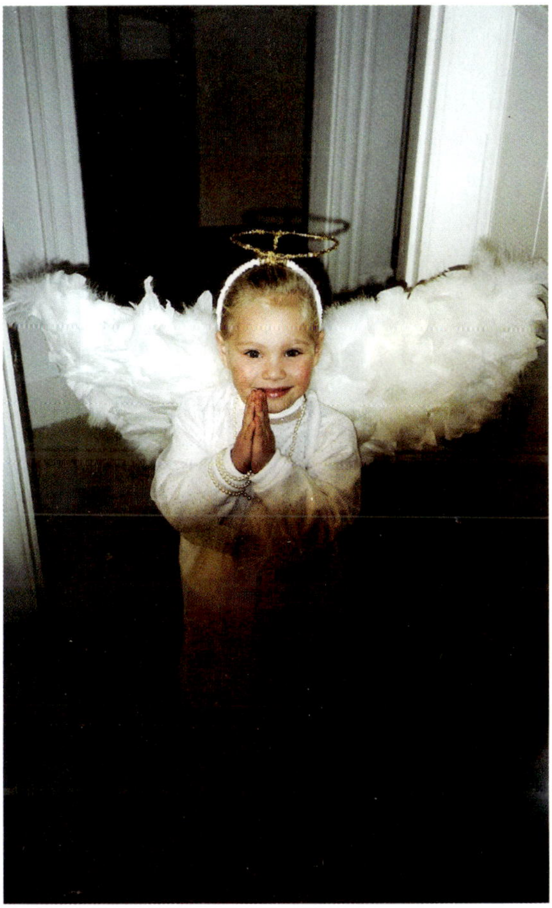

This is the feeling you are trying to capture, like pointing a camera and setting up a shot. Keep reading with one hand balancing the page open and the other flipping through the user manual of your new digital. Look around to make sure you are alone in the room, knowing you are probably not, and turn the page.

You are about to learn how to capture ghosts on film.

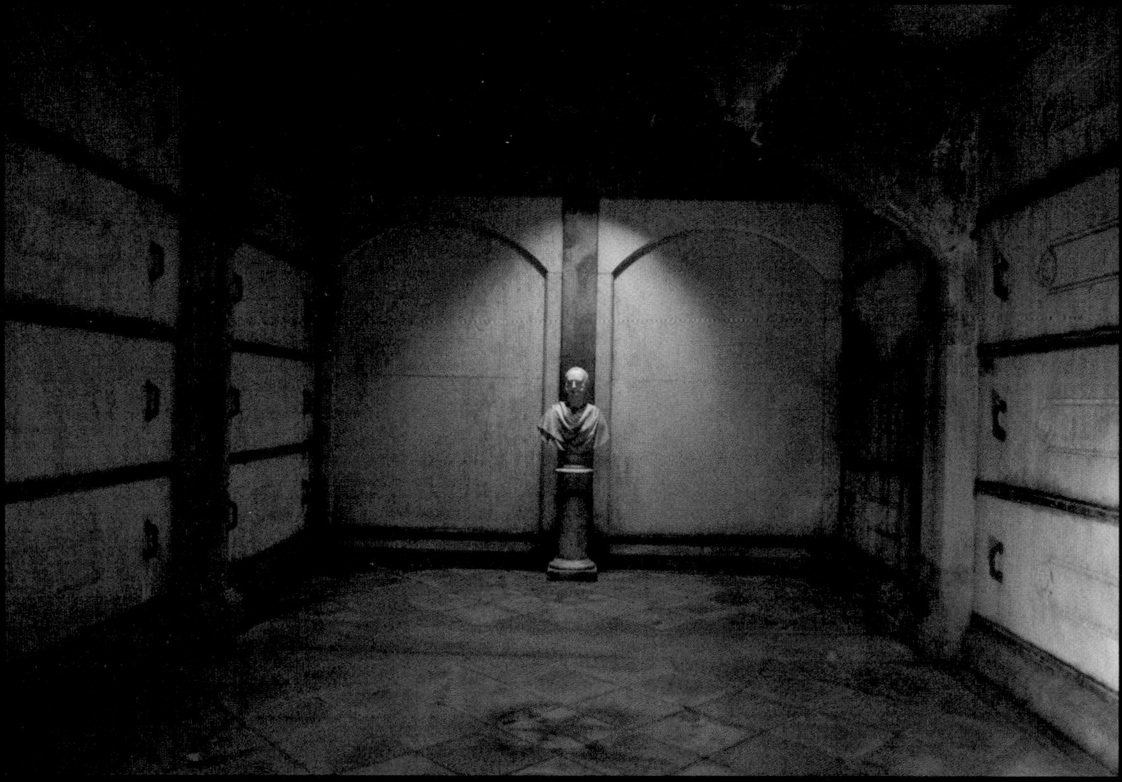

Picture courtesy of Leo Balzano.

1

The Proof Is in the Picture

MY FATHER HAD JUST FALLEN ON SOME ice and cut his hand open. I was in the hospital waiting room while he got stitches, and a little boy I hadn't noticed before asked me what I was reading. His skin was pasty and his eyes had black patches underneath. I showed him the cover and he frowned. "That's too adult for me," he said and stood up. He opened the door he was sitting near and walked out of the room. I was concerned because he looked to be about seven, much too young to be walking around by himself, but as I tried to open the door to call out to him, it was locked. I looked through the window, but the hall was empty.

I still wonder what I experienced that day, and rarely mention it when people ask me if I have ever seen a ghost. I have no proof, nothing to show people so they can trust the moment. If I had snapped a picture, I might be able to hold the moment, present it as being paranormal. I might have a picture of a little lost boy looking sad. Right now, I only have a story.

It's an odd phenomenon I began noticing with my students a few years ago, much stranger than any ghost story I could ever tell. To communicate with them while they were doing their homework, I established accounts on networking websites such as Facebook and MySpace and allowed them access to my pages. Often, while I worked past midnight, they would message me and ask a question they were too embarrassed to bring up in class.

Then I noticed it. While the details of their lives were often thin, and I was proud of this having taught them all about online predators, their sites consisted of page after page of pictures. There were pictures of them in groups striking the same pose no matter who was in it. There were pictures of them giving the peace sign in front of their bathroom mirror. There were pictures of them taking pictures.

There was something even odder about the pages, or more specifically, about the bulletins associated with them. They were constantly asking people to view their pictures and inviting them to comment on them. As a reward, they would then look at your pictures and comment on them. The importance of someone was no longer measured by how many viewers they had or friends they made; instead, their status was built on the number of people who took the time to write on one of their pictures.

I'm Here. I Really Am.

MY GRANDFATHER HAS PASSED away, but a picture of him makes him come alive again. I understand he is gone, but the image confirms he was once alive, and each new digital image my students send out confirms they do in fact exist. Pictures are more than a way for us to see where we have been and who we were at that time; they are evidence in the case that we are someone worth taking a picture of. If you don't believe I was in Paris, just look at the picture from when I was 20 and in front of the Eiffel Tower. I must be important or I would not be posing with such a famous monument.

Pictures are proof positive, and while we can debate what the picture might be of, the physical nature of it, even more than some of the other evidence paranormal investigators gather, they allow us to make the moment real. We see trees and know they are trees, and spot our Aunt Joanne and know she was posing by the trees. That puff of smoke next to her is what we investigators spend our time chasing, but that moment in time did exist, and for all we do not know about the picture, the fact it is there tells us something about the time it was taken.

The Best Evidence?

ONE OF THE MOST STRESSFUL days of my life was the day of my First Communion. I can't remember what triggered it, but I remember there were too many people at my house and everyone wanted something from someone. I didn't want to wear my clip-on tie and my sisters wanted to wear lighter dresses because spring was quickly becoming summer. My parents had yelled at us, and by the time the pictures started the three of us were in tears. All of us now look at those photos and remember that moment and the details surrounding them. The pictures act as the trigger to relive that moment, just like the one of my wife holding my newborn son sparks that moment.

Ghost Photography

The intentional or unintentional taking of a photograph or video that may contain a ghostly image or some other unexplained element.

That is the power of pictures, and the reason we take them. Our memories may be imperfect, but a picture proves something. It defies age, acting as a link between when something happens and when we reflect on it afterwards. That power is in your hands, and how you hit the field and capture ghosts may be the difference to the questions of life after death.

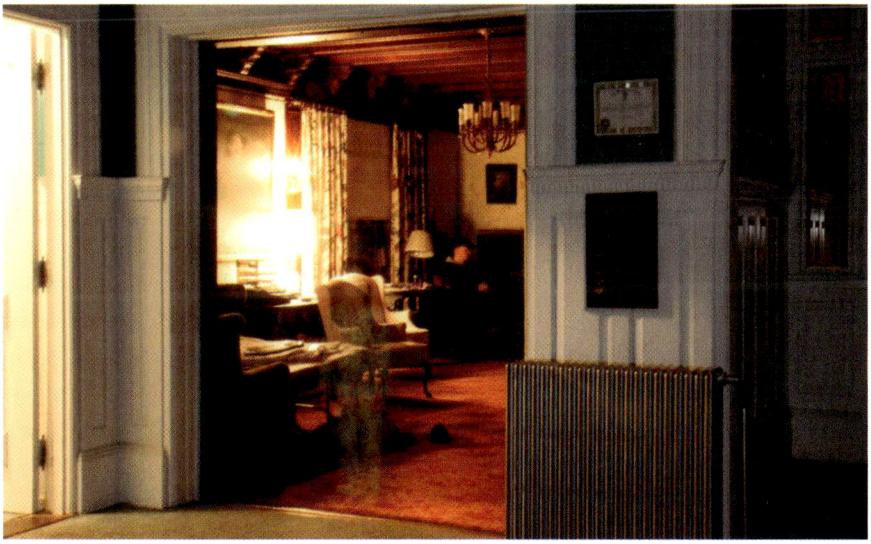

Figure 1.1
Too good to be true? This picture of a ghost child is fake.
Picture courtesy of Josh Mantello.

The Changing Winds

Every technology used to communicate, from the telephone and radio to video and webcams, experiences some level of paranormal activity. Many of these devices are somehow modified to look for ghosts, but more often than that there is just a natural relationship that develops between them. Shortly after the invention of the telephone, people began getting phone calls from loved ones who had just passed. Cameras moved to digital and suddenly there were more unexplained objects floating in the frame. I remember a story of a man who was working on a computer and the letters he was typing in a word processing document rearranged and began a message from his dead grandfather.

When people attack the paranormal as being something completely out of the realm of possibility, I always think about ghost attacks on technology. If they do not exist, how come they keep coming out clearer as we make the better mousetrap? Moving from old-fashioned telephone lines to fiber optics went hand-in-hand with more ghost calls. As digital replaced film, more orbs came about. As video cameras become smaller and expanded their spectrum of vision, we captured more. It has the feel of people lining up on the other side trying to make a person-to-person call and not having enough change for the phone booth. They master and manipulate the new methods almost as quickly as we can invent them, which makes the next few years an exciting time to live for a paranormal investigator.

Much of our modern methods of looking for ghosts revolve around the new technologies and the gap between their releases and our full understanding of them. Instrumental TransCommunication, or ITC, uses these new ways to see and hear to try to connect with the other side. It includes phone calls from the dead, Electronic Voice Phenomena or EVP, and taking pictures of ghosts.

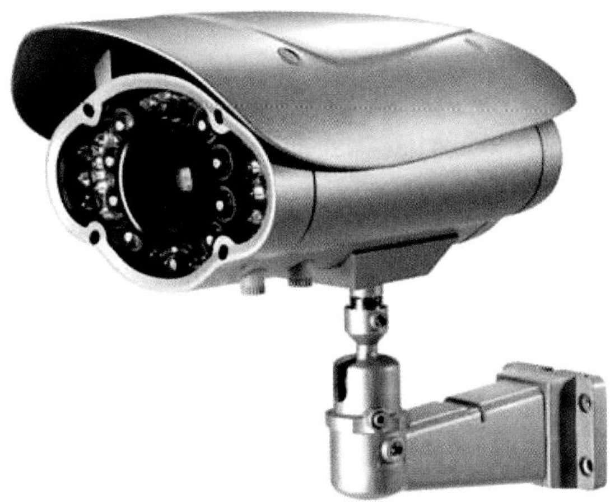

Figure 1.2
A 530TVL Super Hi Resolution.
Picture courtesy of Ghost Mart.

Communication is always moving forward, and despite the fact that you may already have an excellent camera or video camera, you need to stay in touch with whatever else might be out there. With so many paranormal ideas debated about, if you are going to invest in paranormal equipment, it might serve you well to spend more money on your camera and its accessories than some of the more borderline equipment. At the very least, you should be familiar with them so you know how the field is advancing. You can begin taking pictures of ghosts today with what you already own, but there are other ideas you will encounter as you progress.

Another changing aspect to keep track of is the way people take their pictures. In Chapter 10, we will talk about some of the newer ideas entering the paranormal field and experiments that are going on with cameras in the field. Try to connect with these ideas by constantly searching out people who have new ideas. Do not just let a new piece of equipment draw you in. Seek out paranormal ideas and rationale behind why one way to get a picture might be better than another. Despite the "equipment" based society paranormal investigating has become, the best tool is a sharp and critical mind.

The False Positive

One phrase you will hear once you enter the world of ghost photography, or really any aspect of paranormal research, is "false positive." The term comes from science, and there is a connotation to it that comes from being used that way, making it perfect for people who hold up their ghost hunting as science. The phrase means, in a nutshell, that you have received a positive result from your equipment, in this case a ghost in a picture, and even though it appears to be positive, it is in fact, not a picture of a ghost. In other words, there is nothing in the picture that is ghostly or unexplainable.

I hate the term. In reality, a false positive means that you have a result, believe it to be true or conclusive, and then upon further review, or in review by an independent source, the result is found to be untrue. There is a difference in the two, and if there is not, you have to change your perspective as an investigator. The false positive puts forth someone taking a picture who thinks the ghost is real and is not looking critically at what he is doing. If this is what happens when you are evaluating the evidence, you are going about it the wrong way. Instead, take each picture on its own merit and then try to come up with a natural explanation for what you think might be a ghost.

Why talk about this at the beginning of the book? There are two reasons to look at false positives. When you look at evidence, you must not assume you have taken a picture of a ghost, but do not assume everything is perfectly normal either. People often talk about being a skeptic when they investigate, but what they often mean is that they are debunkers or paranormal atheists. I do not share their opinion or approach. Instead of assuming things are not paranormal, begin from a place of open-mindedness and then take everything at face value.

The second reason comes from more of a community perspective. Ghost hunters strive to be taken seriously, and in doing this they adapt words and actions they believe promote that image. It makes sense given that investigating still lives on the fringe. The problem is it often gets in the way of getting things done, and there are some techniques and mindsets that get in the way in the field and do not coexist with scientific research. For example, a scientist does not set out to prove a medicine does not work. A hypothesis looks to be proven, not disproven.

As you gather evidence, think of making your methods beyond reproach. I will give you suggestions and methodology, so when investigating try to produce the perfect result. When evaluating, however, think of yourself as a seeker, a human alarm looking for anything unusual and then try to come up with what might be causing it. You should not be skeptical; you should use paranormal common sense, and by the end of this book you will have that sense.

That being said, people quoted in this book will use the term "false positive," so learn it.

Too Much Stone

For much of the book we will talk about the strength of pictures and video as evidence of what happened during the investigation, and for the most part that holds up. Not always, however, and it is important to keep that in the back of your mind as you look at the images you get. There is no substitute for experience, so where a picture might be a representation of a moment, it is by no means the only perspective on what happened. Time taints our point of view, and seeing a picture enough times, and putting weight in that picture, makes it more real than what happened. The farther you get from the moment the picture was taken, the more it takes a life of its own.

Think of a non-paranormal picture. We sent out my son's Christmas picture when he was three and got many compliments back. He was smiling and his cheeks were rosy and he was holding a candy cane in his hand. He was the perfect angel. In reality, he was in day three of a serious cold and had spent the whole day crying. He was stressed out about the hour it took for us to get the picture, and we had just ripped the candy cane off the tree, breaking three ornaments. Those sparkling eyes were the result of crying.

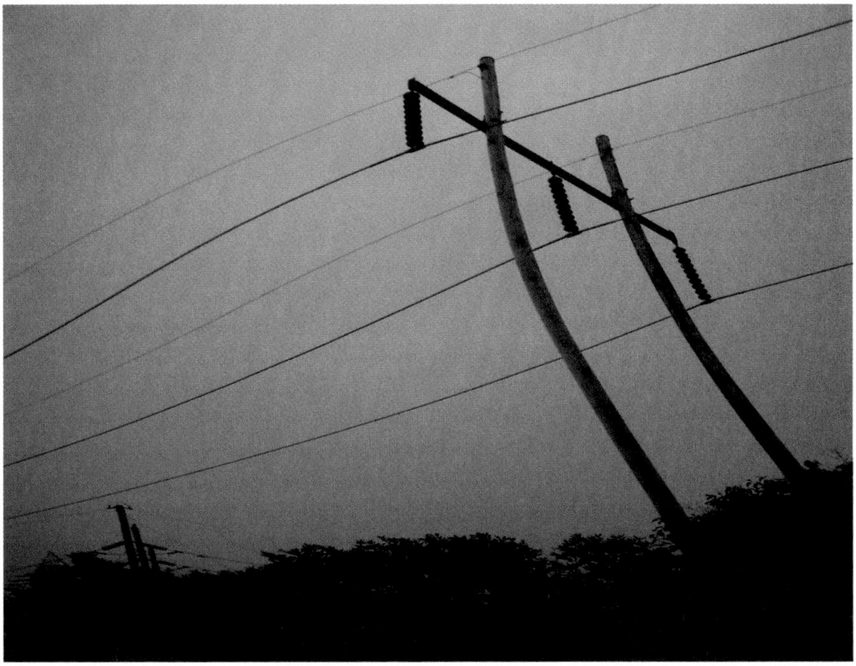

Figure 1.3
A picture in a haunted location known as the Bridgewater Triangle. Would the picture be considered paranormal, especially given the power lines, if it was not taken in a place where ghosts are seen?
Picture courtesy of Jason Lorfice.

Here's a clearer paranormal picture. I had taken a group through the Hockamock Swamp in the infamous Bridgewater Triangle in Massachusetts a few years ago. We had made it about 30 minutes in when the group began snapping pictures. As they reviewed the evidence as they went, they saw what they thought might be a supernatural being hiding behind a tree. I told them it was a trick of light because nothing could stand on the ground in the swamp. "What do you mean?" they asked looking at the picture. "It's solid ground." One of them proceeded to walk off the path we were on and sank knee deep in the swamp. It could have been something unexplainable, but they did not allow for the natural because of what they were seeing with their mechanical eyes. They trusted the picture more than their own eyes.

To counteract living through your pictures, especially if you do not review your evidence until several days after, keep a commentary on what you are doing. If you are taking video, make as many comments as you can on the conditions you are in. If you are making notes in a notebook, and you should be doing that for every investigation, write things down about the environment you are in and things that come up. If you think something might be true in the picture, ask someone you were with. I remember asking someone I was investigating with a week later if the house we were in was really cold. I was wearing a sweatshirt and there was some unexplained fog in the room. He told me no and he had thought it was weird I was so bundled up.

Food for Thought Moving Forward

WHILE THE PARANORMAL field presents many compelling arguments, and many that seem to be self-serving, as to why any evidence can be gathered, there is a fringe idea that is picking up steam among investigators. It began as primarily a concept with people using EVPs trying to get voices of the dead on tape, although it harkens back to century old work in other forms of spirit communication. A ghost will give you exactly what it wants to when it wants to. It is known as the Intention Argument.

The Intention Argument

People who subscribe to this belief argue any piece of equipment, and a human's senses are merely another piece of equipment, can capture evidence of the paranormal. The single biggest factor in coming home with anything is the intention of the investigator and the subject peeking in from the other side. This idea is not very well liked by the more scientific people looking for evidence, as it basically says there is no other way to gather pictures or readings than to be in touch with the ether of the supernatural. That cannot be explained or tested, and leaves many with a bad taste in their mouth.

A ghost may choose to show itself to an old Polaroid camera but not the most sophisticated infrared camera out there. It sounds like a crutch to people who are looking to not deal with the questions of "why" in the paranormal world, but some hold firm to it. Perhaps the most disheartening aspect of it is there is no clear-cut explanation of what the intention of the person gathering the evidence needs to be. It is merely said after the fact.

One of the ideas that counters this, or maybe reinforces it to some degree, is the amount of evidence that is gathered when people begin to get nasty to the spirits they are investigating. At times, it is more of a reflection of the frustration of the investigator, but there are times when pushing a ghost's buttons makes it come out. There are many investigators who rely heavily on this technique, and they get great evidence after doing it.

Use the idea or throw it away, but understand it is out there and some people swear by it. It makes for an interesting peek into the power of the paranormal but will frustrate those who rely on science to explain everything.

The Most Famous Barn in the World

In the book *White Noise* by Don Delillo, there is a moment when the characters discuss the most photographed barn in the world. It's a very nice barn and people began taking pictures of it because it was so darn nice. The more people took pictures of it, the more people wanted to take its picture, until the way the barn looked was no longer important. People picked up their cameras and travelled to it not because it was a nice structure worthy of a picture but because it was the most photographed barn in the world. Its infamy was of more value than its aesthetic value.

This happens in the paranormal world. Think of the urban legends involving haunted houses and then see how many of the families in your neighborhood live in a house that has to be haunted. We expect broken-down houses with an overgrown lawn and a cracked walkway to be haunted. It is the perfect set, but other buildings may be more haunted and overlooked. It is what I called in *Picture Yourself Ghost Hunting* the "supposed to be haunted" factor.

Figure 1.4
Mist or smoke in a graveyard has to be a ghost, right?

Do not just take pictures of places you think are haunted or that you have been told are haunted. Ghost photos can happen anywhere and at any time, and to not try to touch the paranormal anywhere it may be hiding means missing half of your evidence. You can snap a picture in a cemetery, but how about your local park? Can spirits not travel to a place in life that gave them joy? Are they not as likely to be trapped by their own personal demons or have their own desires? Why ghosts haunt us and what makes them remain when they should not be moving on is something wc have never fully been able to explain so do not assume only haunted places have ghosts. By the same logic, do not assume notorious haunted places like asylums or former funeral homes have activity just because they are supposed to.

Take a picture in your house. It may hit you too close, but take a few shots around where you live and ask something to make itself known and take some more. You can learn as much by taking a picture that has nothing in it as you can by trying to get a picture without exploring your camera. There is little to be lost by this experience, but if you take it a step further, you should also take pictures when it is not conducive to taking them. Snap a shot in the rain or after a snowstorm. Also, make sure to get pictures when there is no reported activity. If a family, for example, says they hear a voice at night, go during the day to try to get evidence.

Ghosts have no timeframe. There may be a link between the type of activity and the time and place it happens, but this has more to do with a residual haunting, or one that is more like a psychic burp you happen to witness. They are thought to be stored energy, which replay when the environment triggers it, but other than those moments, ghosts might not have rules for when they can make themselves known. Even if they do, you might just catch one breaking the rules or trying to hide while you take tea in the afternoon.

It Takes a Village

For many years, looking into ghosts was a subset of the science of parapsychology, and while there may have been people who searched for answers on their own, the majority of those asking the questions were scientists working in labs touching upon the subjects of ghosts and poltergeists as they explored the power of the mind and telekinesis. There are still scientists like that pushing the field forward, but there is now an "everyday person" angle to ghost hunting. No longer are the majority of paranormal ideas being put forth by trained professionals, but by people who have taken up investigating as a hobby.

Among all of the ideas that are floating out there about ghost investigators and ghost groups, the one that is the most obvious yet often ignored is the power of connection and community that motivates many people and acts as a confirmation to others. Those out there with cameras and recorders are trying to be part of something, and while the reason for turning to ghosts may be different for each of them, finding that someone who understands them across a crowded cemetery has an impact on how they approach looking for spirits and how the paranormal field is understood. Whether you are looking to just work with a group by tagging along or forming or joining a group, the social drives much of the modern paranormal world.

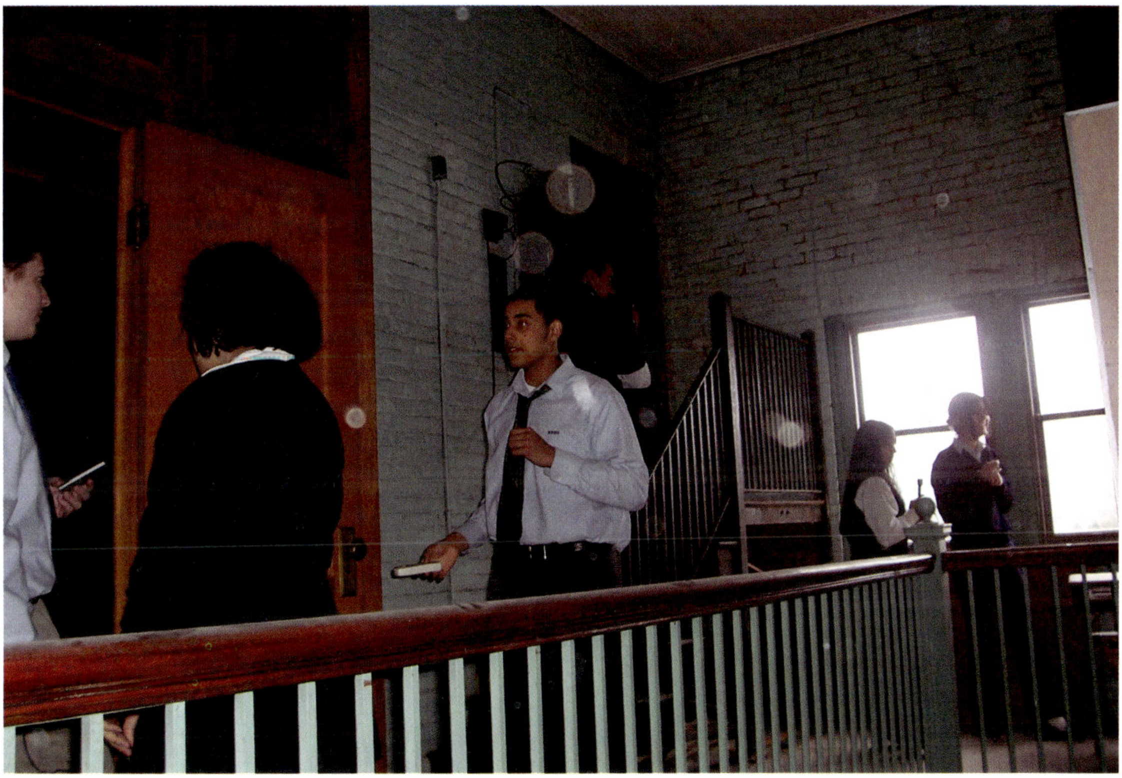

Figure 1.5
These students were bonded by the ghost in their school.

The Butler Report

A recent poll by the Baylor University Institute for Studies of Religion has resulted in two new reports by sociologists F. Carson Mencken and Christopher D. Bader that examine the connection between the religious atmosphere of American Christians and supernatural beliefs ranging from the existence of aliens to belief in ghosts. Their results show many Christian denominations may actually invite open-mindedness to the paranormal because of their deep supernatural traditions. They refer to it as the "small step hypothesis," where religious credence in one thing encourages followers to embrace other ideas that cannot be proven by science. According to Dr. Mencken, "It's a small step between believing in angels to believing in ghosts or devils. Those people are likely to have paranormal beliefs as well."

The results, however, also had something else to say about the state of paranormal ideas in the country. Bader and Mencken do not necessarily see the upward trend in the paranormal others do but rather a larger raw number of people in general. In other words, we have more people in the country today so any numbers have to be adjusted to account for this. There are not more television shows about paranormal topics out now if you look at the number of shows that are out there in general. The percentage is the same. Along the same lines, the number of ghost television shows and books being published does not mean attitudes have shifted. It seems every few months there are surveys that come out that speak of the high number of people who believe in ghosts, but the leap paranormal investigators make is assuming this means they are well supported by the general population.

"Those are deceptive statistics," says Bader. "Just because someone believes in ghosts does not mean people believe in ghost hunters. Those attitudes are not changing dramatically. It is still considered deviant behavior."

That means people with an interest in ghosts will seek out people with similar ideas to justify their own passion. It also influences how people go about trying to find spirits, which may affect how you conduct your quest for evidence.

The Quest for Evidence

When I was writing *Picture Yourself Ghost Hunting*, I sent out a questionnaire asking people their opinions on different paranormal topics. One of the questions I asked had to do with what kind of evidence it would take to convince a close-minded person that ghosts were real. Of the dozens of respondents to the question, every single one said it would take a personal experience to change such a dramatic belief system.

But, the quest continues, and that deviant behavior idea rears its ugly head. You need to ask yourself an important question. If I could offer you a sit down with a ghost who will tell you all you want to know about the afterlife and completely confirm for you that ghosts are real, or I can present you with a ghost photo that even the hardest critic would give a second look, which would you take? Most investigators would choose the second option because they could then try to convince others. Those same respondents of my questionnaire all responded proving that ghosts exist was why they investigated.

Some people in the paranormal field are selfish, but most are not motivated by self-interest. They just want to be the one to come up with the best piece of evidence and be part of a group because they need a sense of community to feel as if they are not deviant. Here, with these people, looking for something they are all looking for, they are a square peg among other square pegs. This is not to say the world is ready to strap them to the stake for believing in ghosts; it just feels like it sometimes.

That inferiority complex also influences how they look for ghosts. The rest of the world will only see these ghost hunts as being legitimate, and the ghost hunter as being sane, if they do not approach it from a metaphysical mindset but from a scientific angle. They must act like a scientist in the field, and they must shrug off non-scientific ideas, to appear as if they should be taken seriously. It impacts what they use to get evidence or even what they consider evidence. The paranormal scientists hate spirit communication boards or the idea of using a psychic, so those who are looking to fit in avoid those things so they do not cause waves.

More related to ghost photography, if you do not take a picture the right way, or even of the right subjects, your evidence will not be taken seriously. Do not even submit a picture of an orb. In later chapters, we will talk about the orb debate and being part of a community, but it is important to know when we start out that the social aspect of investigating, from how we take pictures to how we think about them once we get them, is related to a degree with the paranormal public.

The Ghost Eye

When I was in high school, my dream was to play in a band and become famous. I grew my hair long, picked up a bass, and listened to as much music as I could. Following the lead guitar is easy, but as a new bass player, I had trouble hearing my instrument in every song. Some were obvious, but other songs seemed not to have one at all. By the end of my freshman year of high school, it was hard not to hear the thumping baseline of a song that did not even have a thumping baseline. My ears had become accustomed to focusing on the pitch and tone of the instrument I was playing.

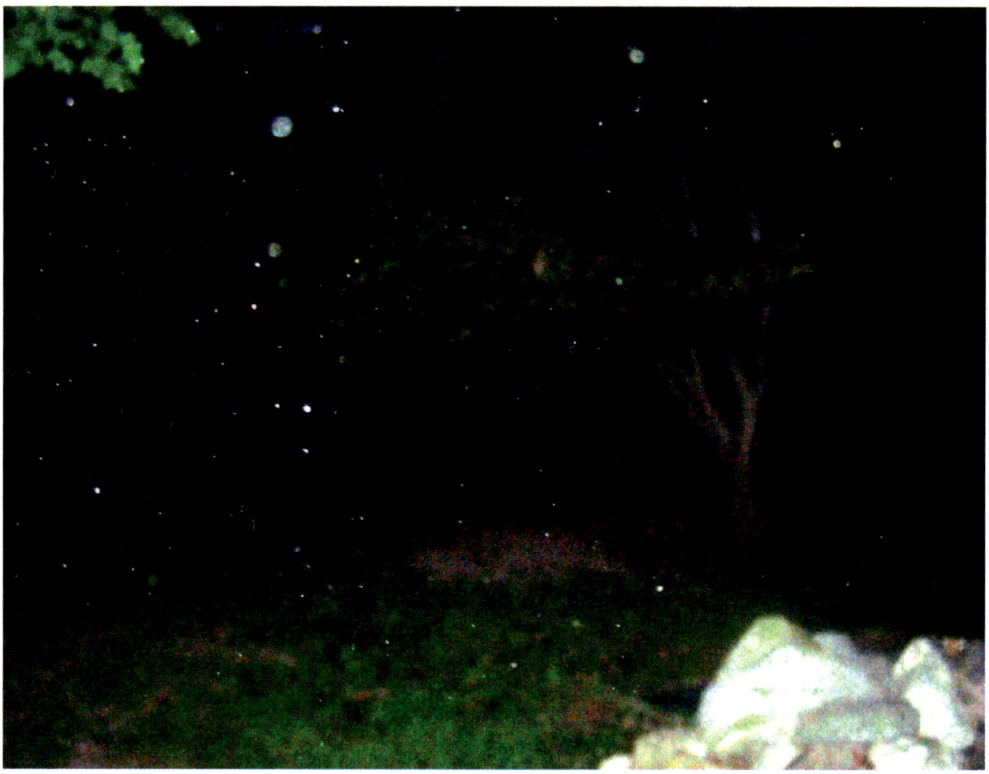

Figure 1.6

A paranormal investigator can tell which of these orbs may be ghosts or some other explanation.

Picture courtesy of Tom Elliot.

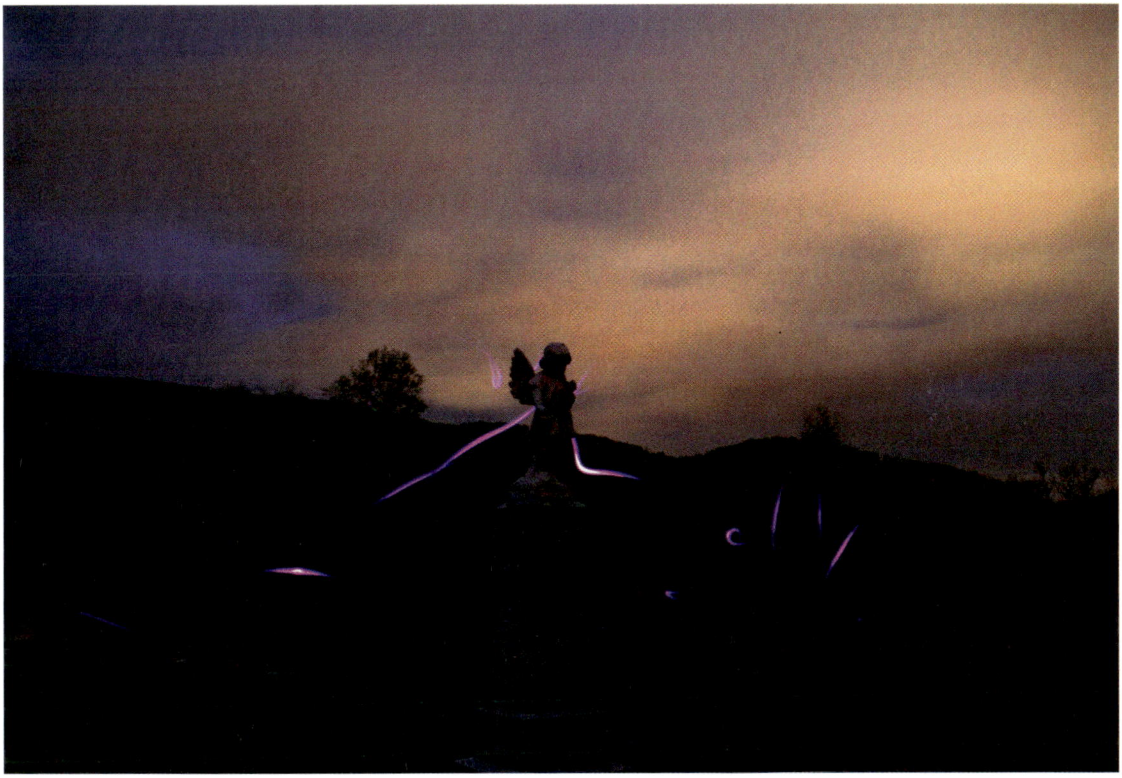

Figure 1.7
Is this picture of a real ghost? After you finish the book, check back and answer.
Picture courtesy of Josh Mantello.

The more time you spend working with people looking for ghosts, the more you will run into people with "ghost ears." You will notice at first that they have bloodshot eyes from staying up all night listening to seemingly endless recordings looking for electronic voice phenomena, or EVPs. They will sit you down and have you listen to an untouched clip and ask you to hear the voice talking. You will shake your head and apologize and they will show you the touched-up version and you will notice a voice from beyond. Either the sound is natural and their tinkering has modified a natural sound to the point it sounds like a voice, or there is something wrong with your hearing and you did not notice it when you first listened.

Both possibilities are present in the paranormal world. As you take more pictures, your skill in getting paranormal results will increase, but your eye for spotting a ghost in a picture will also get better. You will become a computer of sorts, your subconscious firing as it goes over all the pictures you have seen in the past and all of the reasoning you have heard. Your eyes will move over the shot the same way, looking in corners for things hiding and signs of dust to dispel the orb in the middle. You will develop ghost eyes and look at a picture differently from those around you. This may mean you will scan for ghosts automatically in the digital scrapbook your friend sends you with pictures of the new baby, but if you look and do not speak about it, you will be fine.

Of course, the other side may be in effect as well. You may become like an old boxer hit one too many times. You will give anything unusual in a picture a second look, imagining it may be paranormal. This is one of the arguments put forth by critics of the field. They say people see ghosts because they want to see them, and that desire makes mountains out of molehills and ghouls out of grass stains. Know this is coming, but do not try to stop it. It is better to look too much rather than too little if you remember all the rules we will talk about in the book.

How to Read This Book

I'm sure you did it in the store, but I'm also sure you will flip through this book several times looking at the pictures. It's natural, and I highly encourage it. Some of the pictures will seem like obvious fakes, and many are, and others will challenge you. You'll read the caption and ponder whether they are shots of real ghosts or not. Some may even look like ones you have already taken, and you'll compare. This book is odd in that it is the written word explaining a visual medium, so there are certain to be times when you just want to see more and take a few pictures after you flip. This book is designed to be a lesson, like being in my paranormal classroom for a while, so you'll need to experiment a bit before you are done. Please do.

I know the next step because it is almost as natural. You will turn to Chapters 6 and 7, skipping the chapters on why you can capture ghosts, the science of picture taking, and the section on how to pick a camera. I'd do the same thing. It is like being in science class and having a microscope placed in front of you. You do not want to learn why you can see, or even the importance of what you are looking at. You just want to bend over, close one eye, and see something small swimming in the droplet of water the teacher just placed on the slide. Who wants to be stuck on the science when there is a lab to look at?

I encourage this as well. I think the entire book is important, but I am also aware of how ghost hunting works. I spent years in the field getting evidence, good and bad, before I ever learned the reasoning behind some of the things I was doing. Those chapters on the "why" are important and they will make you a better investigator, so do not skip them completely. Do not avoid how to get a good camera, if no other reason than I touch upon the little things that will make a huge difference when you get out there. Chapter 2 is important because you are about to enter into a world that seems fresh and new but in reality is the latest signpost on a well-travelled road. Much can be learned by looking back.

As for how to actually treat this book, I will refer you to the words I have written in other books. Do not treat this book like a holy relic. It is not sacred and nothing about it is etched in stone, and even if it was, I would still want you to get it dirty. I have three copies of a book at home (and do not think I tell you this just because I want you to buy three copies of this book). One remains untouched, and the other I have notes in for when I teach it in class. The last copy is my working copy, the one I get as dirty as possible. This one is marked with my ideas while reading it, times when I think the author was asleep when he wrote a paragraph, and highlighted sections I like to read over and over again.

Please get this book dirty. Reread sections that make sense and ones you do not understand. Make a big black mark on page 78 because you think something I said is too silly or write in big letters, "That's obvious, Balzano." More importantly, I'd like to see actual dirt on it. I do not mention it in Chapter 6, but as you pack for an investigation, throw my book in your bag. This is more of a field manual than a coffee table book. The book should mark the trail you are on in the field, side by side with your actual investigation journal.

So continue on, chapter-by-chapter, or skipping in the way you see fit. Just remember, there is no test on this material other than the quality of your pictures, and no one is grading what you learn.

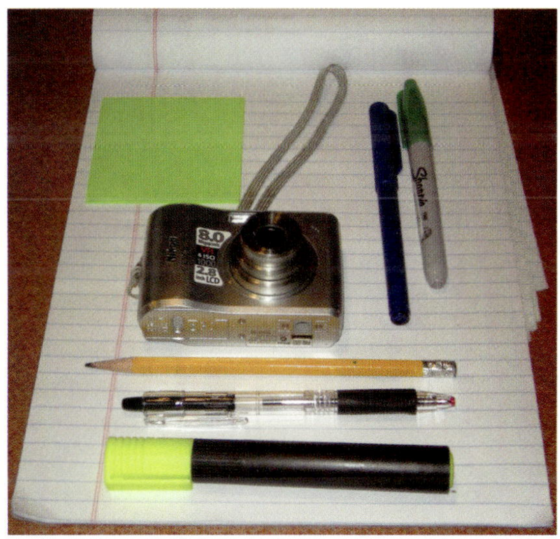

Figure 1.8
Some useful tools for reading this book.

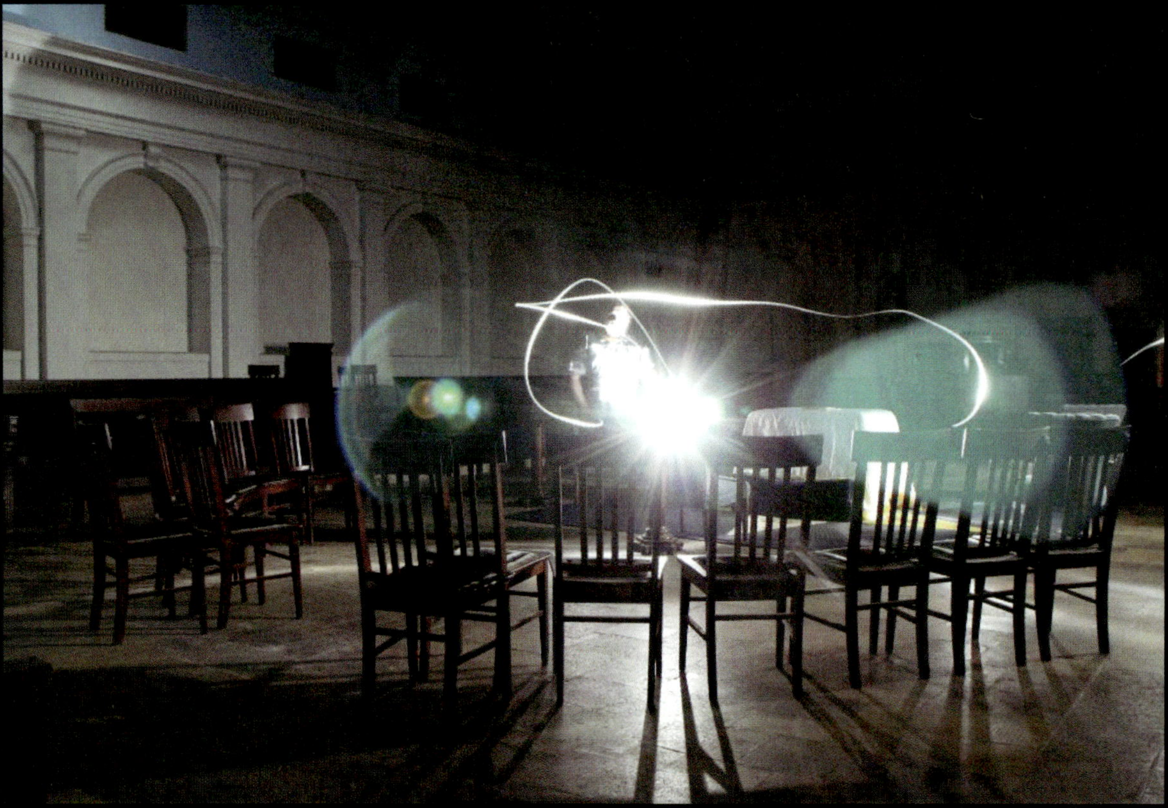

A faked ghost picture.
Picture courtesy of Josh Mantello.

2

Histories and Fakeries

PARANORMAL INVESTIGATING AND USING PICTURES as a way to understand the paranormal have been around as long as pictures themselves. Neither exists in a vacuum and it is important to know the context of the ghost photos we take today. The history of spirit photography is built around and riddled with cases of fraud and imposters looking to make money off of people's need to connect to the spirit world and get their hands around what happens after we die. The two need to be explored together because they have lived with each other for almost 200 years. Much of the history of ghost photography is the history of trying to make money from it.

Histories

IT STILL AMAZES ME HOW things fall on a timeline and give a complete picture of a generation or a moment in time. Art, politics, religion, and technology seem related somehow, as if a common identify unifies them and pins them to each other. No aspect of society can exist in a vacuum, but it is difficult to think of ideas and advances without knowing how they are connected to the other ones of their generation. A complete picture of any time means looking at everything that was the trend of the day.

Photography, while around theoretically for centuries, did not actually become a formalized process until the 19th century, making it a fairly new technology. Almost from the beginning, there were people who found things in their pictures they could not explain, and almost as soon, there were people who began to look to manipulate people with them. The rise of the photo follows the rise of Spiritualism and other spectral-based religions, and when science and energy turned their eyes to explaining God for us, cameras were there to try to establish truth.

The Old Days

The earliest photographs date back to the 1820s and were the result of intentional chemical reactions. Many of the early photos were more like engravings that were then dipped in ink and applied to paper. There was no negative so there was nothing to confirm images, so any questions had to be evaluated for their face value. Pictures were taken by people who became personalities, and each new celebrity touched both those looking to connect with the dead and those who made a living off of pointing out frauds. Whether they produced real pictures of ghosts remains open to argument, but their place in time reminds us that ghosts, or the interest in ghosts, try to sneak into every new technological advance.

William Mumler

William Mumler was a Boston engraver who started a studio to explore the world of photography. While reviewing pictures of himself, he discovered one with a misty woman next to him. She was not in the room when he had taken the picture. After examining it closer he found it to be the image of his dead cousin. Word got out and Mumler was called upon time and again to try to create pictures for other people with deceased loved ones in them. The stardom and the pressure to perform may have gotten to him for he soon found himself to be in high demand and made a full-time job of it.

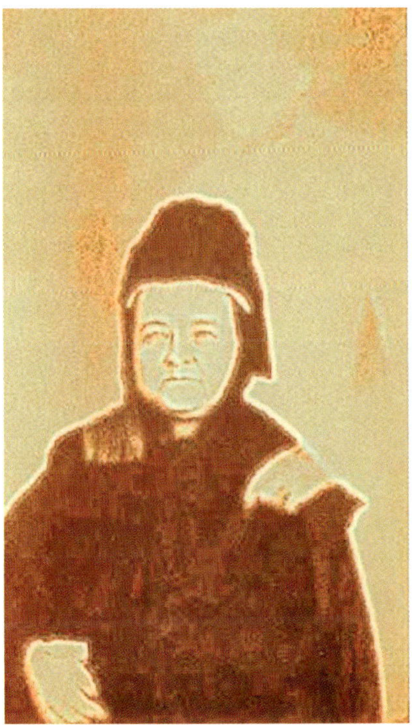

Figure 2.1
The now famous Mumler/Mary Todd Picture.

His rise coincided with the popularity of Spiritualism, a religion begun in New York a few years earlier that still exists today. The foundation of the religion is communication with the other side, including séances, table-tippings, and mediumship. This fit in perfectly with the idea of ghosts on film because they could be used to confirm something was there looking to talk. Spirit photography also found a willing audience with Spiritualists who were more willing to accept that ghosts were present in their everyday life. Mumler changed his focus and marketed his pictures to members of the religion. He had mixed results as he often could produce an image but the person meant nothing to the subject of the sitting. He had enough hits to keep his reputation going and to defend himself against people who accused him of being a fraud.

Mumler seemed too good to be true, and as he continued to make a name for himself, a new picture he made came out. Supposedly, a woman who did everything to conceal who she was, including wearing a veil over her face during most of her time with the photographer, got her picture taken. Later he discovered it was the former first lady Mary Todd and the ghost she was photographed with was her late husband. Several times, he was brought to court to answer questions of fraud, but Mumler was open about his process and allowed people to view his work from beginning to end. No one was ever able to prove he had forged any of his pictures, although some did step forward and say they had witnessed him doctoring pictures. He remains a controversial figure, the victim of rumor and having a skill that defied the belief system of many people of the day.

A Trick of Exposure

In their attempts to prove Mumler wrong, many experts came forth with how he could have faked them. That information, along with the money, may have inspired a generation of frauds who followed him. For the rest of the century, spirit photography's popularity grew, and for every genuine picture to come out of this era, there were dozens that were faked.

There were several ways to do it. One was to place the image on the plate of the picture that was to be taken. Others involved switching out plates or mixing and matching them during the processing step. With so much involved from the snap to the final result, people found it easy to place images over the shoulder of the subject. The most common fraud involved using the exposure of the plate to the trickster's advantage. Pictures were not instantaneous but rather the result of time spent in front of the lens.

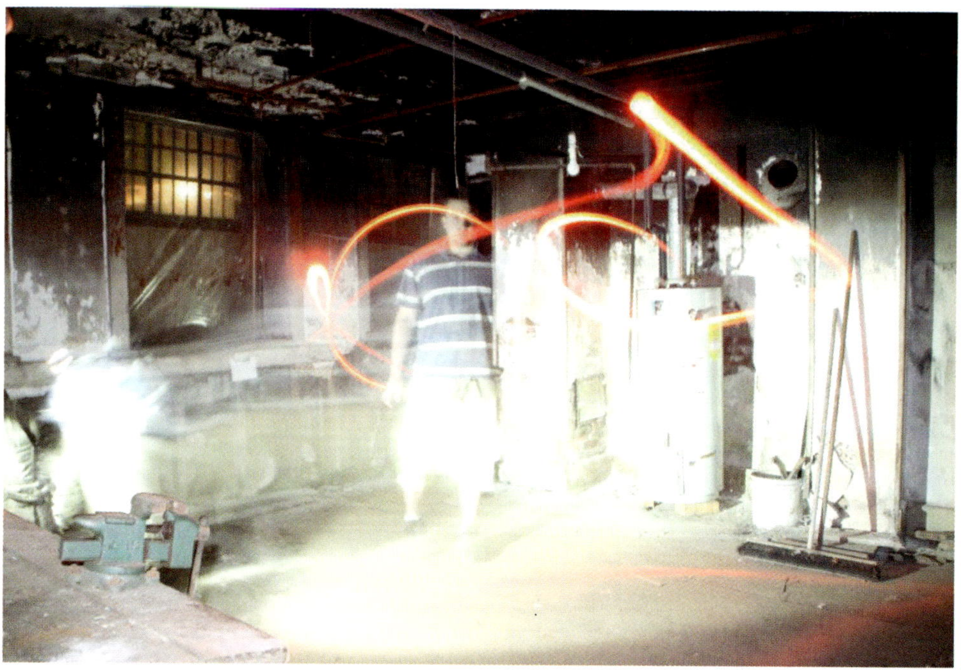

Figure 2.2
Josh Mantello uses a similar method as some of the frauds of old by leaving the shutter open and increasing the exposure time.

A subject would have to sit still for upwards of a minute, giving plenty of time for a person to sneak behind them, pose for a few seconds, and then slip out. Mumler might have made this using an easier method. After someone left him, he opened up the shutter again to get a picture of a second person. The results were the same, a faint figure alongside the original model. A good con man could learn about a person who was coming, set an assistant up with something he might relate to, and take a convincing if blurred picture of a spirit he might be able to relate to.

Unfortunately, the practice of robbing the public was so frequent, and the original material so self-contained, there is no way to separate what might have been a real ghost picture from a fake one, so most of the pictures of that time are dismissed. What is interesting to note, however, is the idea people had about ghosts in their pictures. They believed you had to set up for a spirit photo, almost as if your intention to get one was the main reason you received one. There were very few images of ghosts outside of these sitting sessions that remain today for us to question.

The more relevant issue for paranormal investigators of today is the attitude about what a ghost was. These frauds could have produced orbs, streaks, or mists easier and without getting caught, but the public did not seem to be satisfied with that. Even if they could not identify who was in the picture with them, they believed a compelling ghost to be nothing short of a person with a face and body parts. Their high standards may have led to ghost pictures being lost forever.

Snapshot

There is another connection between the spirit world and pictures during this time. Many people believed a good death was the only way to move on to heaven. One had to be surrounded by loved ones to pass peacefully or their spirit might not find rest and become a ghost. Soldiers far from home in the Civil War would carry as many pictures of their family members and houses back home as they could. If a soldier was wounded and near death, the people around him, sometimes his enemy, would search for these pictures and surround the body, creating the impression he was in the presence of people who loved him, so he would not come back as a spirit.

20th Century Images

This continued for nearly 40 years. People came forward in the early 20th Century with similar claims and similar results. In 1911, James Coates published the book *Photographing the Invisible* in which he laid out experiments and results. People like Harry Price and Harry Houdini worked to discredit frauds and the early parapsychology groups worked to get results in the labs. Then something changed in the photography world.

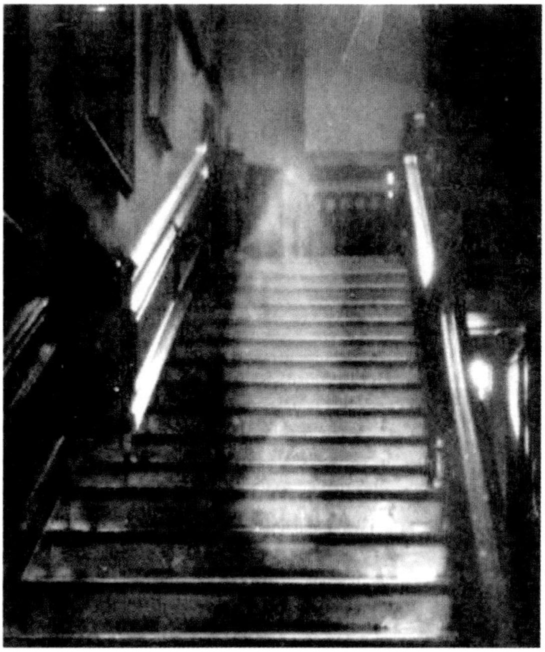

Figure 2.3
The famous Brown Lady who has made an appearance on book covers and the paranormal media across the globe.

Film was developed. This not only made the process of capturing a picture quicker but also made carrying a camera around and snapping a picture easier for the everyday person. This could be called the "time of the famous photo" as some of the most popular pictures came out of this new time. Type "spirit photo" into a search engine and the same pictures will come up time and time again. The Brown Lady of Raynham Hall, perhaps the most famous picture of a ghost and the cover of several paranormal books, comes from this time, along with a hooded figure on the steps of the altar at England's Newby Church and the famous woman sitting at a cemetery.

It should be noted that ghosts were not the only subjects of these pictures. There were also pictures of faeries and monsters, as well as a cryptids like Bigfoot and Loch Ness type creatures. The whole supernatural world seemed to explode on film.

A Changing View

On July 8, 1947, a UFO was reported in Roswell, New Mexico. There had always been unexplained lights in the sky, but the incident sparked a shifting of public focus. People became more concerned with aliens from another planet than people from beyond the grave. More and more images of lights in the sky were being distributed, and the idea was somewhat more plausible to people. Ghosts were still in the realm of religion and spirituality, while an alien may be science, or at least science fiction.

The result was not a dying off of the ghost photo but a changing opinion of what a picture of a ghost may be. No longer did people just look for a full-bodied apparition to say a ghost had been present. Taking a page from the ufologists, people began noticing the lights in their own house or the streak across a graveyard.

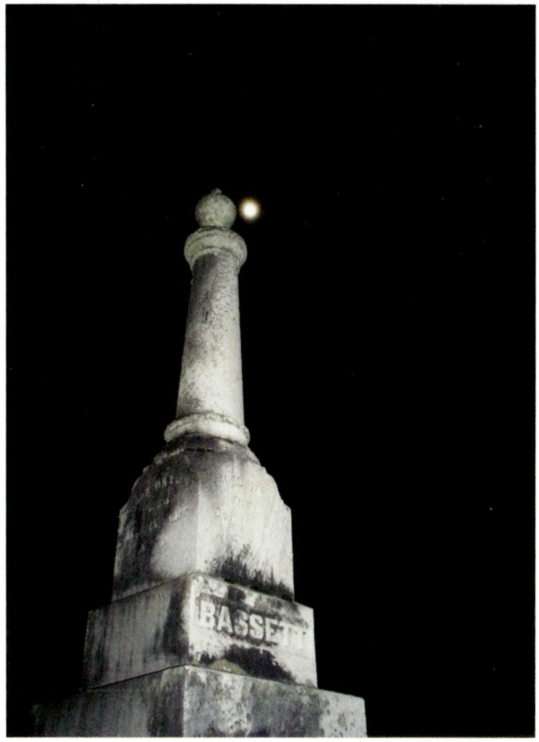

Figure 2.4
Lights in the sky at a cemetery. Ghost, UFO, or something natural, like the moon?

> **Snapshot**
>
> **The time between the 1940s and 1980s marked another type of spirit photography. Psychics and people who experimented with the telekinetic power of the mind began to take their own kind of pictures. They would place the camera to their head, often a camera that offered an instant picture, think about someone who had passed, and snap a shot. The result was often a blurry image of something slightly resembling a person. They may also think of an object or a place they had been to. This type of experimentation continues today with mixed results.**

Paranormal investigators were pleased to get an unexplained shadow because it pointed to something they did not see with their own eyes and therefore something potentially ghostly. Anything that was not deemed natural was fair game.

Some can argue this merely coincided with a different technology that could produce these unexplained elements in a picture, but the attitude shift was noticeable. Now a ghost was not just a ghost but how a ghost may exist in an environment. The move was away from the spirit and towards energy that could be captured on film. Ghosts became science.

Television Changes Everything

GHOSTS HAVE MADE waves in all aspects of the media, mainly because it touches upon questions that are crucial to whom we are as people and because they remain unanswered. Folklore and oral traditions often had a paranormal element to them, and when languages became solidified and stories began to be written, ghosts and monsters found their way onto the page. Radio and movies captured the imagination of those interested in the paranormal and supernatural with shows like *The Haunting Hour*. One of the most popular early television shows was *The Twilight Zone*, and as television grew, you could always count on ghosts to be a popular theme. From the *Ghost and Mrs. Muir* to *Buffy the Vampire Slayer*, people saw the narrative power of specters, and there were always shows that documented the real side of paranormal investigators, from *Sightings* and *In Search Of* to *The Scariest Places on Earth* and *Fear*.

In October of 2004, the television show *Ghost Hunters* premiered on the SciFi Network. It was a sign of the times, taking the popularity of paranormal shows, and mixing the human side of reality shows by following a team dealing with looking for ghosts while trying to get along with each other. The show was a hit and brought looking for the paranormal into people's living rooms every week. The focus was not on the haunting like the previous shows. The hunters were the stars of the show.

Ghost Hunters did raise the profile of paranormal investigators, but the more lasting and impressionable effect of the show is that it solidified to many how to look for ghosts. People had always investigated, and there were people out there who put forth some best practices in the field, but for the first time people were able to make the link between what a group did and the results they got, and many who watched considered everything TAPS did to be representative of what investigating was. The result was a generation of ghost hunters who reflected the practices of the group, molding how they went about getting visual evidence and what that evidence meant.

Soon other shows sprang up to try to capture the public's imagination like *Ghost Hunters*. Each had its own angle on looking for ghosts and each became more specialized to try to distinguish itself from other shows. Followers of one show adopted those methods and beliefs. Today you can chose from any number of angles into looking for the paranormal, and each show will offer some opinion on capturing ghosts on film. The shows become investigations themselves because they seek to document what people are doing to try to find spirits. They are not harmful, but the fraud that has hurt the paranormal field in the past can resurface from time-to-time as television shows become highly edited paranormal events and mundane moments become supernatural to break up the hour of seeing people walking around looking for something and finding nothing.

Fakeries

EVER SINCE THOSE OLD Spiritualist images were proven to be fake, people have tried to fool the world into thinking they had captured evidence of some kind. Whether their motives are for profit or fame they have caused undue pause in the public in believing in any picture that comes out. We develop a thick skin to lies when we are lied to time and time again, and a legitimate investigator will always be thought to have produced fake evidence when he comes forward. Ghost hunters are guilty until proven innocent, and with each new manufactured picture that comes out, the odds of convincing people inside and removed from the paranormal community gets harder.

I am still surprised when I find a fellow investigator who comes across an old picture that has been proven fake and believes it to be of ghosts. Great fakes become like little urban legends, the back-story known by heart, and the evidence good enough to make someone want to believe. We have gotten better at noticing when something is fake, but we have also gotten better at making pictures that show nothing more than ingenuity to deceive.

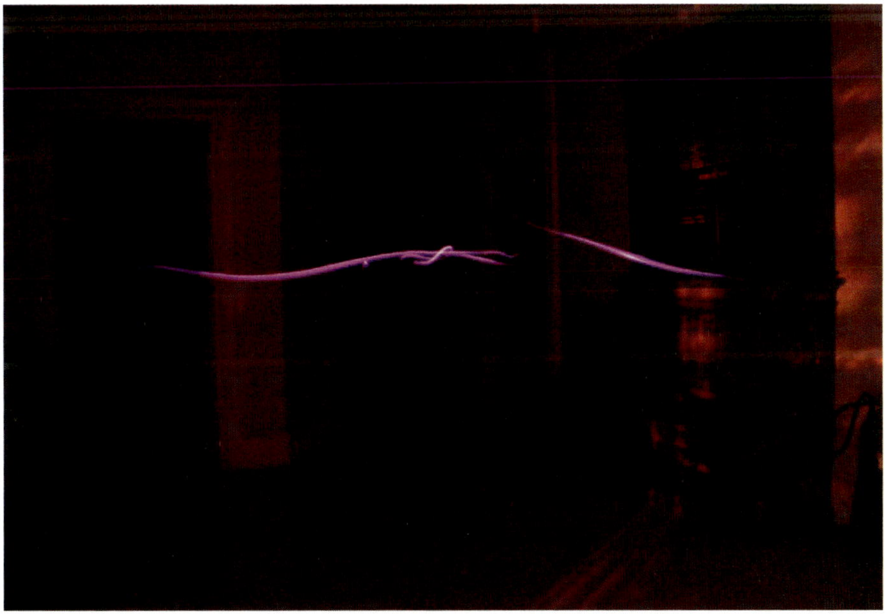

Figure 2.5
Josh Mantello makes another ghostly picture using shutter speed and a light.

It's a Simple Mistake

The majority of bad evidence out there comes from investigators, not snake oil salesmen. They believe what they have gotten is the real deal and pass it along to others. Two things help to mold respectability among peers in the paranormal world: evidence and the quality of that evidence. A good investigator realizes not all of his evidence is worth revealing to the world and holds some back. If someone has a strong name and has given good evidence before, we assume all of their pictures are real. We are more willing to accept their bad pictures. In a rush to get the word out, people allow things to fall through the cracks.

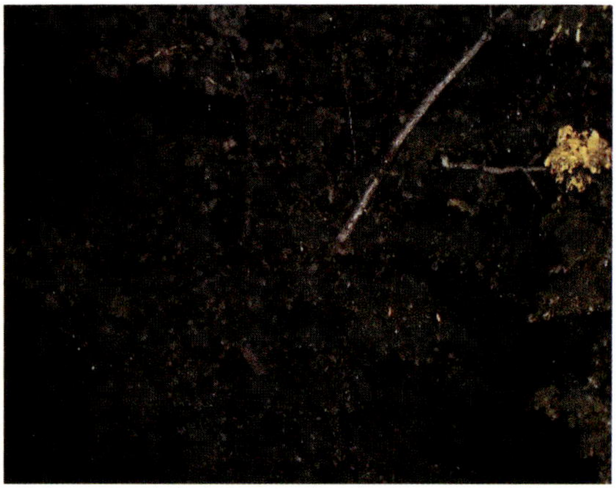

Figure 2.6
I was sent this picture from an investigator. Not only do I not think this is a ghost, I'm not sure what I am supposed to be looking at.

This becomes an even larger problem with newer investigators. You can make your bones on a good picture, and to some quantity means experience. This is the gold with which investigators buy and sell. To build the foundation, individuals and groups throw everything they get up there hoping some of it sticks to the wall. When other investigators do not know the difference, a bad picture becomes an example for others to follow.

Most of the pictures out there that can be dismissed are of orbs, which we will discuss in much detail in Chapter 9. Other pictures have to deal with double exposures, reflections, and improper storage. In Chapter 8 when we talk about evaluating the evidence, we will get into what to look for, but for now think of this as a warning. Step carefully when you look at other people's pictures, and maybe be a bit slow to think you have captured a ghost on film.

Teaching Through Deception

Many investigators create bad evidence intentionally to prove a point. Getting paranormal evidence involves understanding the elements that can make dust or bugs take on supernatural importance, and becoming a good spirit photographer means seeing these things in every picture you look at. Paranormal investigators who consider themselves teachers produce these fake images to show people what a dust orb looks like or how an overexposure looks so they know them and avoid them. On the DVD, you will see an example of this when researcher and author Jeff Belanger creates pictures of dust, and people across the country are doing the same thing. Sometimes these pictures are taken out of context and passed as evidence, but for the most part, they are a teaching tool as useful as the camera itself.

Figure 2.7
Fraud picture made by blowing smoke at a cemetery.

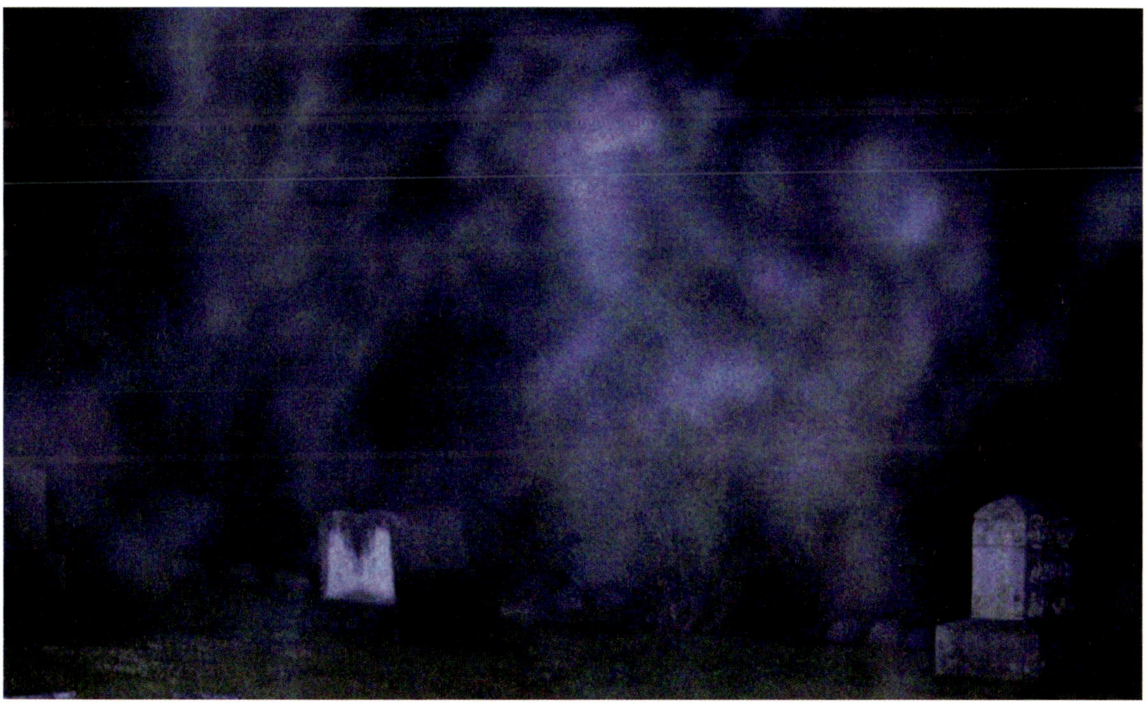

Figure 2.8
The picture is made even creepier with some editing.

Snapshot

Create your own fake pictures. It's fine to see the ones other people have posted, but each camera is a bit different. Note how your camera makes them, and the conditions surrounding the fakes, and store them. When you evaluate the images from your ghost hunt, compare them to see if they can be eliminated as evidence.

Intentional Deception

Paranormal investigators can be like rock stars today. With the popularity of paranormal television shows and the proliferation of ghost radio and Internet radio shows, someone with evidence and a story to tell can hit the circuit and make some money. A hobby can become a career, and with enough exposure, one might be able to turn that around and get a book deal and speak at conferences at hundreds of dollars a pop. With even good investigators feeling pressure to have the best evidence to get their name out there, the temptation to create something hot and fresh can become overwhelming. Imagine the person next to you being asked to be on a television show for a paycheck and a chance for another payday. What would you do?

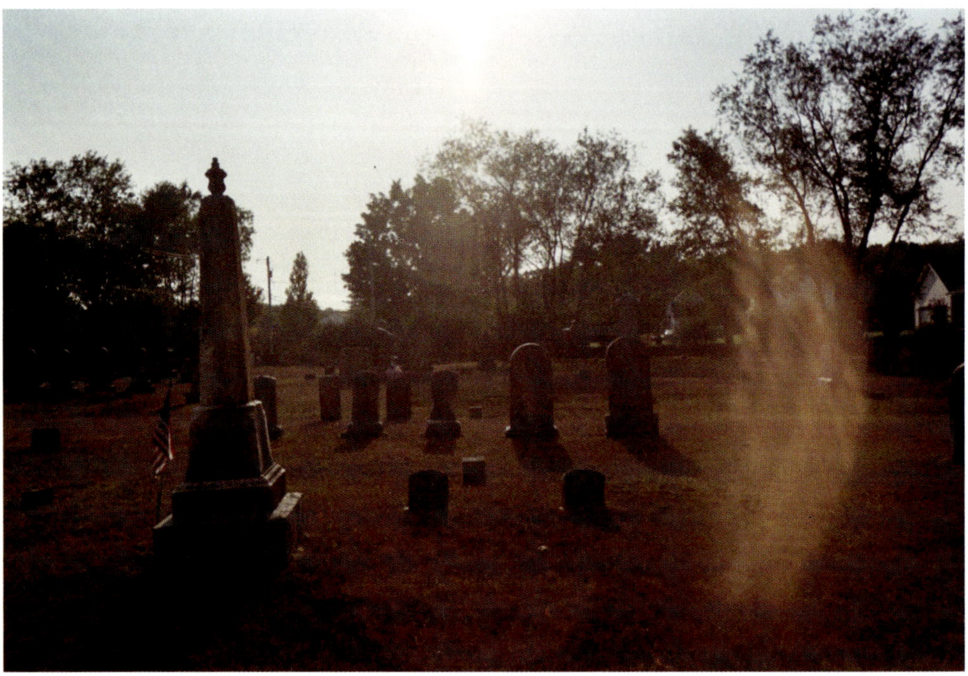

Figure 2.9
I did this fakery with a mirror bouncing the light up to the lens.

Getting the Dirty Job Done

As a teacher, I feel obligated to give you a homework assignment, so let's get it out of the way early on. Create your own fake ghost picture and send it to some investigators to see their response. The fortunate angle is that we have become so cynical we do not allow pictures of ghosts to penetrate our walls. The unfortunate part is that today such a convincing picture can be created that someone who wants to believe will. Here are some of the classic approaches people can take:

- **Innocent birth:** An investigator comes across pictures all the time they should disregard as being created by something natural or a mistake. They identify it, but it also has a certain appeal. They keep the picture and polish the edges to make the picture more acceptable. This is often accompanied by the statement, "I'm not saying it is a real picture, but decide for yourself."
- **A staged event:** There are moments during an investigation where the opportunity comes up to fake evidence. Someone looking to fool others might whisper into a tape recorder using a different voice or throw something across the room and respond to it. I have had the fortune to investigate with someone who enjoys using a laser pointer to drive other investigators crazy. There are dozens of ways to fake a picture, my favorite being the open shutter method, which is a recreation of the old spirit photos. You set up for a picture in a room and set the shutter speed to a slow setting. Then you allow someone to walk through. Another involved flashing lights through when taking a picture.
- **The Blair Witch Syndrome:** When the *Blair Witch Project* came out people were mesmerized by the way it was shot and promoted. A website was established to tell the fake back-story and convince people it was real. The real beauty lies in the shot selection. You have something happen off camera and then a reaction shot by the three students. The same thing can happen in the paranormal world. Investigators set up a scenario, turn on the Nightvision to make it even more cloudy, and walk through a ghost hunt. At some point one of them says, "Did you see that?" or "What was that?" and everyone else reacts. They then spend the next few minutes talking about what happened, and by the time they move on, the viewer forgets he did not see it himself.
- **It's all in the editing:** There has been a rebirth of editing fakes recently, although some might say it never went away. In this form of fakery, the deceiver just takes an image and edits it to look the way he wants. Think of computer software that allows you to cut the head off a picture of yourself and paste it on some famous body. Same idea, but you add a ghost in the corner of the room or a shadow walking through towards the window. These are perhaps the hardest to identify, and these are the main reasons why it is hard to get any picture taken seriously.

Some Classic Angles on Fakes

Like I said before, some altered or fraudulent pictures are like urban legends. They take on a personality or a motif and can be seen time and time again by investigators from all walks of life.

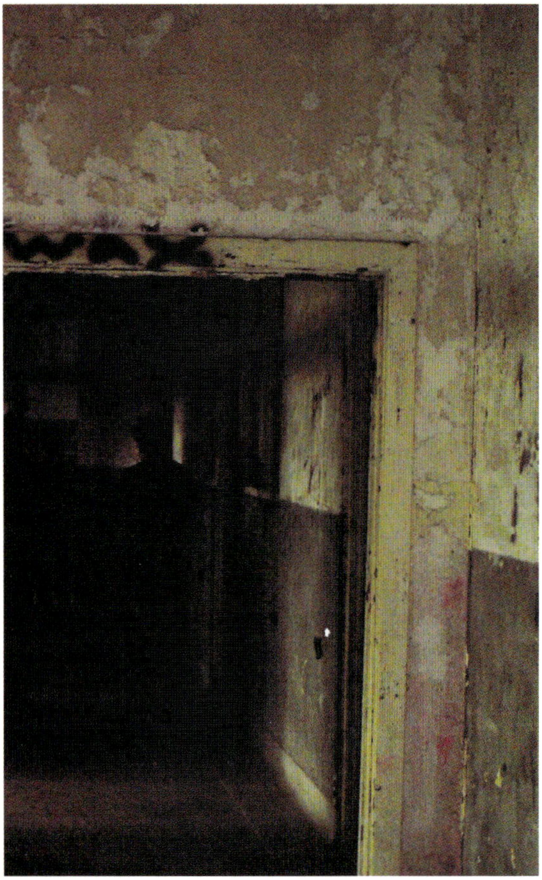

Figure 2.10
This dark and lonely figure is actually a member of a tour group. I cropped him and made the scene darker.

They survive like this because it makes for the best story and at times it's done with an effort to draw in those outside of the paranormal community. Other people who look into supernatural events run into pictures of Bigfoot and the Loch Ness Monster or UFOs, and that evidence is faked with the same frequency. Here are some of the most popular ghost motifs, many of which may be real paranormal occurrences but have to be questioned based on how often they are captured:

- **Pictures of children**
- **Pictures of people, usually women or children, in cemeteries taken during the day**
- **Orbs flying around through Nightvision caught by video tape**
- **Demons in smoke, although some of these are a trick of the eye**
- **Angels near car crashes**
- **Orbs on people who are said to have passed shortly after**
- **Shadows in the corner of the room**
- **Mists captured in cemeteries**

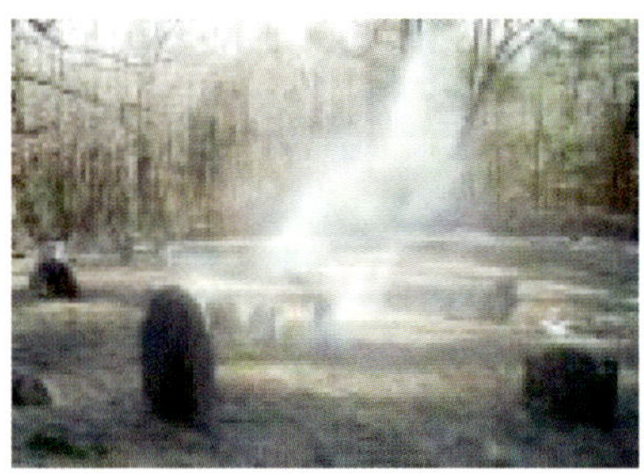

Figure 2.11
Another fake cemetery mist.

Snapshot

In 2008 and 2009, the following locations had cameras running when a ghost made an appearance:

- **A hospital**
- **A fitness center**
- **A funeral home**
- **Larry King Live**
- **The set of a reality show**
- **A school**
- **Seven parking garages or parking lots**

These stories come over the newswire and are picked up by the normal newscasts. They make for a perfect story because they are quick, are never followed up on, and promote the place that found them. They appeal to people's belief in the paranormal and drift away, keeping the paranormal in people's mind without taking it too seriously.

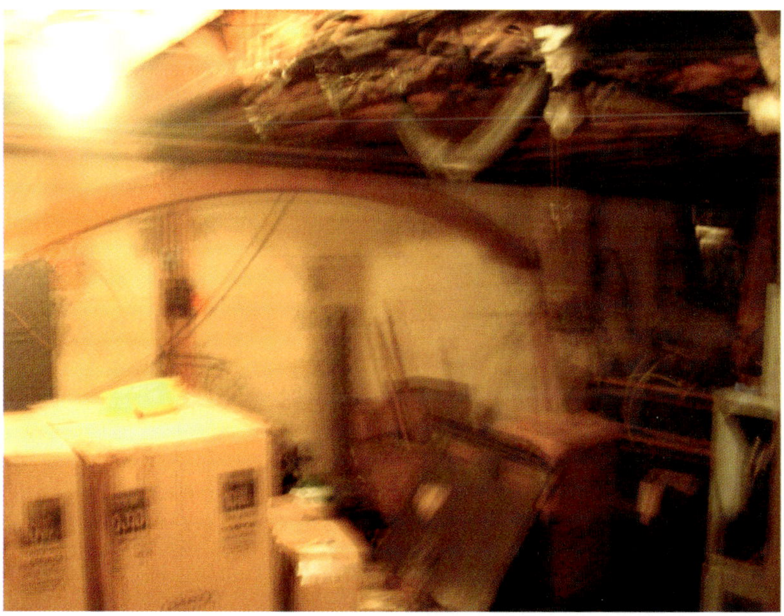

Figure 2.12

A picture caused by shooting at a light with Nightvision on.
The right story and this is something paranormal.

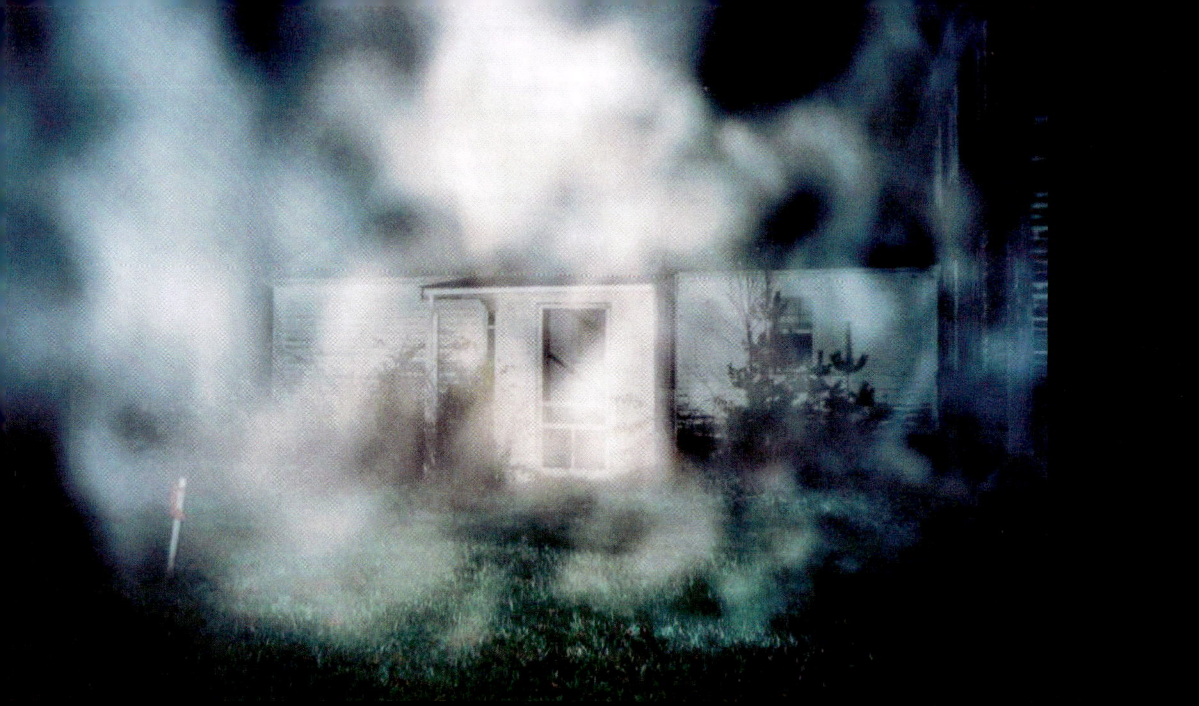

Picture courtesy of Sheryl Vartanian

3

The Why and the What

I WAS INVITED TO SIT IN ON a meeting of a local paranormal group in Florida and decided to just sit back and see how they approached the evidence review. They were reviewing some pictures they had taken during an investigation and began to argue about some of the things they had captured. I remember one picture of a shadowy figure, which looked as if it were trying to hide behind some stairs. One investigator claimed it was a demon because of the dark nature of the figure, while another stated it was a dimensional creature that could not be photographed in light because of the dimensional shifts. Another said it was a shadow person and that they really could not define what it was because there was so much conflicting information about them. The conversation quickly degraded into a full-blown argument until I stood up and raised my hand.

"I think I see something paranormal in the picture," I said.

"What do you mean?" one of the arguers said. "Of course it is something paranormal."

"I know. I just thought we should admire that for a while before we moved on."

There is a tendency to over-classify and over-categorize the paranormal, which can be both frustrating and exciting. Ghost hunting brings together people of conflicting ideas and approaches, so the meaning of evidence brings out the angle with which someone is looking through the camera. This should be true. I am constantly asked if I think differing ideas and disputes hurt the paranormal field, and recently I changed my opinion. Arguing and bickering is absolutely necessary, when directed on the evidence and not the investigator, because it opens up ideas that may be missed. The problem is, we need a baseline from which people can start, some basic understanding of how to get ghost photos, and some working vocabulary to begin the discussion.

The Why

GHOST INVESTIGATORS are split over why cameras can pick up ghosts, and many put forth an aspect of the science behind ghosts they buy into when explaining how they come to be on film. No investigator has ever given me an answer that satisfies me completely, although aspects of some explanations make sense in at least a limited way. At some point, the science will always fail the scientific paranormal investigator, so I prefer to think of it in terms of common sense; and in this case, it is an idea we have touched upon and will continue to explore as we move forward. Your camera is an extension of your eyes, only better.

The "why" of the capture is important because getting familiar with the best way to capture spirits will increase the quantity and quality of your pictures, but it is also important to understand that getting evidence does not prove that the science is not flawed. For example, one of the ideas behind ghost pictures is that ghosts register on a frequency lower than what the human eye can register and a digital camera, which can pick up those lower frequencies, can capture them. Now, it may be true that digital picks up ghosts better, but getting the image does not mean ghosts vibrate on a different frequency.

Just Because It Is There

When I was in high school, the mother of my best friend passed away. It was a hard hit to us all, but within a year, her husband had found a friend of a friend of a family member to find comfort in and they eventually married. While moving some of the pictures of his first wife, he came across a picture from a Christmas party. He and his first wife are smiling and holding up their champagne, and in the background, his second wife is smiling and pointing at the camera. There was nothing suspicious about it; they all just happened to be in the same place at the same time, even though they did not know each other. Getting a picture of a ghost works the same way sometimes.

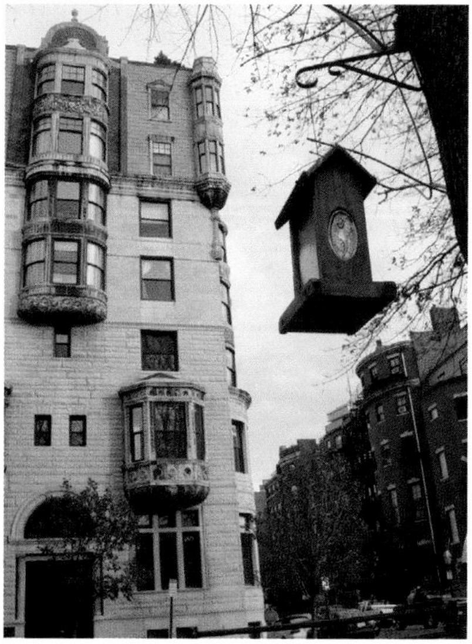

Figure 3.1
This random shot of the Charlesgate Hotel in Boston yielded a ghost picture.

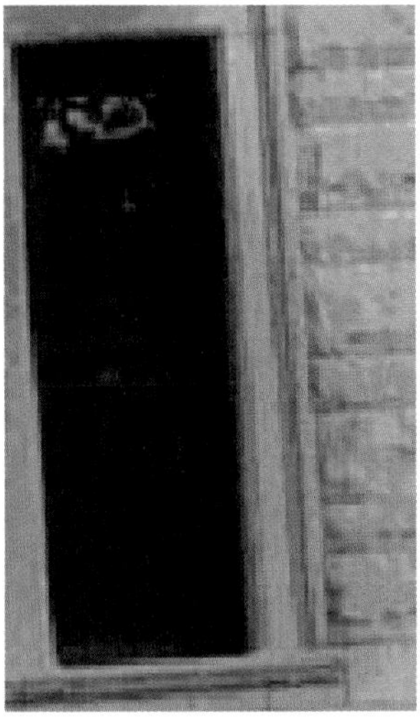

Figure 3.2
A close-up of the figure in the window.

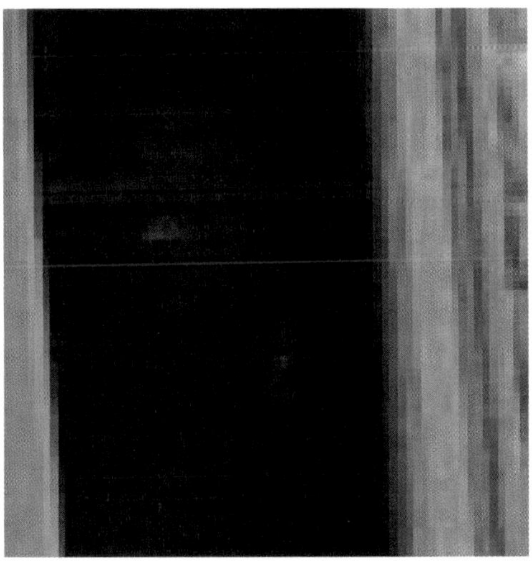

Figure 3.3
And even closer.

There are a certain number of ghost pictures that are just the result of being in the right place at the right time. These specters may even have had the possibility to be seen by the human eye; it is just that no one was looking. A friend of mine from junior high believed she lived in a haunted house and would see an old man looking out the window. The same ghost was seen by other people, especially those who had no idea of what was going on in the house. Several of the pictures they took in front of the house had the shadow of a man in the room he was thought to live in. He was always there; they just happened to get him in a picture of something else.

Ranges

I spent more time working with EVP in my early years of investigating. Before I ever tried to record any of these voices, I would turn an old radio to low-ranged AM stations and try to pick up voices during an investigation. I also carried a sound meter used by bands to test their levels before a live show. I had no real reason for using them other than they both concerned themselves with picking up lower ranges of sound. I was never able to record evidence, but I sure was able to confirm the presence of something based on them.

Light works in a similar way and may make more sense than the wave ideas of sound because they are both part of the electromagnetic spectrum, which also includes microwaves and x-rays. On one end of this spectrum is an AM radio wave, which may be as long as one mile, and the other is gamma rays, which are only microscopic in length. Between those two is everything we hear and see, and much of what we don't see. The visible spectrum is only a tiny fraction of that and the more we investigate that spectrum the more we realize the lack of power of our eyes. We are at a loss to even see the waves our remote controls give out. We turn the channel and never see the wave of light that makes the commercial go away. We know and trust it is there, and the channels change, but we never see the light that does it. We go outside and get a tan, seeing the rays of the sun and feeling the heat, but never actually seeing the ultraviolet light browning our skin.

Snapshot

You can test your digital camera's sensitivity to infrared by aiming a remote at your camera and holding down a button while clicking a picture. If that little light bulb comes out green in the picture, the camera is sensitive to infrared and can see more than the eye.

Our eyes are actually quite limited in the range of light that they can see and are prone to failure in certain conditions that happen naturally. Take away the light we need to process anything and it gets even worse. One truth that can be said about cameras, especially digital cameras, is that they can pick up a range of light well beyond that of the human eye. A camera gathers evidence simply because it captures more of that range. It can not only process the gaps between what our eyes see, but also extends the ends into the other ranges of that electromagnetic spectrum that are next to what we know as visible light. Infrared is one extreme and ultraviolet is the other, and digital cameras specialize in having at least a small toe into those ranges.

One reason for this might be the nature of ghosts. If we can assume, which we obviously can argue with, that ghosts exist the majority of time in the realm of energy and not mass, we would not be able to see energy the same way we see mass. We cannot see electricity without something to convert it to a viable form or microwaves even though we know they are cooking our food. A camera might be able to get a little further into those energy spectrums and see what we cannot.

Speed

If our eyes worked the same way as a camera, or at least could process information as quickly as a camera, movies would be horrible. We would see 32 frames per second, and they would exist as a series of thousands of still pictures. Instead, our mind is fooled because of the lag time and we see it as animation. There is a series of promotional pictures of Zelda Rubinstein from 1982 taken in quick successions for the movie *Poltergeist*. Out of all of the pictures that were taken, only one shows her surrounded by a field of smoke, which some claim to be the ghost of relative who died at the moment the pictures were being taken. Held up as one by one, there is no paranormal evidence, but because of the spray method, something is caught in the net.

A camera can capture a moment in time in a fraction of a second. If we could access our own mind and slow it down, maybe even freeze it for a few frames, we might see ghosts all around us that can be seen for only a portion of a moment. A camera does that, so every once in a while the appearance of a ghost coincides with the speed with which the camera takes a picture. That crossroads is where paranormal evidence exists. Some investigators take this idea to the extreme and set their cameras to take multiple pictures with one click. While this may result in thousands of pictures to look at later, it may produce evidence that has some level of context to it.

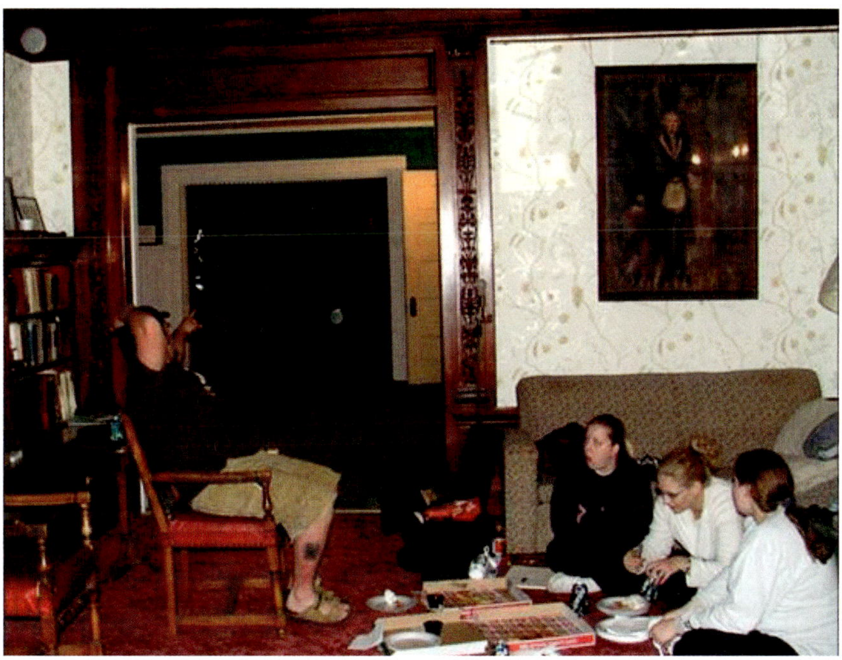

Figure 3.4

In this picture some people were sitting around and talking in a haunted location. They heard something and the investigator pointed to where the noise was coming from. His human eye did not see the orb, but the camera picked it up.

Picture courtesy of Josh Mantello.

The What: The Major Suspects

THERE ARE FEW TIMES when getting paranormal evidence means seeing a picture of a full-bodied ghost in the middle of the frame smiling and holding a sign telling you its name and date of birth so you can confirm it. In fact, the bulk of ghost hunting gold in the evaluation process has nothing to do with what the majority of the people in this world think of as a ghost. As we discussed in Chapter 2, the more like a human the image seems, the more likely someone faked it. Those instances are just too few and far between, and we are not even sure that they can be captured on film like that. We see them with our own eyes, but even when a picture can be snapped, the film usually ends up getting something different. Think of the movie *Poltergeist*. One of my favorite moments is when the movie camera captures the people walking down the stairs. With the human eye, all the people in the room witnessed were orbs, but when the film is played back, the full image of a person is seen. Real paranormal investigating works the opposite way.

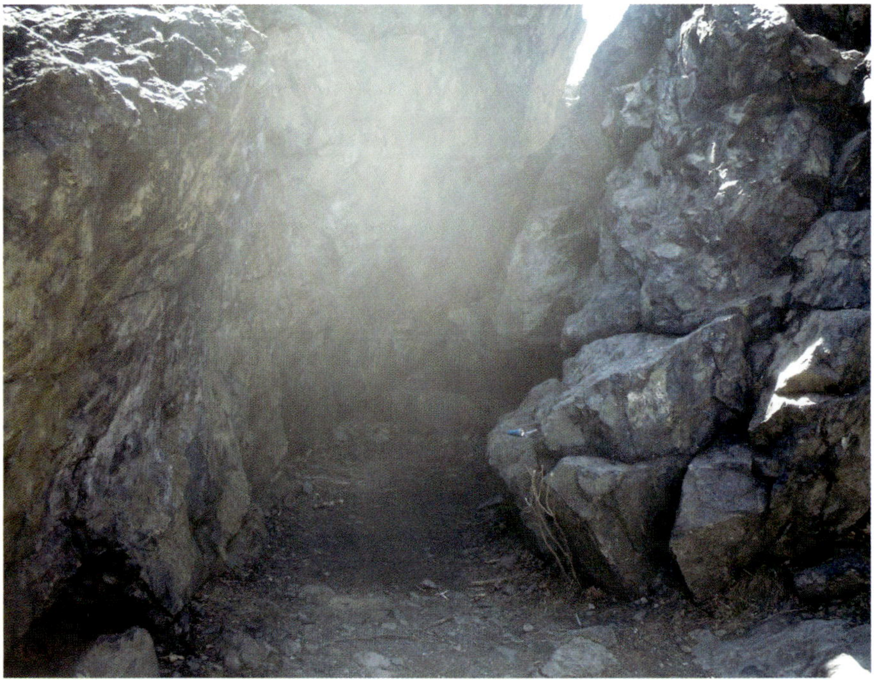

Figure 3.5
Hard to nail down...is this the sun, paranormal smoke, or a light shadow?

It then becomes more important to be familiar with the other types of evidence that are out there. Most beginners have seen pictures of orbs before, but how about a vortex? Each has its own features, but each also has its own natural explanation that needs to be taken into consideration and a possible paranormal importance to those who see it when you share your evidence, as we will go over in Chapter 12. Think of paranormal investigating like real investigating. You may even know what kind of evidence to look for before you are in the field because certain images are associated with different types of hauntings. So like a good investigator, let's look at the suspects.

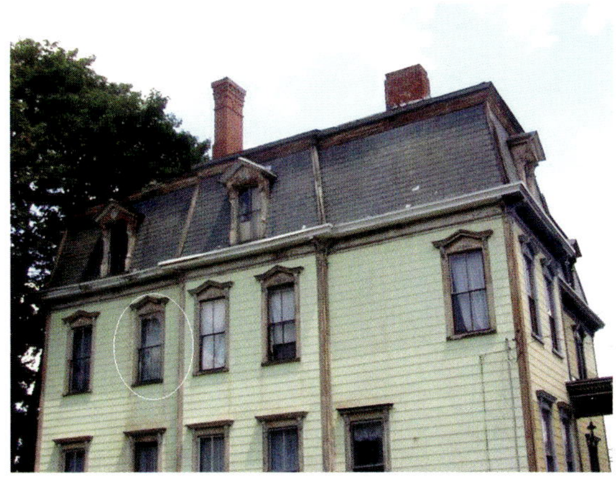

Figure 3.6
The Victorian in Massachusetts.
Picture courtesy of Tom Elliot.

Suspect: The Full-Bodied Apparition and the Ghostly Body Part

What It Looks Like

Consider this the Holy Grail of evidence, which is why it is so rarely captured in the field and why when it is people assume it to be faked. The best evidence would be a full-bodied apparition, which is just a fancy way of saying a picture of a whole ghost. There are few if any clear pictures of the full body of a ghost, and even fewer that are beyond reproach. Instead, the majority of these pictures are of the body parts of a spirit. You get a glimpse of one small part, say a hand, and there is no explanation for why it would be there. One of the more compelling photos I have seen of just a body part came from an old investigator who got the picture of an arm around one of his friends during an investigation. Keep in mind that a ghost does not get bigger when it dies, just as it does not get smarter. This holds true for body parts as well. If you get a picture of a giant hand, it may be the hand of God, and I cannot help you.

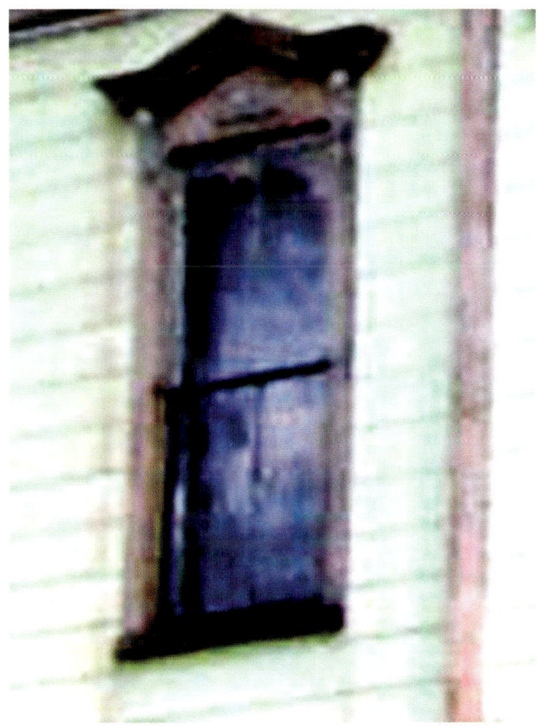

Figure 3.7
With a full-bodied apparition in the window.
Picture courtesy of Tom Elliot.

The general appearance of an image of a human, full bodied or not, is generally translucent and does not seem to belong in the picture. There may be fading in parts, especially as you get closer to the extremities. The person may be seen only in patches or in varying degrees of intensity, although paranormal investigators report the fading seems, like the extremities, like someone starting to erase the image from the outside in.

The most frequent body part people see is the face, which people have seen in smoke and mirrors, literally. During an investigation, I suggest shooting near mirrors, although not directly into them, for this reason. The large number of faces may be due to matrixing, which we get into more in Chapter 8. For now, think of it as your mind needing to make what it sees make sense. Human faces being the most common thing your eyes have to read, it sees faces everywhere.

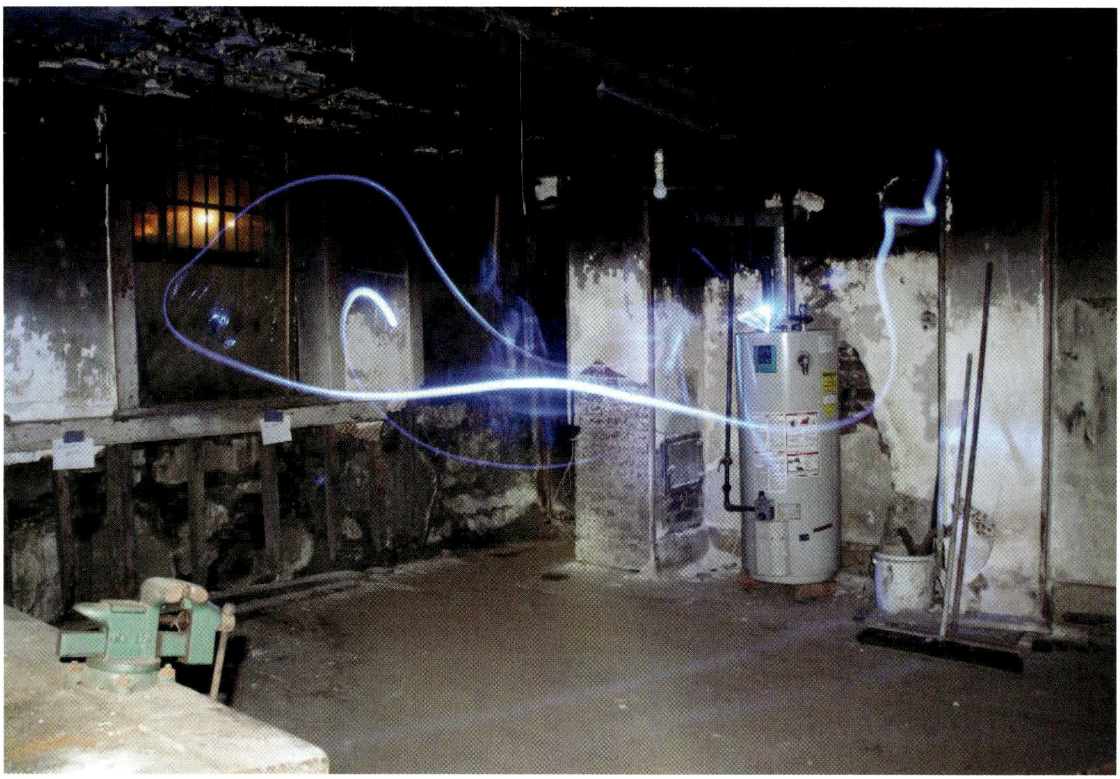

Figure 3.8
A full-bodied apparition surrounded by orbs and streaks, but in this case they were produced intentionally.
Picture courtesy of Josh Mantello.

What It Is Thought to Be

This one is easy. A picture of your little brother who passes away is your little brother. If you see a person in your picture and that person is not supposed to be there and you have eliminated any other possibility, it is a ghost. Enjoy, because you have something most people will never get. Due to the nature of some ghosts and the energy they are associated with, you are more likely to capture the body of a residual haunting than an intelligent one. It would appear the energy they use traps the picture, but also helps create one.

Natural Causes

If you are using a film camera, the most obvious mistake is a double exposure or a processing error. If you are using a digital camera, a picture of a person may be the result of keeping the shutter open too long. As we discussed in Chapter 2, this would mean someone moving into your frame for a short time would appear ghostly. If the picture is the result of the investigation, the evaluation is easier. Does the ghost look like someone on the team you investigated with or someone who might have been present? If not, you are in business.

The Best Way to Prevent a False Positive

If you are shooting on film, get the right speed film and shoot evidence with as few bells and whistles as possible. For both kinds of cameras, follow the basic rule of right of way. If you are shooting, you have the right of way. People should pass behind you or wait to cross the camera. If they do cross the camera, make a note in your notebook or document it some other way.

Snapshot

The most famous full-bodied apparition caught on moving film may be the suicide victim caught during the filming of the movie *Three Men and a Baby.* During several scenes, you get a glimpse of a person who may be the young man rumored to have killed himself in the apartment shortly before the movie started production. However, this is only an urban legend. The ghost is actually a cutout of one of the actors used for lighting that was not taken completely out of the camera range.

Suspect: Paranormal Smoke

What It Looks Like

There is not much of a mystery behind what paranormal smoke looks like. It may not reveal itself as being ghostly, but it does look like smoke. It may come in more than one color, although the most popular color is white, which is one of the ways you can distinguish it from natural smoke. Smoke from a fire or a cigarette is dirtier looking than paranormal smoke, which is almost immaculate. It also wafts in long streaks, as opposed to smoke or fog that clumps and travels as a whole. The spirit kind extends out from a middle source.

Many people describe a darker form during hauntings that is compared to black smoke but with more substance. This lies somewhere between smoke and shadows, which we will talk about later this chapter. This generally accompanies a more intense and scary haunting, although not always. When you are documenting this as an investigator or evaluating evidence after the fact, make the judgment call on which it is closer to. Ultimately, it does not matter which it is because noting it in the field is only so you know what to look for when you examine the evidence.

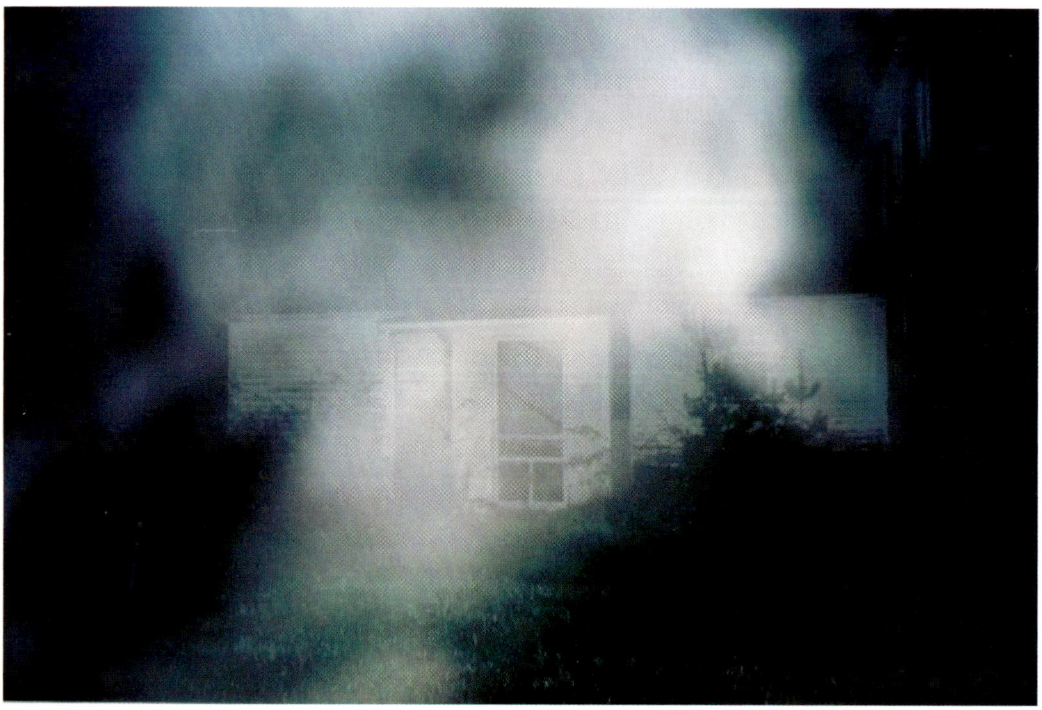

Figure 3.9
Ghostly mist with a face.
Picture courtesy of Sheryl Vartanian.

What It Is Thought to Be

Imagine two worlds and something that can go between them. Better yet, think of a good magician who suddenly appears on stage with an explosion and a cloud of smoke. There are two popular ideas about what paranormal smoke may be, and both of them are related to making a flash moving from one place to another. Of course, no one in real life is smoke or fog, so this state of ghost matter represents that transition. The first idea is that a spirit does not have enough energy to go from energy to mass or to transform pure energy into visible human form. Fog has less mass and order so it comes first.

The second idea, which is closely related, is that the smoke or fog is what happens before energy can become a full-bodied apparition. If you catch it on film, you have seen the ghost before it becomes a wholly visual ghost. This idea is reinforced by the number of faces people see in paranormal smoke. Most have some area that can resemble a human face, especially when you consider matrixing.

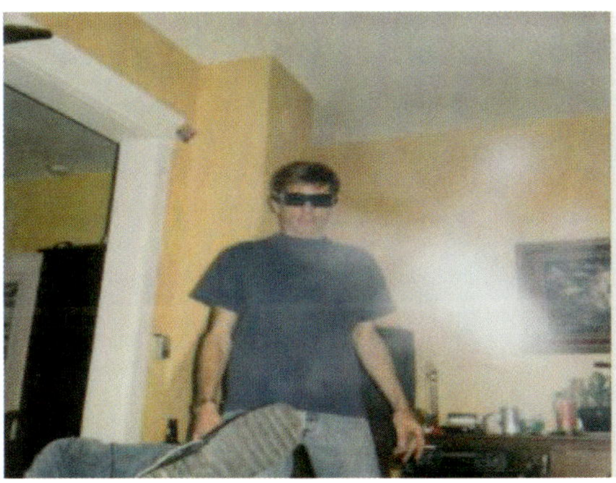

Figure 3.10

This was sent to me as potentially being paranormal smoke, but the gentleman in the picture is clearly smoking. Picture courtesy of Clarissa Vazquez.

Natural Causes

The most obvious reason for a natural picture of smoke is someone is smoking, or there may even be a fire nearby. People often claim they went out on a warm night and they still got this fog in their pictures, but what they fail to realize is that anything leaving your body can be upwards of 96 degrees. Just about any night, especially if it is not the middle of summer in the South, will have a drop in temperature between the moisture in the breath coming out and the air near you. It might not be cold enough for that moisture to become fog, but you would be surprised how high the temperature can be and still see your breath.

Some investigators believe the fog you pick up on your camera, especially when it is located above the heads of the people who are the subjects, might be the release of oxygen from the trees. This release happens at night and many times these types of pictures are found during investigations where there are trees. Remember, oxygen is a colorless, odorless gas, so it would not show up on a camera. A better reason might be the gases that are released from dead bodies, including methane. This might be why paranormal smoke is seen so much in graveyards.

The Best Way to Prevent a False Positive

The best way to get rid of the majority of non-paranormal fog pictures is to leave the cigars and cigarettes at home and know your surroundings. Document the temperature often, even if there is no change, and keep your nose open for people with chimneys or fires in the area. If you can smell it, it is close enough to get in the way of an investigation.

Suspect: Ectoplasm

What It Looks Like

Ectoplasm is a word coined and widely used long before the rise of paranormal groups and the sharing of evidence. It also came before we had so much classification, so the word was originally a very broad term for many of the suspects on this list. As the field advances, the clear definition for ecto becomes as easy to hold onto as paranormal smoke. It has the look of orbs and streaks, but functions more like smoke in pictures. It shows up on the image like smoke, but more solid and with different colors. It is like the classic expression about pornography: I know it when I see it. If there is something that falls outside of what you can classify, it is probably ectoplasm. Think of it more as being defined by its relationship with things in the picture. If it is in the top corner of the image, it's paranormal smoke. If it seems to be coming out of someone's head, it's ectoplasm. Ectoplasm is thought to have more of a function, perhaps draining energy or showing where a ghost has left energy behind.

Some of the most disturbing paranormal pictures are of psychics and ectoplasm. Many are faked photos, but a few are still unexplained. They look like a person is vomiting a ghost or the ecto is trying to thrust itself down the person's throat.

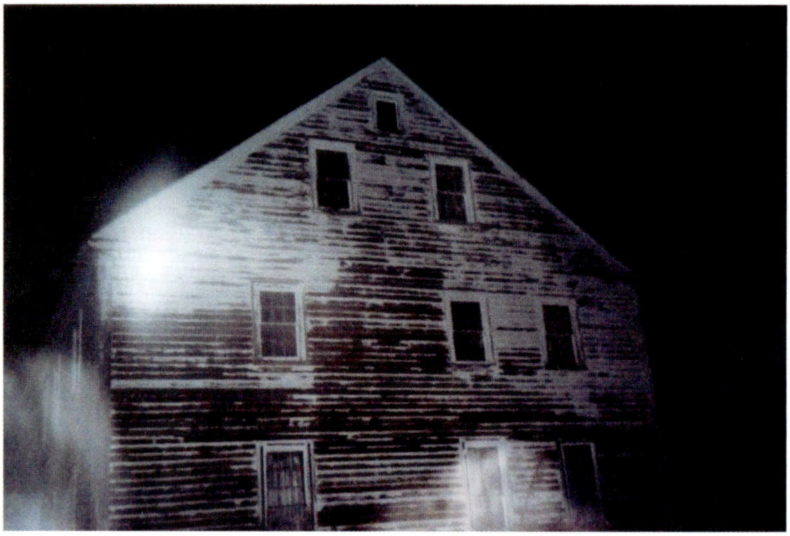

Figure 3.11
One form of ectoplasm.
Picture courtesy of Sheryl Vartanian.

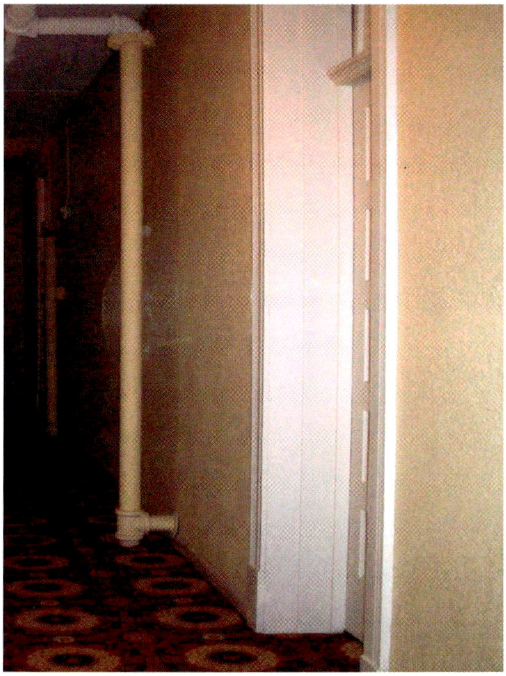

Figure 3.12
Another form of ecto.
Picture courtesy of Clarissa Vazquez.

What It Is Thought to Be

Ectoplasm is actually a French term. Spiritualists claimed it came out of their orifices during a séance. In more modern times, the definition of ectoplasm has changed, and of all the suspects here, it may be the one people will disagree about the most. Investigators may argue over whether an orb is a ghost, but for ecto they argue over what it is. The prevailing argument is that ectoplasm is what is left over, like a paranormal fingerprint or snail trail, when a supernatural event has happened. If an orb may be the collecting of energy or the eating of energy, ecto may be the ending part of the digestive process. This becomes important when you think of what might have been or when there is something that happens during an investigation and after a long row of pictures you get one that looks like ecto.

Natural Causes

If the ectoplasm you pick up on film does not have a paranormal origin, chances are it resulted from any of the other mistakes you could make when dealing with our suspects. There is also a good chance it could be from a developing error if it was taken with a film camera.

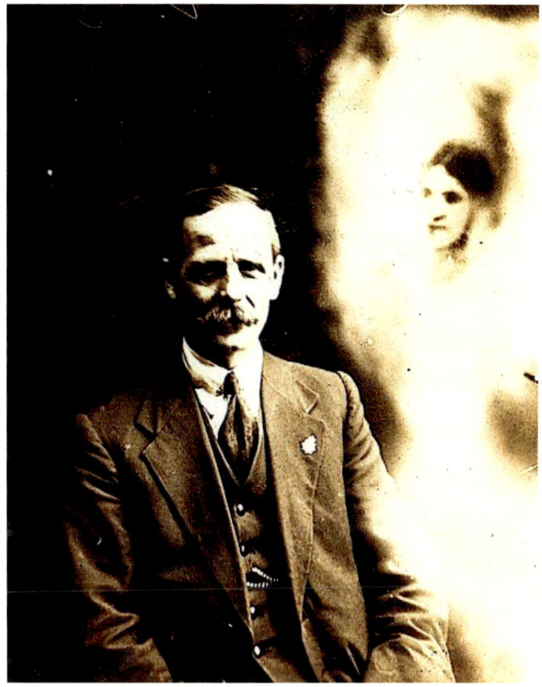

Figure 3.13
An older idea on ecto. Notice this is a result of some of the methods we looked at with older spirit photos.
Picture courtesy of Wikipedia.

The Best Way to Prevent a False Positive

The only real way to minimize ecto in your pictures is to take all of the steps you would to prevent the natural causes of all of the other suspects.

Suspect: Orbs

To anyone not in the paranormal world an orb is a round sphere. They take on a whole new life to people looking for ghosts. Orbs are balls of light people see with their eyes or when they develop pictures. They are one of the most fiercely debated topics in the world of ghosts, although most people tend to not even consider them evidence of anything. Whether you do or not is up to you, although I suggest learning all you can about them before deciding, and I strongly suggest evaluating each piece of evidence on its own merits, which means every picture needs to be held up and looked at.

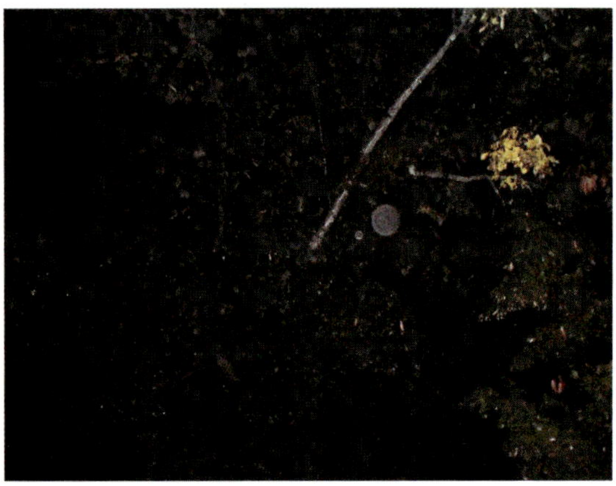

Figure 3.14
An orb in the trees.

With all of that being said, it also is one of the most common paranormal anomalies you pick up with cameras and warrants an entire chapter on its own. Chapter 9 is all about orbs, so if you need more information before you continue, please read it before finishing the lineup. The chapter is more closely related to evaluating them as evidence, but it is worth going over now.

Suspect: Streaks

What It Looks Like

Every Fourth of July we went to a park the next town over and watched the fireworks. I was amazed by the explosion in the air and by the reactions of the people watching, but my favorite part of the evening was always when my parents would buy me a glow-necklace. Of course, the glow-wand was a tradition during Halloween, but the necklace, also known as the glow-bracelet, had the added ability to be used as a whip. My sisters and I would take them apart and try to find as much uncovered skin as we could to smack, and in the dark of summer waiting for the next explosion, the spaces between us looked like a string of lightning bugs doing a conga line.

That is pretty much what a streak looks like in the paranormal world. There is a light source with a head, although it is not usually round or orb-like, and a tail, and can run for the entire length or width of the picture, although they usually seem to travel horizontally or from the foreground to the background. Again, they can be about any primary color, but most often they are whitish or yellow. In their most spectacular form, you will feel like you have just seen a laser light show.

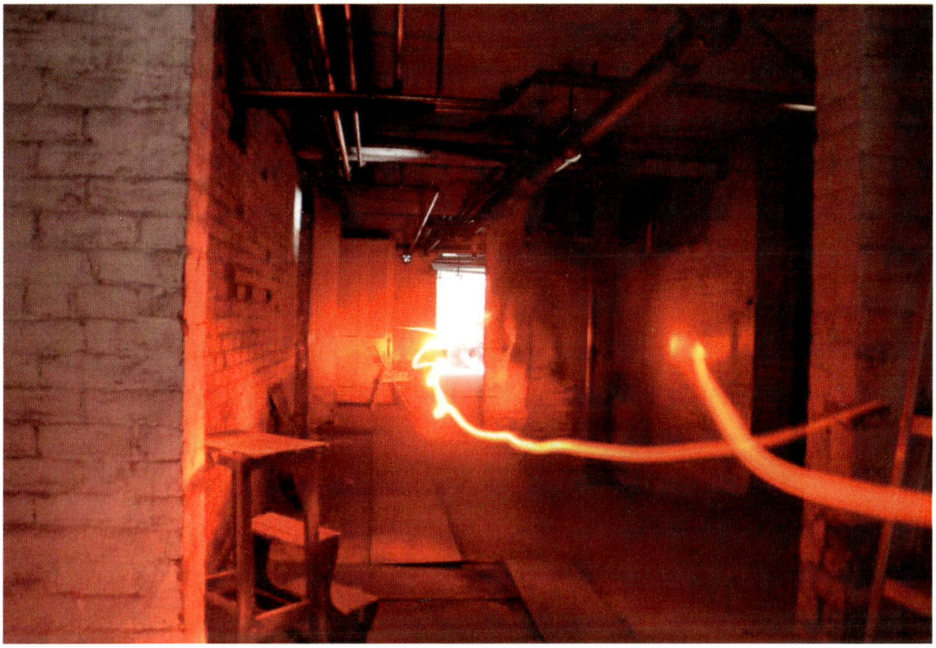

Figure 3.15
Fake ghost streaks.
Picture courtesy of Josh Mantello.

What It Is Thought to Be

Streaks are the part of the cult of traveling ghosts. They are thought of as spirits that are on the move and the camera picks them up as they travel from one area to another. Rather than the "smile and say cheese" ghosts that make up many of the other categories, streaks are the action photo, which may be why the faster cameras get less of them. Do not think of them as more powerful or more active. You just caught them during an active time.

Natural Causes

The reason streaks invoke thoughts of the old glow-bracelets is that most of them are something very similar. Cameras are dumb, and they often capture movement and present it as a blur, and the more you use the features on your camera that reduce the shutter speed, the more action a still picture will look to cram into a single image. There is a reason most are white and yellow. Those are the most common colors for flashlights and flashbulbs.

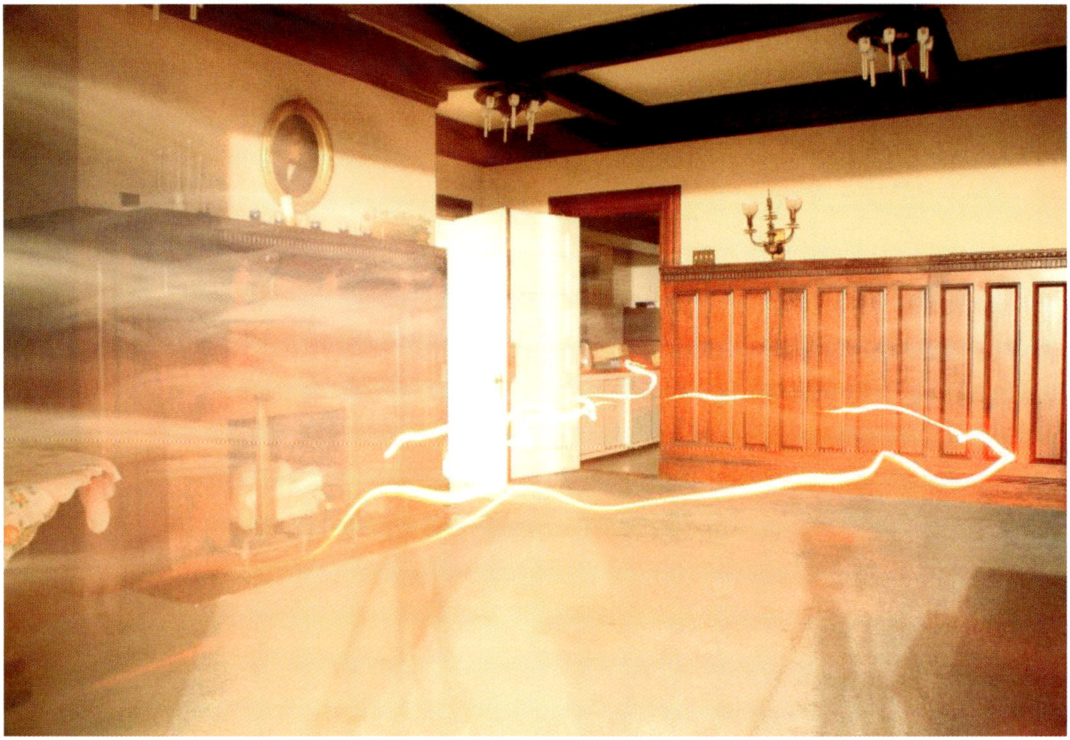

Figure 3.16
Fake ghost streaks.
Picture courtesy of Josh Mantello.

The Best Way to Prevent a False Positive

In Chapter 4, Josh Mantello defines and explains many of the features of a camera and how to adjust your camera to get good evidence. Much of it deals with how to stop getting those pesky streaks, so read it well. When you look at the picture during the evaluation look at the light source nearby. If it streaks from something common, like a flashlight or streetlight, the streak can be explained away.

Suspect: Vortexes

What It Looks Like

Vortexes are another paranormal element that combines other elements we have looked at but is defined mostly by its shape and appearance. It is separated by the implication of its appearance. In some respects it physically looks like a rod, and some people might even classify some smoke and orb pictures as their idea of a vortex, so it becomes hard to separate them from other images. For our purposes, a paranormal vortex is any anomaly where there appears to be a second level to the object, implying something more inside the object itself. Think of a curtain drawn back a bit, but I have never seen that dramatic of a vortex before. One of the more comfortable definitions for most paranormal investigators, so it is safe and necessary to say it here, is any object that has a funnel shape or comes to a straight point at the bottom. This includes an orb picture where the tail has a defined point and does not just dissolve.

What It Is Thought to Be

One of the reasons many ghost hunters keep the idea of a vortex at arm's distance is that they are thought to be gateways to another dimension, a passageway to and from the paranormal world. Imagine one world where the living inhabit and another for the dead, and ghosts are people or spirits who can travel in between them, or are stuck in between them. There is another theory that ghosts are people who continue to live but in a parallel universe to our own. Alive or dead, there are intersections where we go back and forth between the two worlds. These would be vortexes.

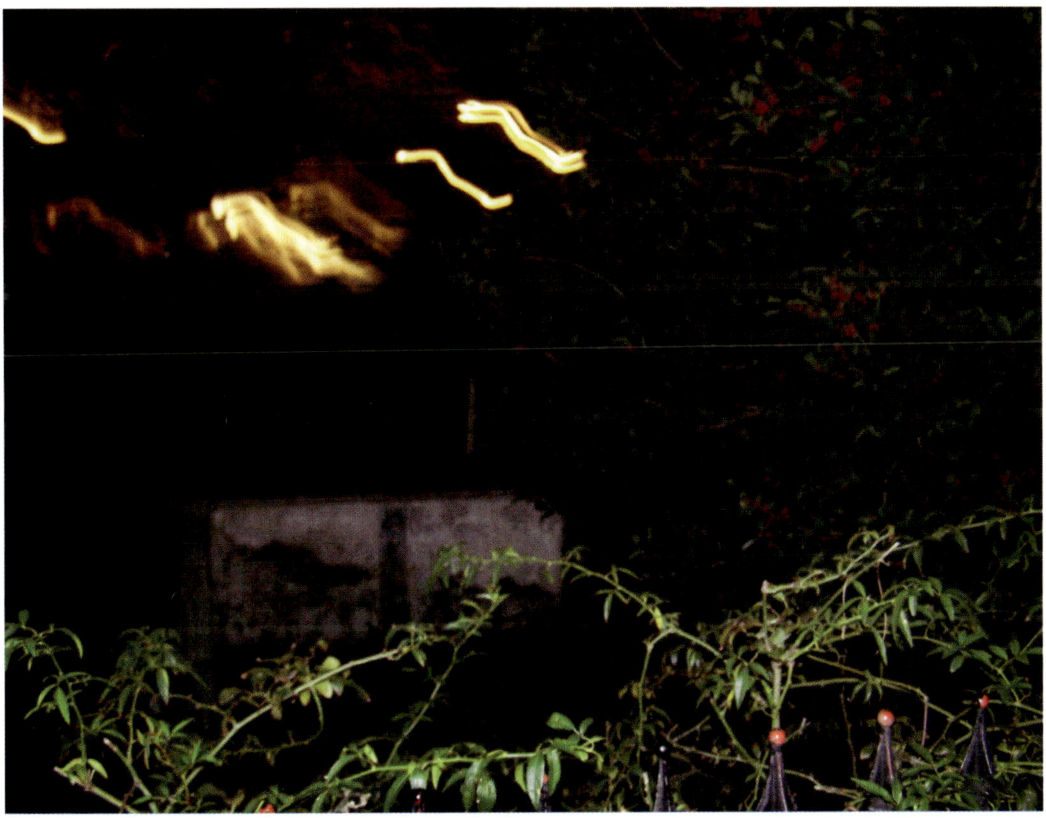

Figure 3.17

A vortex with some rods surrounding it. Often paranormal anomalies appear together.

Picture courtesy of Sabina Besic.

It is a general idea that vortexes are not spirits but mark where spirits come and go, so think of them the same way you would coming in and finding a locked door unlocked. Like the bears coming home, when the picture was taken, someone was eating your porridge.

Natural Causes

The "two places at once" effect can often be caused by a double exposure on a film camera. This may be the reason so many vortex pictures were taken before digital cameras and why the idea of a door between worlds became so popular. This idea would conflict with some of the more science-based groups even though it is an idea explored by mainstream science. Newer examples of the effect may be the cause of overlapping images due to the shutter speed and f/stop. This would also account for the streaky cone or funnel type vortexes as well.

The Best Way to Prevent a False Positive

Follow the methods in Chapter 7 and natural vortexes should be all but eliminated.

Suspect: Rods

What It Looks Like

Once a very popular paranormal motif, the rod has lost some of its popularity in recent days. It appears on camera as a glowing stick of any length. Characteristically, the paranormal rod is defined by its straight lines, as opposed to the glob aspect of an ecto or the roundness of the orb, although they may also have undefined edges, which appear like blur. They are often bent, although only at the top or the bottom but standing straight up, vertically. They are rarely seen horizontally. There are a few instances of them being dark, but the majority of them are yellow or orange. There is an entire subclass of rods that are dark, but these are maybe better classified in the shadow section.

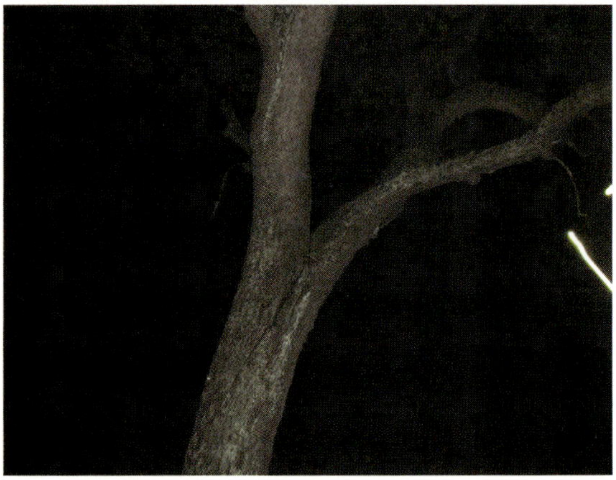

Figure3.18
Rods in the trees?

Think of a rod like an orb in rectangular form. Many of the same problems arise when trying to evaluate a picture, although they are often seen in several pictures over the course of an investigation, implying some type of movement. Rods are also caught on video cameras and webcams where their movements can be recorded and studied. Instead of the meandering and switching of direction of orbs, rods dart, moving through a picture with some speed. They sometimes interact with the environment they are in, moving to where there is empty space but not through solid objects.

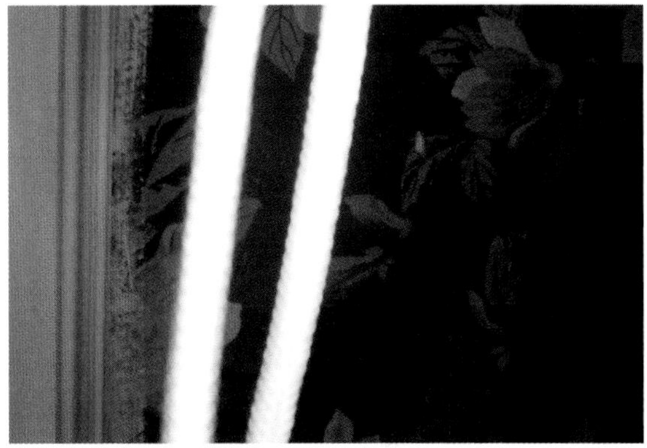

Figure 3.19
Another version of a rod, although this one is a camera strap.
Picture courtesy of Josh Mantello.

What It Is Thought to Be

There is one end of the spectrum that talks of rods being small alien or trans-dimensional travelers. I try never to discount any paranormal idea, but let's move that to the back of our minds for now. Because they seem to move with purpose and seem to be bound by some rules of physics, rods may be energy that has taken on some mass. Unlike a mist or even a full bodied apparition, you are not seeing energy but matter.

Natural Causes

Rods are the physical manifestation of the haunted reflective object across the room. In other words, at their worst they are the reflection of light off of a reflective surface. Think of an orb as a straight shot reflection off that surface, but there is another way light comes back. Imagine taking a picture with your running shoes, or better yet, one of those vests road construction workers use, in the background. The reflection comes back like a line and not a ball. The farther away the object, the more likely the image will bend.

Of course, the most dominant idea on rods is that they are insects, or at least the reflection of parts of insects as they move into and out of the path of a flash. This explains why they do not have wings but appear as streaks with defined lines. This also accounts for some of the fuzziness surrounding the outline of rods.

The Best Way to Prevent a False Positive

If you are taking steps to prevent other false positives, you are going to get fewer bad rods.

Suspect: Shadows and Glowing Lights

What It Looks Like

Think of shadows and glowing forms as two sides of the same coin, with shadows being the physically dark version of the light form. This may have something to do with their nature, and it does have an effect on how many untrained observers view them. They both can look like anything from smudges on the film to a human form.

What It Is Thought to Be

For those who put some kind of weight into the color of things, glowing lights may be angels and the shadows are demons. That is probably too simple, but there is a type of paranormal phenomenon known as shadow people. While not all shadows look like people, even a dark, thick cloud or smudge may be a glimpse of one of these paranormal watchers. A bright glow is also thought to be a ghost gathering energy or releasing it, and others have speculated it might have something to do with the light at the end of the tunnel people see in near-death experiences. This is the place souls must find to be at peace, and capturing it on film might mean the ghost did move on at that moment.

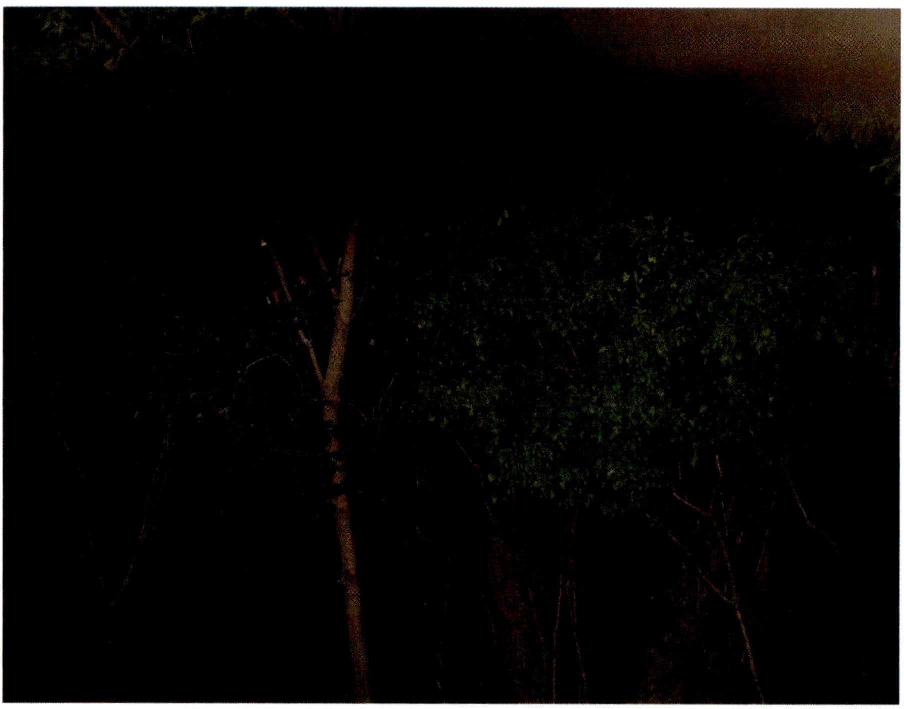

Figure 3.20
This shadow is almost like black smoke.
Picture courtesy of Allen Dunski.

> **Snapshot**
>
> **From a spiritual and esoteric angle, the color of glowing lights and orbs has meaning. Aura readers believe, for example, that a yellow glow means inspiration or optimism. A bright red correlates to survival. A certain color in a spirit picture might have something to do with how the person died or their existence in another world. I have even heard the color of orbs might have something to do with how the person died. A blue orb, the color of the throat, might mean the person died of throat cancer.**

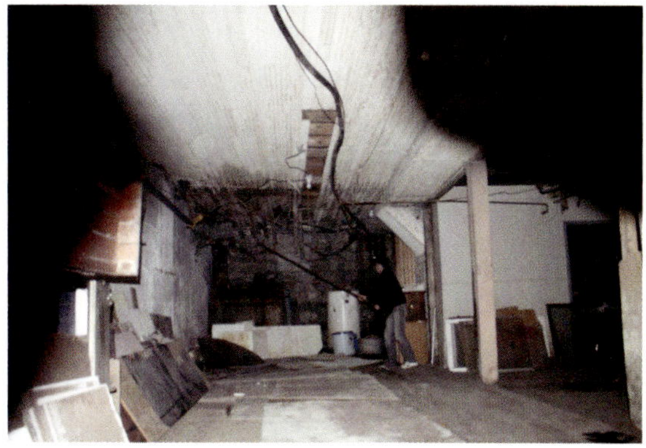

Figure 3.21
This shadow has more form to it, but it may just be something natural obstructing the lens or the flash.
Picture courtesy of Allen Dunski.

Natural Causes

The glowing light may be the result of too much flash or light in the room, but also the light's reflection off one of the most abundant surfaces in an investigation. Many do not realize the reflective power of wallpaper, and something similar can be said for rocks, especially headstones in cemeteries and graveyards.

The shadows are usually caused by something in front of the camera that should not be, like the camera strap. The object appears dark because it is too close to the lens to reflect any color. If the object has a more defined human form, it may be the shadow of something you cannot see, which does not need to be a person. With the first mindset and approach almost anything can look like a person, just like when you were lying in bed as a child and your chair or desk lamp looked like a monster's head. Of course, the more human it looks, the more likely it is you caught the actual shadow of someone with whom you were investigating.

The Best Way to Prevent a False Positive

There really are no new ideas behind how to not get false figures, so the trick lies in eliminating the pictures once you get them. If the shadow or dark figure is completely in the frame of the picture, it's likely not something hanging from the camera like a strap, though it's possible it's a bug or dirt on the lens, which gives me another opportunity to stress keeping your equipment clean. Follow light sources to see if there could be an object off camera that would cause such a shadow or find common particles that could be in the air that resemble what you find, like an insect.

The Unexpected among the Unknown

I AM NOT A BIG FAN of the paranormal reality television movement, but I do listen to radio shows about ghosts and the supernatural just about every night. The audience is a bit different, especially in the way they already know about the topics. Anyone can sit on their couch and come across a television show, but to actually seek out and find one of the Internet radio shows takes some commitment on the listener's part, so you know they come to the table with something. One thing I am also intrigued by is the commonality of the paranormal in these arenas. It is not a question of whether ghosts exist, but the details, and while I was on one show, I found myself uttering a phrase I thought I would never say. "It was your average haunting..." As soon as the words came out of my mouth, I knew they sounded ridiculous.

As soon as ghost hunting becomes average or mundane to you, stop. You are dealing with questions and mysteries that have yet to be unlocked since the beginning of human history; do not think you can create an all encompassing approach or idea about it. That can also be said about your paranormal evidence. If you go into an investigation thinking you may get a full-bodied spirit and you don't, that does not mean you got nothing. This chapter has addressed some of the ghostly suspects people have recorded over the years, but that list is inexhaustible. There is no average or normal evidence, so think outside the box when looking. More accurately, forget there is a box.

Picture Yourself Not Seeing a Ghost

The most haunted location I ever investigated had a problem with the third floor, which was a converted attic. There was activity on the first two floors, but the bulk of the happenings took place on top where most of the rooms were used for storage and offices. The man who rented the second floor has issues with the ghosts in the house, mainly because they would tug him at night. We had been investigating and had laid down some talcum powder to check for rodents to try to get other evidence, and the renter went into the room the next night. He was frustrated because we continued to get EVP evidence from the location and he was tired of them hiding from him. The stress of the haunting eventually got the better of him. He began yelling at the ghosts, asking them why they never materialized in front of him. He asked if they were scared of him, left, and when he went back up to the attic a few hours later he saw the word, "yes" written in the powder.

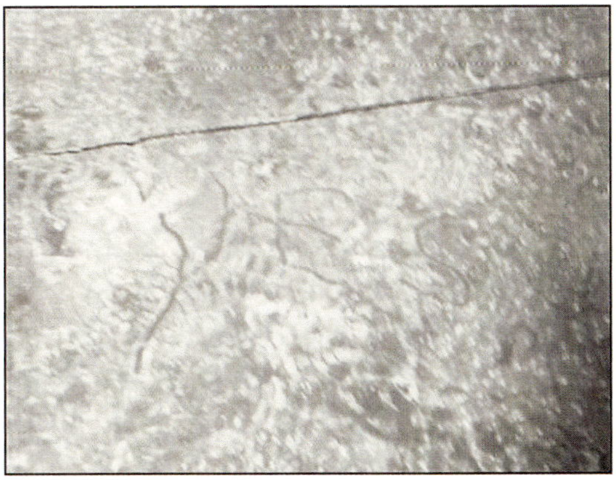

Figure 3.22
The ghostly answer.

Investigating the paranormal is about getting evidence at the time, but it should also be about recording what has happened. Looking for the suspects is only part of the job. Sometimes ghosts make themselves known in other ways. I was investigating a house attached to a restaurant and was recording the whole thing on video tape. When we left the second floor we shut off the lights and went into the restaurant, which was closed. We left a few minutes later and I took come pictures of the outside for a story I was writing, and when we were looking at the pictures afterwards we realized the light we had turned off was on. No one else had access to it, and the owners, who left with us, were not trying to fake something or make a big deal of it or they would have mentioned it at the time. Using pictures we were able to record the light was on, and going back on the video we could document it had been shut off when we left.

They might not be as dramatic on their face, but these kinds of pictures sometimes tell you more than evidence that can be disputed. The paranormal is not just about moments, but also effects. Many investigators lose this, and it is one of the lessons to gain from the techniques of ufologists and cryptozoologists who spend all of their time tracking the evidence left behind. When you look at your pictures afterwards, make sure to note things in the room that might be important or places you have focused on. Are mirrors backwards or is the television on? You may have noticed these things at the time, but you might have missed it as you worked on other aspects of the investigation. If you mention something, or it has a history of occurrence, give it an extra ten seconds when you review evidence. A ghost we were investigating liked to ring a bell, so we asked it to ring the bell during one of our hunts there. It didn't but when we looked at pictures weeks later the bell was turned around.

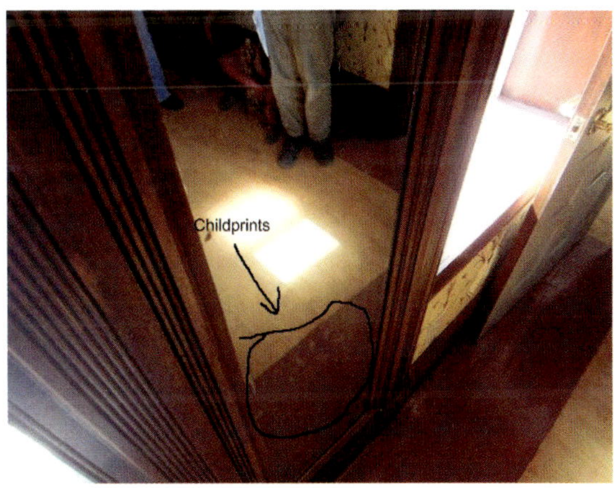

Figure 3.23
This time a child's footprints appeared in the powder.
Picture courtesy of Gary Manley.

Odd Pictures or Oddities in Pictures

Ever open up your film when it has been processed and wonder why a strange picture is there? Maybe it is just a red blur, or maybe a yellow streak through the middle of a black picture. You really do not remember when the picture was taken, or what picture you are missing, so you toss it. Maybe it is a picture of someone you don't know or a place you have never been to. Something probably happened during the processing of the film, and most likely that is just what happened. Yet, maybe something else is happening. Sometimes we are too quick to call ourselves or others idiots.

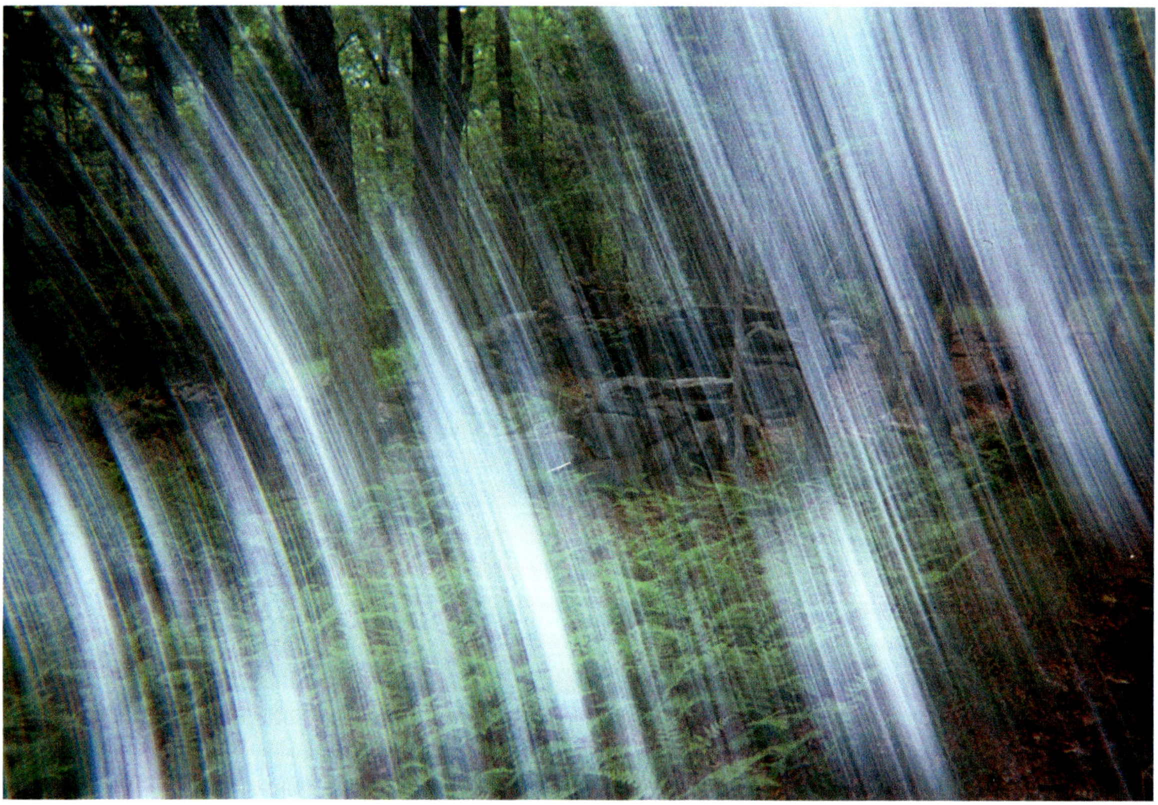

Figure 3.24
Something unexplained picked up.
Picture courtesy of Jason Lorfic.

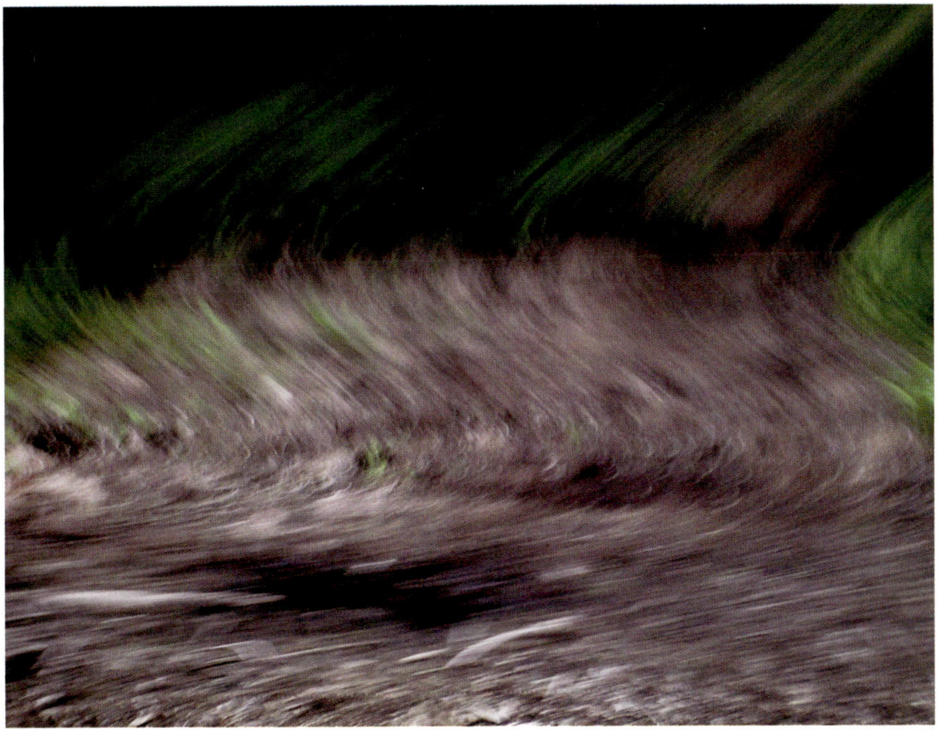

Figure 3.25
Another image with something unexplained on it.
Picture courtesy of Jason Lorfic.

It can be discarded when something like this happens at a graduation ceremony, and I am not sure it should, but when it happens during an investigation, it should give you a moment of pause. I have seen faces become distorted or blacked out or pictures that seemed to be of nothing that anyone ever focused on and clicked. Some of this may be due to error, and these can extend to digital cameras as well as film. Imagine for a moment you are videotaping an investigation and have some EMF equipment running. The meter spikes and you mention it on the video camera and snap a picture. When you review the evidence afterwards you get a shot of a completely distorted scene. Is it a mistake now?

The fact is, nothing should be tossed away if there is context to it, even a black image when you know you took the picture. These can be pieces of the puzzle that may be put together afterwards. Just because something does not fit into the suspect list doesn't mean that it is not a ghost. Much of this has to be taken into account in the evaluation, which we will cover in more detail in Chapter 8, but it is important to put into the back of your mind now. Ghosts can be interactive, so be willing to communicate on any level.

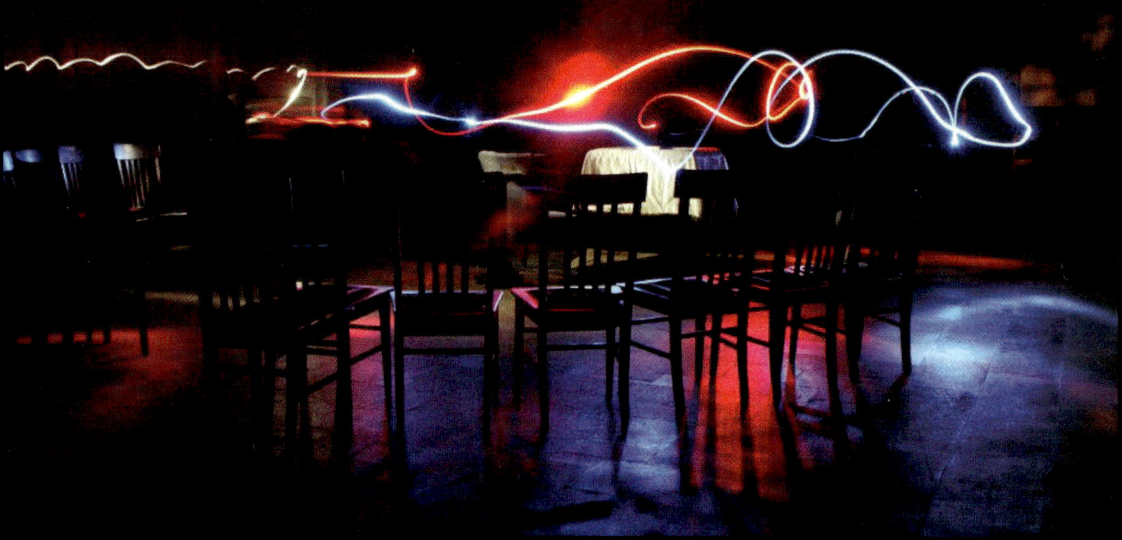

With a long shutter speed and some colored lights, you can make intriguing, but not necessarily ghostly photos.
Picture courtesy of Josh Mantello

4

Taking a Picture for Granted:

A Crash Course in How a Camera Works

WHEN I FIRST GRADUATED from college, I had the pleasure of working for a successful literary agent in Boston. Twice a week I would go into the office and the agent would sit me in front of three or four dozen manuscripts and ask me to eliminate all but two to take home with me for further review. I was only in the office for three hours at best, so this meant I was crushing the dream of 40 people while only giving the story a few minutes of my time. I was a new graduate, and I was rejecting Harvard professors, MIT graduates, and poets from the best schools around the country. I felt bad about this, especially not being a very good fiction writer myself, but the agent consoled me.

"Chris, the computer is going to kill literature. Every person with an idea and a laptop thinks he can write."

It is much the same way for photography. For years, the expense made taking pictures the role of someone who was trained in what they were doing. Your Uncle Wally was still taking pictures of his retirement party and having them developed, but he knew his place. There was a difference between taking pictures and being a photographer, and much like a good writer, someone who made his living capturing the world knew the ins and outs of his instrument.

That line is blurred now. The cost of a digital camera and the ease with which someone can process and publish pictures makes everyone an expert. The value of the photographer is in the quantity and not the quality. Left in the dust is the skill and the knowledge a professional has when he hits the field, which is why so many mistakes are made by ghost hunters trying to gather evidence. How can you know the limits of your camera, or even what you are taking a picture of, without the understanding of all of the little gadgets and buttons on your equipment?

Imagine you travelled back in time 500 years. You take a step out of your time machine and snap a few quick shots to show your friends back home. A local comes up and asks you what you are doing. You laugh and say you are taking a picture to bring home with you. The local thinks you are taking his soul by photographing him, but you assure him that is not the case. "Why?" he asks. "How does it work?"

Could you answer his question?

The everyday nature of shooting with a camera never challenges us to ask how it works. We just take it for granted that when we hit the button a picture will appear, but it is important to know the basics of how a camera works if you want to gather the best evidence.

The United States entered World War II with an advantage other countries did not have. Many of the young soldiers grew up working on cars in their driveways and had more than a passing knowledge of how one worked. Other countries, Germany for example, did not, and would often abandon a vehicle once it stopped working. American troops would come in, mix and match parts, and drive it away. Some battalions ended up with more vehicles than they had when they entered the war.

Knowing how a camera works will help you understand how best to use it, but it also has a trickle-down effect in the rest of your investigating. Once you know how a camera takes a picture, you will be able to see how some pictures just are not a message from the spirit world. Like many of the best pieces of paranormal equipment, a camera is an extension of one of your senses, in this case, sight.

Camera 101 by Josh Mantello

The Mechanical Eye

The best way to start this is to first think of the camera and its lens as the human eye, with the human eye being the lens of the camera and the light receptors of the brain being the camera or film. Light is received by both and then processed and turned into an image. Much like the eye, a camera is sensitive to different light levels, brightness, and the amount of time your eye is open and looking at an object. All of these influence our perception of an object, but not the object itself, so changing any of these factors can create a completely different image. Think of a tie that looks great at the store, but when you get it home in never looks quite as sharp.

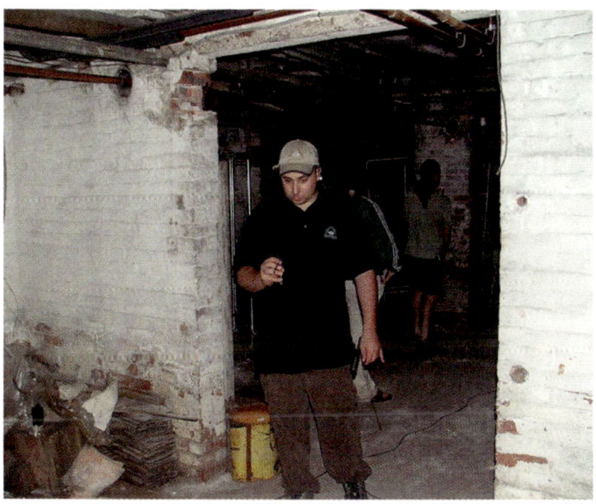

Figure 4.1
Paranormal investigator and picture expert Josh Mantello of the Berkshire Paranormal Group during an investigation at the Houghton Mansion.

However good a picture looks, however well it captures a moment or a ghost, you have to remember it is a distortion. You are taking objects that exist in a three-dimensional world and reproducing them on a two-dimensional medium. It may appear to have rounded edges and everything in its place, but you are counting on the camera to set things in order. It does not always make the right decisions, and so no picture can be trusted completely.

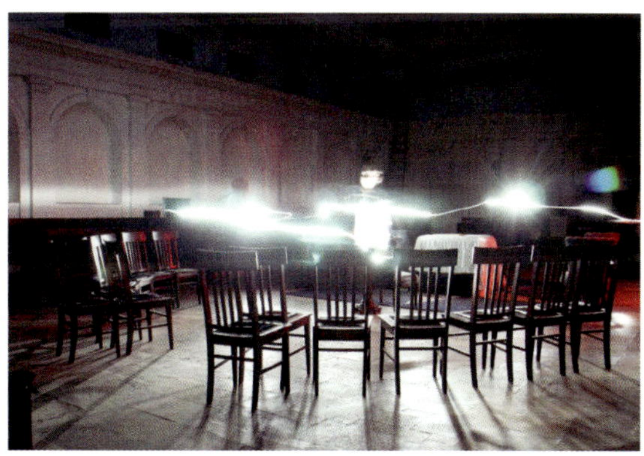

Figure 4.2
An extreme example of a common mistake from not knowing your camera.
Picture courtesy of Josh Mantello.

The major difference between a camera and the human eye is the fact that we have two eyes or lenses and the camera contains only one. This is important when we start talking about depth of field in a picture or depth perception. We as humans are able to perceive depth because we have two eyes. Lose one and you lose your depth perception, and images take on a completely new meaning and relation. There is some adaptation and your mind compensates a bit, but seeing depth is still an issue. When you look at a picture, you can figure out where everything belongs, but this is only because your brain is guessing where things belong based on its size and position in the picture. More importantly, your mind takes longer to process distance and relationships with only one eye, which is why you can have a baseball pitcher in the major leagues with only one arm, but a player with one eye would find it almost impossible to hit a 90-mile-an-hour fastball.

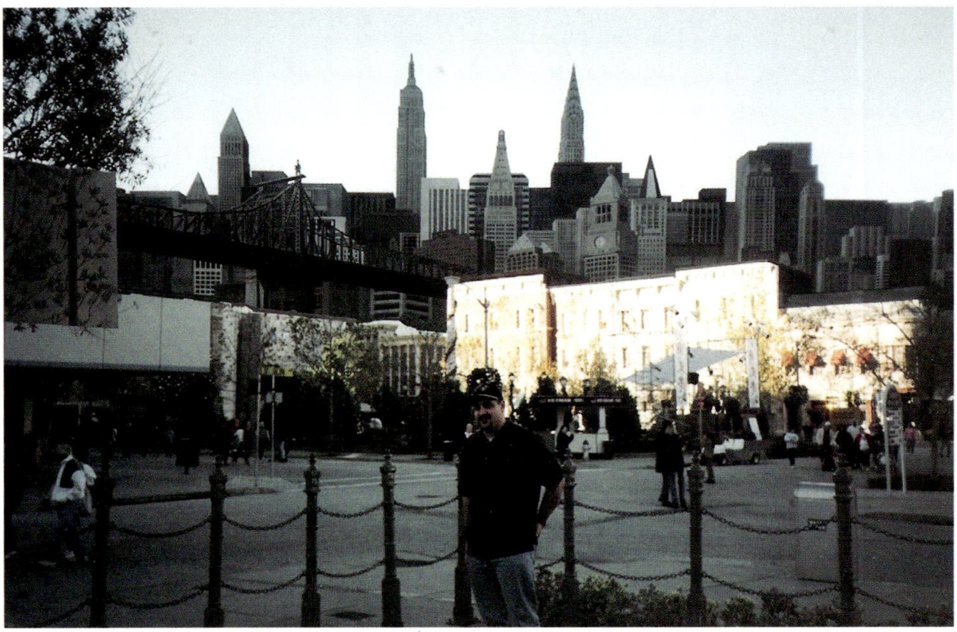

Figure 4.3

An amusement park makes use of the problem with cameras and perspective.

Your brain can be fooled when looking at a picture when you start putting things of different sizes in different places. The best example of this is the old camera trick where someone takes a large landmark that is off in the distance and then takes his hand and places his fingers over the top and bottom of the landmark and has someone take a picture.

In the picture, it appears that this obviously larger landmark is being squeezed between the person's two fingers. Better yet, think of all of those tourist pictures of people holding up the Leaning Tower of Pisa by positioning themselves in the right place. This is basically explained by the fact that the brain assumes things that are smaller are far away and things that are larger are close, but when the two of them start to interact or overlap then it gets confused.

The other major difference, which relates more to the evaluation of evidence after the fact, is that the mind quickly tries to make sense of what it is seeing, where the camera takes an unbiased picture. Two people are walking down the sidewalk towards each other. The mind is working at an incredible pace to process information. Do you know the person? Are they dangerous? Do you need to move? It might shift perception several times in the course of seconds as new information enters the field of vision. Try waking up in the middle of the night with only a little light in the room. You process all of the information through your memory of the area during the day as well as the information you are getting at the moment. Things that should not make sense do because your mind puts them in some kind of order.

A camera can't do that. Assuming you have the autofocus off, you the picture taker are the one who determines the relationship, and the image is a direct representation of what is in the field of vision, accounting for increased light spectrum, of course. With no special features on, the camera just captures the scene without analyzing it. With a feature like the autofocus on, it will look to make a spot in the picture clear while sacrificing the surrounding objects, much like your eye, and depending on the quality of the camera, you would lose information your brain would have processed and moved on from. We'll talk more about this in Chapter 8.

Burning the Image

So how does the camera actually capture a picture? It's really not as complicated as some may think, and the basic idea has not changed for more than 150 years. The process and equipment has only become refined. All of this is true for traditional film cameras as well as digital ones, with a few notable exceptions.

The first process of taking a picture is deciding what you want to take a picture of and then pointing your camera in that direction. You play with any of the features you may have on the camera, adjusting the focus and allowing more light in or deciding to use a flash or not. You then push the button on the camera, take the picture, and hear a click or two. Those clicks are the shutter at work, and when we later talk about shutter speed, we will talk about how fast or slow those clicks happen. When you push that button and the shutter opens, it is like opening your eye and then closing it.

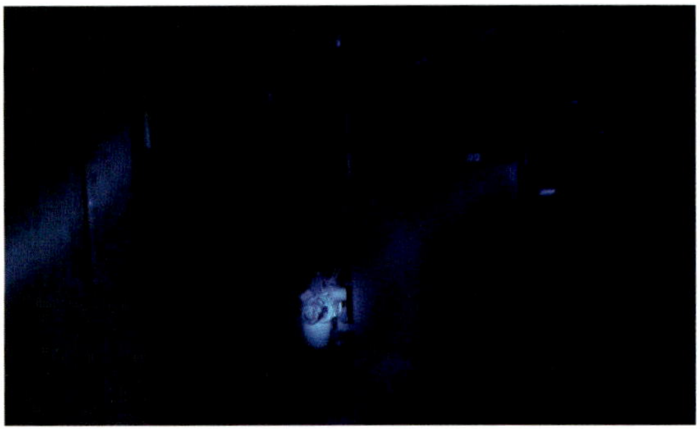

Figure 4.4
The camera eye is open for an extended period of time so it can pick up the low light that is in the room. Picture courtesy of Josh Mantello.

When the shutter opens, it allows the light that is focused through the lens to hit the film. That light is recorded onto the film as an image. With digital cameras, instead of light hitting the film when the shutter is opened, it instead hits a light-sensitive chip in the camera. Keep in mind that unlike the human eye, film can't continually be exposed to light. This is why in most cases shutter speeds, or how long the shutter is open, are measured by fractions of a second.

The Importance of Your Features

There are a few other simple camera functions that you need to familiarize yourself with and learn how to use and adjust. Knowing these will not only help you to capture more in the field, but also eliminate false spirit pictures. These functions are found on most newer handheld digital cameras as well as your higher-end digital and film single lens reflex, or SLR, cameras. These settings are not usually found on the older point and shoot or instant film cameras and are rarely found on digital or film disposable cameras.

Most groups and investigators, as well as the average person taking a picture, don't use most of the functions that their camera comes with. Many simply rely on their camera's ability to point and click. Our goal is to understand how a camera might be able to capture something we do not see with our eyes, so we must take pictures with different settings to get the complete picture. Most people in the field are using a camera that is set to "auto," which means all you have to do is point and hold the button down halfway to focus and then shoot. They do not really know what the camera is doing during the time you press the button down halfway.

One of the most significant advances in cameras recently has been the development of the single lens reflex camera. Basically, a picture uses a single lens allowing the viewfinder and the film lens to share a reflective surface; the image seen in the viewfinder is the same as what comes out in the end, allowing for a better representation of what the photographer wanted.

The camera is not just figuring out how far away the object you are photographing is and focusing on it, the camera is also deciding the best way to take that picture. It will take a light reading of the area and then decide all the camera functions for you. It decides the perfect f/stop or aperture, the right ISO to use, and the right shutter speed. It's most important decision is whether or not to use the flash.

If you are taking pictures using the "auto" setting, take the time to look and see what the camera is setting all these options to and maybe make a note of it for future reference and to look back on as to whether or not any of the pictures with anomalies may be caused by the setting the camera used. Some computer operating systems can read this when pictures are downloaded and display them on the screen during a review or playback mode. Make sure you compare this to the information you recorded during the same session.

Shutter Speed

The shutter speed can dramatically affect your pictures, and it is one of the least understood functions of the camera. It is one of easiest to manipulate, but most amateurs do not know how it works or what it does, and as a result, many faulty pictures are due to a slower shutter speed. A slower shutter speed allows your camera to take in more of a scene, taking away some of those confusing objects it blurs because it can't quite make them out. There is debate over whether the shutter should be changed at all during an investigation, but it depends on who is using it and the setting.

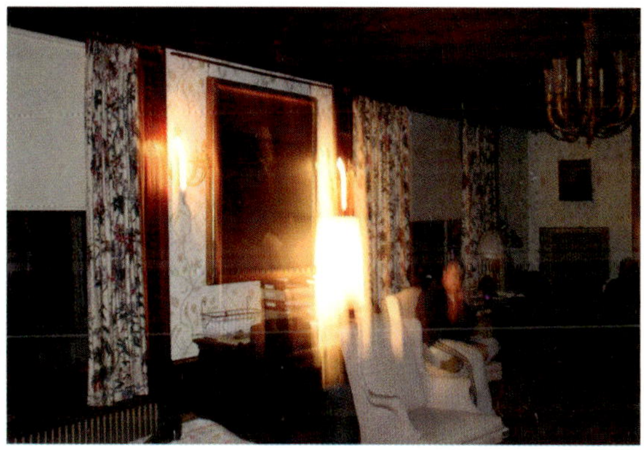

Figure 4.5
The shutter left open to create light and the fuzziness is caused in part by hand movement over the extended shutter time.
Picture courtesy of Josh Mantello.

I would suggest playing with the setting before using it during an actual ghost hunt. It will help you to see the difference in the two pictures you get. There is also something to be said for the nature of the investigation and the type of ghost that has been recorded in an area. If you are taking an establishing shot of a room said to be haunted or filming in a location where you need little or no movement of the camera, a slower speed may work for you. If you are in the middle of a cemetery shifting your camera from side to side, trying to catch something you think you are seeing out of the corner of your eye, a quicker shutter speed might be needed.

To fully use the feature, you need to know about it. When the shutter is open, and for the duration that it is open, the camera is recording all the light in its view onto the film. If there is no light at all, the picture will be black, and if there is too much light, the picture will be white. This is another reason it appeals to the paranormal investigator. If you are in a dark situation with only a little bit of light, such as ghost hunting in the dark, you might want to use a shutter speed that is longer. This allows more light to be exposed into the film.

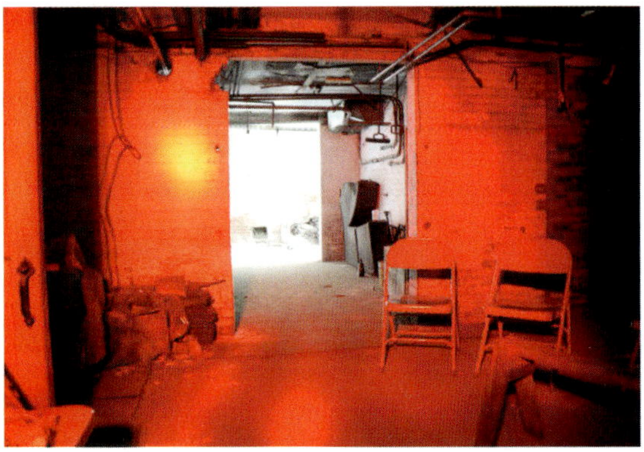

Figure 4.6
Making light where there is none.
Picture courtesy of Josh Mantello.

There is one very important thing to remember, and this is where the inexperienced photographer makes his mistakes—movement while the shutter is open. The camera is pressing everything onto the film so the camera needs to be still. When we are using a shutter speed that is relatively fast, less than a quarter of a second, which is standard setting, keeping your hands still isn't a big deal. Chances are you are not moving your hand that much during that quarter of a second.

What about a half-second or longer shutter speeds? Your handholding the camera may make very small and subtle movements during the time the shutter is open, and the resulting picture will be blurry or streaked. Many of those streaks are points of light. A simple half-inch movement of your hand may make a point of light 20 feet away appear to have moved a significant distance, and people will believe you have captured a moving ghost.

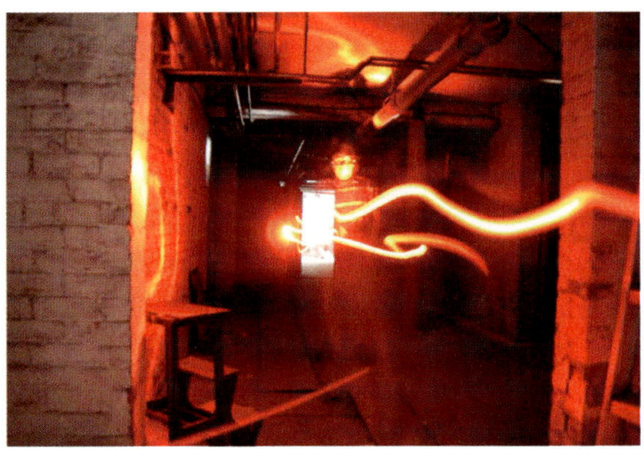

Figure 4.7
But then natural light goes through it and makes a ghost.
Picture courtesy of Josh Mantello.

To help prevent such movements of your hand and the camera, it is recommended that you use a tripod when using a camera that is set with a slower shutter speed. We will discuss the benefits of a tripod in Chapter 6, but it is worth mentioning here. This will stop any movement of the camera and those light streaks from occurring in your investigation pictures.

Other Troubles with Shutter Speed

There is one more cause for these light streaks in pictures, even while using a tripod. During a paranormal investigation, other investigators might walk through your picture with a flashlight while the shutter is open or shine a flashlight across the picture while the shutter is open. One of the methods we will talk about in Chapter 7 is identifying when another investigator uses a flash while you are taking pictures.

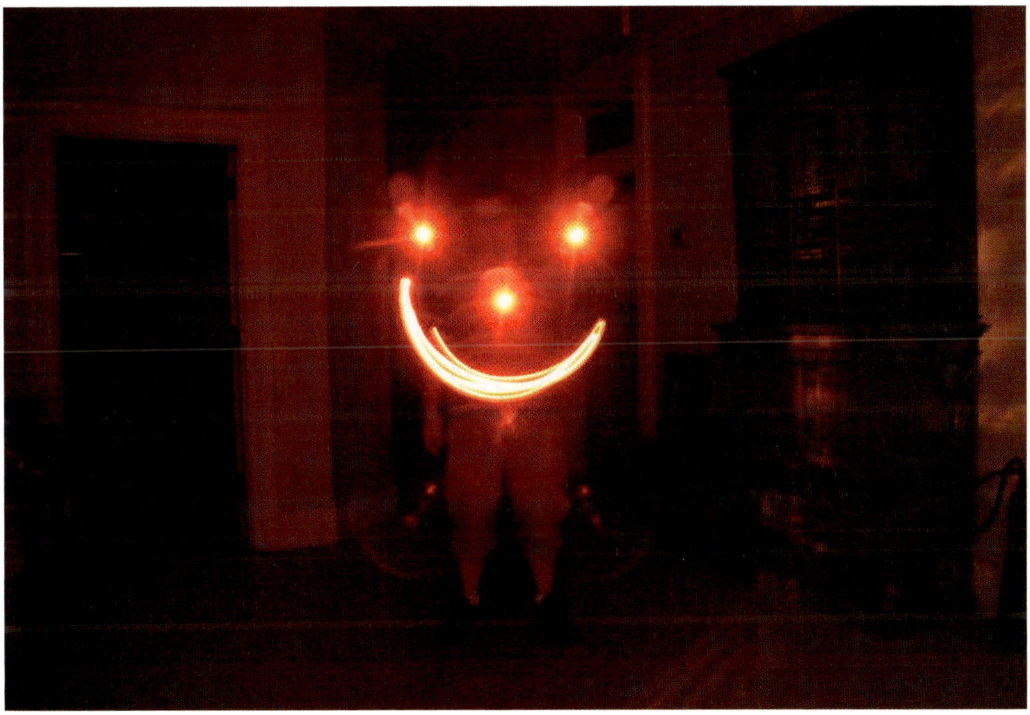

Figure 4.8
An example of catching the light but missing the investigator causing it.
Picture courtesy of Josh Mantello.

One thing people find very surprising when this happens is the fact that the light is captured in the picture, but you hardly ever see the person holding the light. Upon review of the pictures, there is a bright streak running through the picture that looks like a shooting orb or a vortex and no one around to possibly cause it. It is immediately ruled a ghost. The person holding the light is not visible for the simple reason that the camera doesn't see him. Usually, a flashlight is held in front of the person and its light is projected forward not backward onto the person. Think of an old detective film where the police are interrogating a suspect by shining a light in his eyes. In a dark room, the light of the flashlight does not illuminate the person holding the light, and the camera doesn't capture him, but it does capture the light coming from the flashlight.

The best way to combat this is to keep track of your shutter speeds while taking your pictures and document them. This will allow you to understand the picture, and anything that shows up in it, in the context of the whole environment. You may also want your team to know when you are slowing down the shutter speed. An investigator rarely will take ten minutes of pictures with the shutter open, so ask the team to put out any light sources during your brief time or have them point the lights to the ground.

ISO

ISO stands for International Organization for Standardization and originally referred to the standard for film's sensitivity to light. Most people who remember when we actually had to buy film for our older cameras will remember that you had different film speeds you could purchase. The film speed number was the ISO. It was usually 200, 400, or 1600, and most people didn't really understand what the difference was. Now many of the newer digital cameras have a setting on them to adjust the ISO from 200 to 1600, and in some high-end cameras, you can even set it to 3200. So what does this do to our pictures?

The ISO or film speed determines how sensitive the film or camera is to light. If you are taking pictures on a bright sunny day, you are not going to want an ISO that is overly sensitive to light. You would choose something in the 100-400 range. If you are in an indoors or darker situation, you will want a setting that is more sensitive to light—800 or higher. The wrong setting might cause overexposure or dark pictures, although the range for the ISO to best use is large enough to not matter when taking a picture of your cousin's high school graduation. In paranormal investigating, when the accuracy and range of the camera is pushed to the limit, it matters a great deal.

This will affect pictures during paranormal investigations in a couple of different ways. Since most of us are investigating at night and in the dark, we would probably want to use a setting that is more sensitive to light. Using a setting that is lower and not as sensitive to light will end with producing pictures that appear abnormally dark and seem darker than you remember it actually being. We don't want to pass this darkness off as a demonic entity being present or any other paranormal reasoning.

The same thing might occur when a picture is taken when all the lights are on in the house and the investigator is using a higher ISO. It appears very white and brighter than expected, but this is not because it was some sort of invisible light not seen when the picture was taken. The camera just overreacted to the light that was present at the time of the photo.

Keep in mind ghosts are energy and light is the easiest energy for us to comprehend because we can see it with our eyes. Manipulating the ISO on a digital camera, or even using the wrong film on purpose during an investigation, may produce results. Purists will tell you your evidence is tainted, but think of it as pushing the envelope or even applying the trial and error aspect of science back into the investigation. As always, make note of what you have done, but feel free to experiment.

F/stop

Light is controlled in the camera world another way. The f/stop, or aperture, is basically the iris of the lens, much like the iris of the eye. It opens and closes to allow in more or less light depending on the situation. Just like your eye, when the iris or pupil is wide open, it allows in more light, and when it's closed, it lets in less light. Think about your eye. You don't want your pupil wide open when it is very bright out because it burns your eye, and you don't want it small when it's dark because you won't see anything. The same goes for the camera. A smaller number f/stop means the aperture or iris is more open, and the larger the number the smaller the iris or aperture of the camera.

When taking pictures in a low-light situation, like ghost hunting, you want to be able to allow in the most light you can so you will want to use a lower f/stop and the exact opposite in high light saturations. Just like the different ISOs, the different light levels will affect pictures. A wide-open aperture or low f/stop in a high light situation will cause the picture to be too bright and a smaller aperture or higher f/stop will cause the picture to appear abnormally dark.

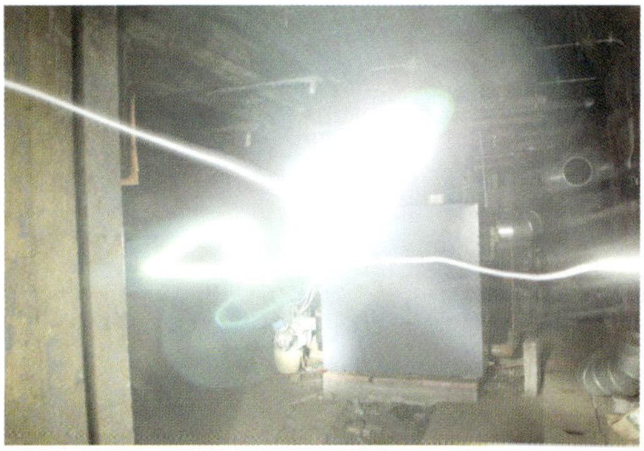

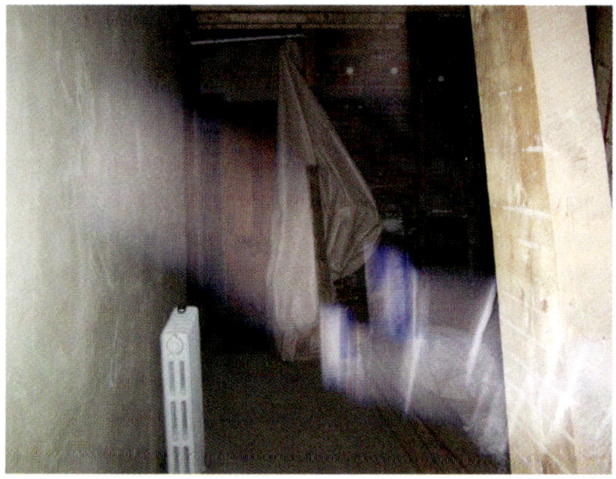

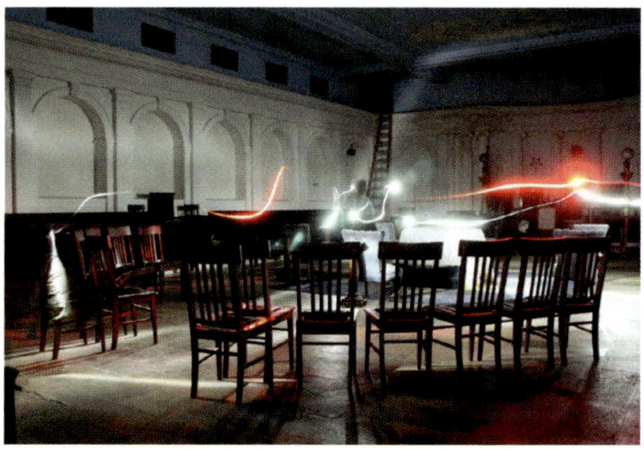

Figure 4.9 to 4.11

Three examples of shutter speed and f/stop issues.

Pictures courtesy of Josh Mantello.

Flash

There is no need to go into too much detail about the flash of a camera, but it is important to understand its place in making really good evidence that is useless and misleading. A bright light goes off and the camera can see in low light for a split second. That's about it.

To help understand how a flash will affect your picture while the shutter is open, think of it as being nothing more than a strobe light. Obviously, we don't really need a flash in situations where there is a lot of light. The flash's common use is to light up a dark situation for just the split second the shutter is open and light up the area enough for the camera to see everything and capture it onto its film. But it gets complicated when the flash goes off for that split second and the shutter stays open. Picture a completely dark room where you and the camera can see nothing. You go to take a picture and you either purposely set the camera to a long shutter speed or it does it on its own due to the low light situation. You push the shutter button and the flash goes off, and suddenly you and the camera can see everything for a second and then go back to seeing nothing. For the split second the camera got a clear picture and recorded it onto its film, but the shutter stayed open and is still exposed to nothing.

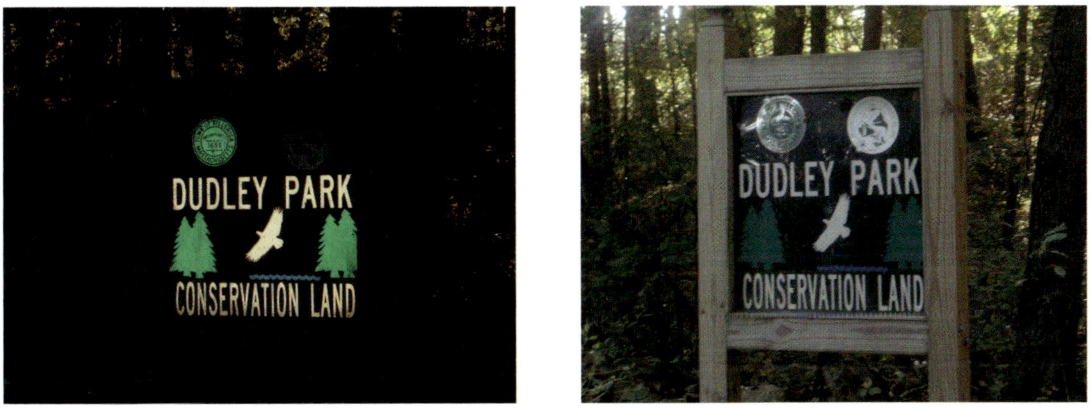

Figure 4.12 and Figure 4.13

Two pictures taken at the same time of day at a haunted location.
The first uses a flash and causes a light backwash. The second does not.

Now what if someone else in your group takes a picture in the same room and his flash goes off? You and your camera just got another blast of light and the camera just recorded it all. What if something or someone moved during the time in-between or even if your camera moved? The two bursts of light will conflict with each other and create a double exposure of sorts. If someone was standing in one place when the first flash went off and moved out of sight when the second flash went off, he will appear transporting and ghost-like. Or, if no one was in the room and the camera moved because you weren't using a tripod, then objects will start to appear transparent or streaked or disappear. With your flash going off, you always have to be mindful of your surroundings and any reflective surfaces that may be in the room. A mirror, window, or any shiny surface can bounce the light from that flash and cause flares or light streaks in your pictures, and I think we have all seen this passed off as a spirit picture at least once.

Conclusion

I have gone on and on about how all these settings can be used to rule out spirit photos, but is there a way to use these settings to our advantage and maybe use them to capture a spirit? I feel there is, but it just takes some different adjustments of all these settings to get the right result. First, when we are trying to capture the essence of a spirit on film, we are basically trying to capture its image or any light it might be emanating to make its presence known. What if this light was so quick we couldn't see it or so dim the camera couldn't pick it up, or simply a light the human eye just does not register. In many cases, more modern-day digital cameras are known to be able to pick up a wider range of the light spectrum than the human eye can see and one of the leading theories in the paranormal field is that spirits and their light are light range we cannot see. Maybe using a digital camera is allowing us to take a sneak peek into their realm of light, whether it is small or not.

If a spirit is emanating a small amount of light, how can we really get that to show up? Think about all the settings I just discussed. You choose the settings to determine how much light is brought into the camera. If the spirit is emanating a small amount of light for a long period of time, maybe setting up a camera on a tripod in a dark room with a long shutter speed, say 10 seconds or longer, will give the spirit more time to burn into the film and be visible. Maybe try busting up the ISO to 1600 and know the camera will be more sensitive to any light, including spirit light that is present. It may capture it even though you might not be seeing it. The same goes for the f/stop; open up the aperture to allow that spirit light in and give it time to burn itself into the film.

Be mindful of what is going on around you while doing this and take notes if someone walks in front of the lens or shines a light into the room while you are taking the pictures. Play with the different settings and look at each picture after it's taken and then try a different setting and see how it has changed or if there is something you notice in one but didn't notice in the other. There are new ideas and technologies being created all the time that challenge the paranormal field and the investigator. Advances come in the form of experiments with the equipment we all already have as well. Stretch your camera and your eye to the limit, and good luck in the field.

Other Special Features

Autofocus

Perhaps the biggest crutch the modern amateur photographer uses is autofocus. It has become so common most people do not even think about it, and it has become as common on film cameras as digital. We all remember the images of the old professionals frantically twisting their lenses as they try to get the perfect shot. It is a great feature for someone who has little experience taking a picture, and when you want your subject to be the central figure in your picture, it is a great feature.

This is what is important to remember about autofocus, and focusing your camera in general. When you take a picture and hope to gain evidence of the paranormal, you do not have a subject. You may see something you want to get a picture of, but most times you are pointing at the air and hoping to get something.

I once was filming a séance at the Lizzie Borden Bed and Breakfast with a lower-end video camera. In addition to the Nightvision feature, I allowed the autofocus to run during the entire event. As things happened during the course of people holding hands and trying to contact the dead, my camera would lose focus and work to regain a subject. This happened most when something stirred the room and all of my subjects reacted. The camera was trying to refocus on the moving subjects. In reviewing the evidence, an amateur would connect the activity with the loss of focus and use it as proof something happened.

Figure 4.14
This picture was taken during the séance and the focus made it appear something paranormal was happening.

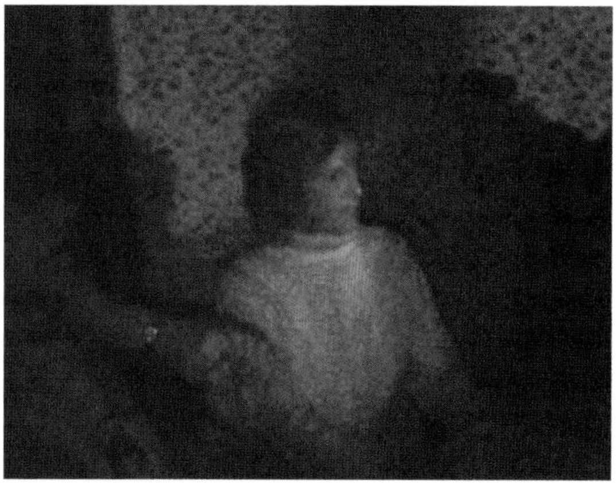

Figure 4.15
The autofocus, and the washing out of facial features by Nightvision, made it appear this woman was becoming possessed during the séance.

The same issue can happen with still photography. Why use a focus, especially an autofocus, at all? There is something to be said for having a clean shot that establishes what is in a room, but other than that, a nice focused picture just looks good on a website or in a book. Instead, try to take a picture of where you are with autofocus, and then shoot the rest with it turned off or attempt to focus on different objects in the room manually. You are not trying to make order out of chaos but rather see things that are in the room on the same playing field. With nothing to take attention away, you might just capture something.

Size

Digital cameras allow you to choose the size of the image to be produced. This really has no impact on whether you catch a ghost on film, but helps in the evaluation process. Always shoot with the highest resolution and the largest picture size. This will allow you to have the most to consider when looking at the picture afterwards, and can be reduced later in the process. You also have a better chance to see something a lesser resolution will miss. Think of the difference between a disposable camera and a $300 digital camera. The digital can get a face with so much detail it can tell where you missed shaving.

The downside to a higher resolution and size setting is that you will have fewer images in your data storage, but that can be remedied by bringing more data storage into the field, so why not have the best image possible? There will also be an impact on your battery life, but the effect is minimal.

Zoom

The zoom feature on your camera, while used with frequency in the field, may be the one feature on your camera that makes you feel like a professional. Watch bad home movies, especially of parents who are filming their children in plays. There is the wide establishing shot and then the close up of their child as she delivers her one line, and then back to the establishing shot. There may even be a reaction shot here or there. A zoom, whether it is with film or video, is seductive because it makes us feel like we control the action. In reality, it may distort things a bit because when our eyes look at something outside of their range, they compensate and readjust. A zoom does not have a brain so it cannot establish context while getting in close. In a paranormal investigation this feature may be utterly useless.

As I said before, shoot big and reduce later if you need to. If you zoom in too tight on a subject, you lose the context the subject is in. This makes it harder for you to realistically tell what is going on in the shot, and it also makes it harder to see elements within the scene, just off camera, that may account for the weird glow in the corner or the puff of smoke that appears to be drifting in. Try to focus on the whole picture.

The Best Feature

It has already been said that the camera, or any tool you may use in the field while looking for a ghost, is an extension of the user. The user may be the best tool, especially when you consider he is responsible for framing the evidence and for the precision of the picture. Do not let yourself be overwhelmed with all of these bells and whistles. They add to an investigation, and like Josh explores, they may even establish a new way to see things. Remember to also rely on your instinct, both in thinking about whether a ghost may be present, but also in how to get evidence from any given encounter. In the next few chapters, we will explore just how much the human element controls the technology, not the other way around.

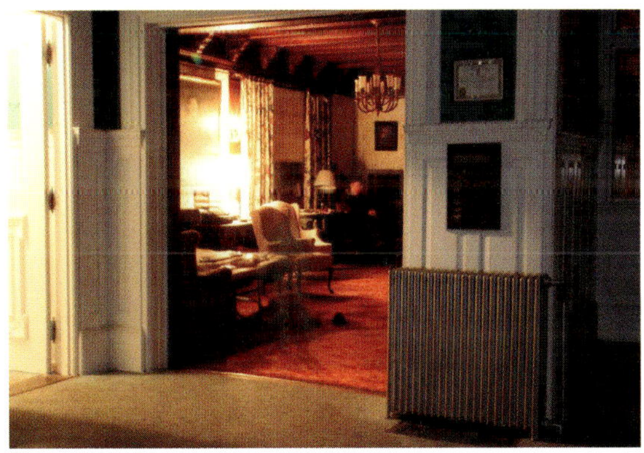

Figure 4.16
Ghost children created by using real people and an open shutter. People running through your photographs can cause all types of inaccurate pictures.
Picture courtesy of Josh Mantello.

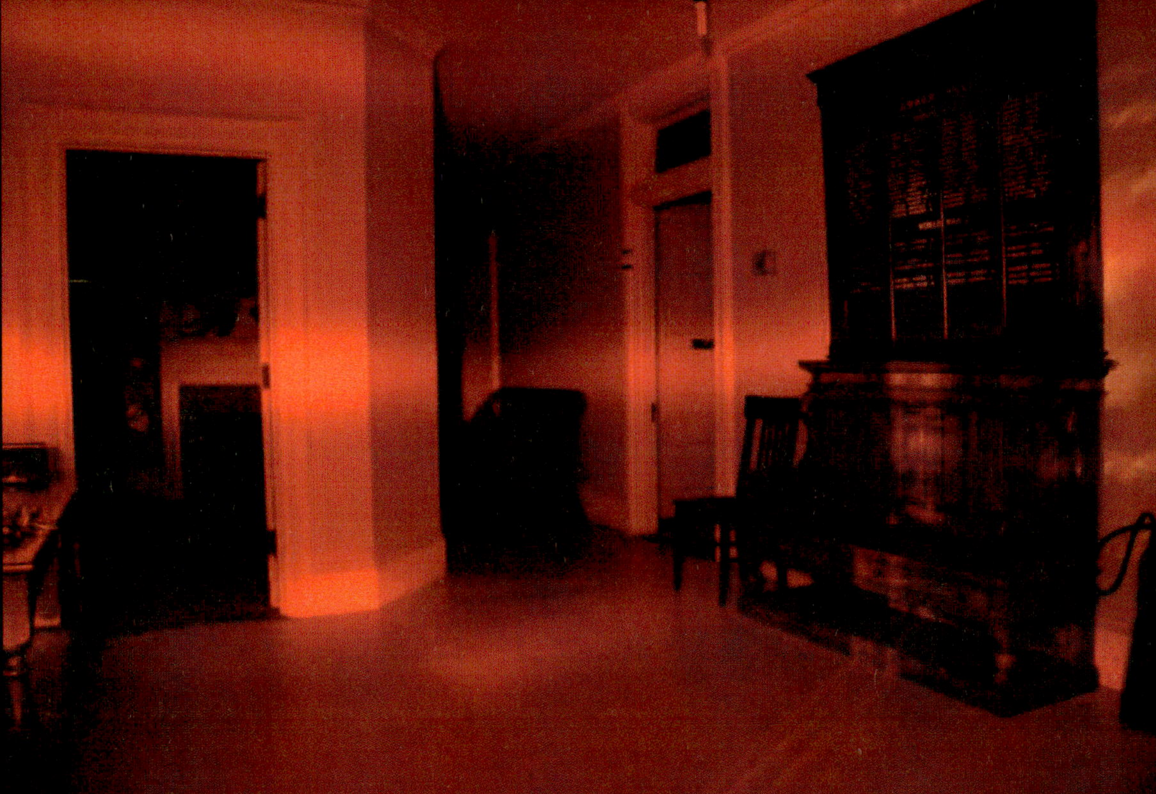

Picture courtesy of Josh Mantello.

5

Finding What's Best for You

PARANORMAL EVENTS ARE ALWAYS interesting to attend, although you don't always get the best evidence if there is an investigation involved. I ran one myself through the state forest in Freetown, Massachusetts, one year, and after I spoke for an hour and a half, we went to the forest to hit some of the more haunted locations. I allowed a bit of time in each location and watched the attendees investigate, and then I answered questions. Then I noticed a trend.

A woman who was walking down one of the paths in the woods came back and asked me about the spirit energy and my theory on its connection to crime. Another with an EMF meter asked me about the potential ley lines and the magnetic power of the rocks at one of the locations. A third person did not speak to me at all but walked around talking into his digital voice recorder and then holding it to the air. All three, it should be noted, had cameras around their necks and frequently snapped off pictures.

Their questions reflected their approach to the field, what they were concerned with, and what they brought into the investigation as important knowledge. Their equipment did the same thing. You can determine what a ghost hunter thinks about the paranormal just by the tools he uses, and while a camera of some kind seems a primary tool for all of them, the kind of camera he uses can say as much. Some use traditional film cameras while some believe going out in the field with anything short of an instrument with infrared or Nightvision is a waste. There are some basics all investigators need, and at some point, the path diverges in the woods. The interesting thing is the paths keep crossing when you try to capture ghosts on film.

Cameras

IF YOU HAVE A GOOD Geiger counter, you can check for radiation in your house, usually in your basement. You can check the levels and make sure your family is safe. Other than that, and looking for ghosts, an investment in a Geiger counter is pretty much useless, so making the investment in one means you are going to have to justify its use in the field. And checking your basement every once in a while. Is it worth it?

The best thing about obtaining a strong toolbox filled with equipment is that it can be used more outside the field than in. I was able to justify new cameras for investigating by telling my wife we needed a handheld monitor for our new baby. It is also the way I got my new camera, and those moments of her first meal of whole food and her first step will be captured alongside that ghost I just got a call about three towns away.

Of all the equipment, the camera is the most basic. You probably have one right now, and regardless of its quality, you could go out right now and try to get your first image of a ghost. Paranormal investigating began with trying to get visual evidence, and while some other equipment has entered the field to improve the search for ghosts in other ways, it is still the camera that sees all that is going on and preserves it for review later.

The Great Debate: Film or Digital

One of the first questions I am asked whenever I meet people looking to get into paranormal investigating is whether they should be using a film camera or a digital camera when out in the field. I always decide to give the noncommittal answer that they should be using both to get the best range of evidence and experience in the field. While it is true that the more you can bring into the hunt the more complete your investigation, the two kinds of cameras are useful for different reasons. It all depends on what you are looking to capture and, more importantly, what you are looking to do with the evidence when you are done.

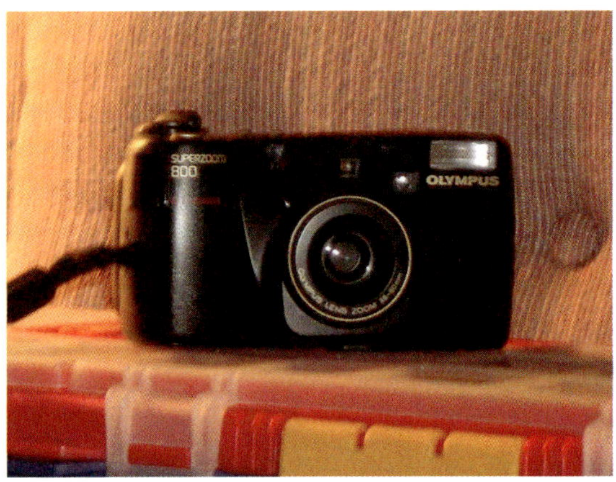

Figure 5.1
My trusty old Olympus.

Double Vision and Little Rips

A woman once sent me a picture of her son riding his bike. There had been paranormal activity in her house for years and the unexplained had become part of her family's life. In the corner is a face bearing down on him, almost as if it was going to take a bite out of him, and when she added the two things together she was convinced it was a ghost or demon. I researched the location, even going so far as to find an unusual number of power plants near her house that might result in some kind of hallucination. Then I looked at the picture more closely and noticed the ghostly face was actually in the exact opposite location in the picture as another blur she thought was a second ghost. I printed the picture out and folded the paper in half, proving they lined up. Somehow in the process, the image had stuck to itself, like tearing something off the wall that had been taped. The material has part of the wall and wall has part of the material.

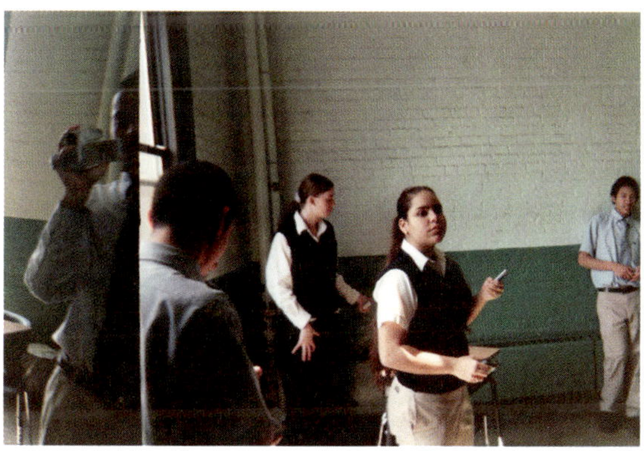

Figure 5.2
The film pictures of this investigation were ruined by a shifting of the picture.

This would never have happened with digital. So many of the anomalies captured by film cameras are the result of double exposures, and the more human it looks, the more likely it is that the camera caught two images together. How many times have investigators been awed by a ghost standing in the middle of the room only to notice in a moment of clarity it was another investigator she had taken a picture of earlier. Film cameras also have that half field effect where there is a black or yellow line through the image with different scenes on either side.

The fact is film is very sensitive and can be damaged in any number of ways during an investigation and on the way to get it processed. It needs to avoid violent movements and is affected by heat and light. It has to be loaded and unloaded, and depending on your camera, this process may involve gears that have to be turned to make it work right. All of that adds to the potential for user error.

Winner: Digital

Ease of Evaluation

This is a hands-down round for digital, and when we go into great detail about how to do this in Chapter 8, you see why more clearly. The image in a digital camera is stored and transferred to a computer through a cable that comes with the camera when you purchase it or in any number of ways using a memory card or stick. These devices all talk to each other, and even my mother-in-law can get the pictures of the picnic we went on into her computer with no problem. There was even a commercial recently that showed a three-year old downloading pictures off of her camera. Once in a useable place, evaluation and manipulation can start.

When you have a film picture, you are limited in how you can look at it. To do any serious evaluation or sharing you need to scan the picture into a useable format, which is not as accurate a transfer as with an originally digital image. There can be small imperfections on the screen you are using to scan. There can be a contaminant on the picture you did not notice before you put it down. Assuming you have a clean scanner with high resolution, you are still taking something and turning it into something different. It's like taking an old record and running it into your computer to make an MP3. Most film processing stores will offer you some type of digital version themselves for an additional fee, but all that consists of is a slightly better process than you can do yourself with your scanner. Nowadays you can also use a digital scanner that accepts negatives, which will give you a better digital image assuming the negative is still in good shape.

Winner: Digital

Number of Pictures

The best advice I can give any investigator when he is in the field is to shoot everything and sort it out after. This sometimes means taking five pictures in a row of the same thing just to see if there is anything different in them. This makes being able to take hundred of pictures during an investigation essential. This cannot be done effectively with a film camera. You have a limited number of pictures before you have to unload the used film, store it, and then load the next roll of film. This all takes time and can become expensive. The price of a multiple gigabyte memory card drops daily, with an 8GB card pricing in at $10 at one store. Once loaded, you can shoot the appropriate number of images without having to worry about reloading, even when you set your camera to take the largest pictures possible. Imagine there are 1,000 megabytes in a gigabyte. That would mean an 8GB card would have 8,000MB, and if the average high-resolution picture takes 4MB, which is a high estimate, that would mean you could take 2,000 pictures on one card. Try loading film 83 times during an investigation.

Winner: Digital

Power

I'm not quite sure if this category is a head–to-head battle or more of an argument to have both on hand. Power is an ongoing issues in the paranormal world. Time and time again, investigators have reported having their power drained when ghosts are nearby, but even if there is no supernatural drain, there is always the normal usage, which can be a drain. Digital cameras are notorious for how much power they use, even without using special flash or filters.

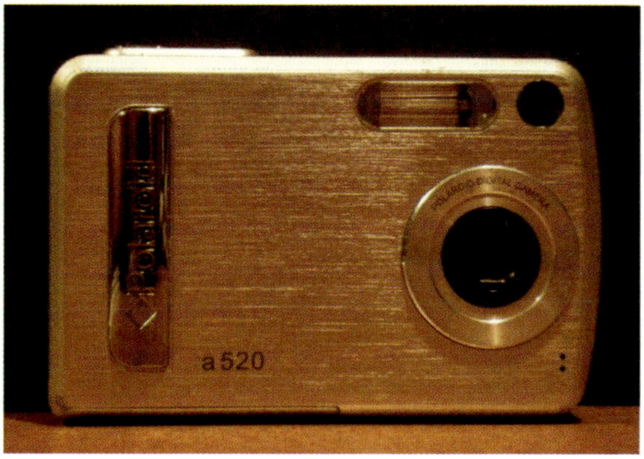

Figure 5.3
My trusty old digital Polaroid. I bought this three cameras ago and it still works as my backup.

They even make special batteries that are designed to handle the load and special rechargeable batteries that last longer under those unique conditions. Newer film cameras use very little battery power to work, and older film cameras, which can still be useful in the field, use no batteries at all.

On the Go Video

A good investigator should be ready to use anything in his arsenal to get the job done, which often means being able to use something for more than one purpose. While I am not a strong believer in using the video features of a digital camera during an investigation, I can understand having an easily accessible alternative on hand if your video camera fails. This is a feature you obviously do not have with a film camera.

Price

This is a tricky spot because you have to think long term to really understand the cost of each kind of camera. A film camera will be less expensive than a digital camera of the same quality, although as you start to think of what makes a quality camera that may begin to slant. You can buy an inexpensive film camera and be off and running for much less than a cheap digital, and the price of a digital rises more dramatically as you start adding improvements on resolution, memory, and range. You can buy a disposable camera on the way to an investigation for less than $5, but they now also have digital disposables in stores for slightly under $20.

After the initial cost, the digital pulls even with the film camera. If you want to add any special lens, like a zoom, you may have to pay for something new to attach. There is also the constant buying of film and the cost to get the film developed. If you want that digital version, it will mean even more money. With film running at least $5 for 24 exposures, you might have to spend $20 before you get to the field.

Winner: Digital

The Negative

Andrew Lake, a paranormal investigator from New England, once said something that made complete sense to me. I had been telling people for years that to be a good investigator they had to become best friends with their local librarian. A ways back Andrew had another idea. He claims being a good ghost hunter means having a personal relationship with the person who develops film at your local processing center. When something unexplainable appears in your image, this person may be able to diagnose it. If you wanted to know how to cook good egg-plant parm, you could go to your Italian friend's grandmother, but you'll probably get a better recipe from the person who cooks it every day in a restaurant. For the grandmother it is the result of a hobby and the other it is part of his livelihood.

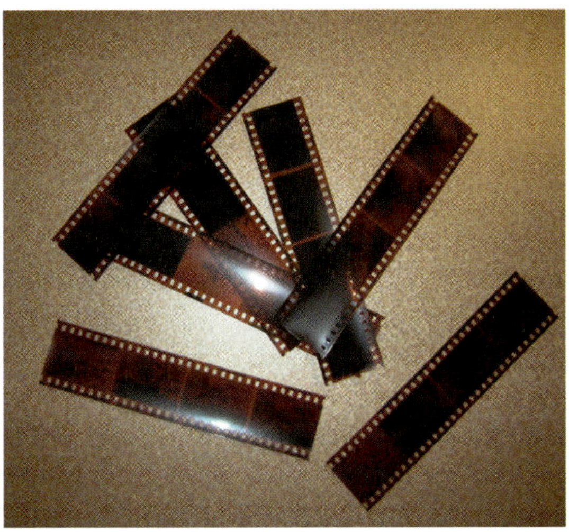

Figure 5.4
A picture of negatives from an investigation.

With digital you lose this connection with your local Photomat, and film cameras offer you something else digital cannot. The traditional camera offers a negative—an untouched, exact account of what the camera saw. There may have been a problem with the processing or a double exposure, but having a negative can solve this problem. At the very least, you can see how the picture went from inside the camera to the picture you hold in your hand. You also can go back and change the development process and see if you get a different result. Of course, there is always a chance you can lose the negative, but if you follow my suggestions in Chapter 6 you should be able to handle that.

Winner: Film

The Best Camera

The best and most popular camera is the best one you can afford. There are really no cameras that are designed for looking for ghosts. Here is where your commitment to getting evidence is tested. You could go out on an investigation with a disposable camera and good intentions or you could spend thousands of dollars on a camera with all of the features and bells and whistles and add-on equipment. I am a firm believer in using what feels comfortable to you and what fits into your budget. Lastly, the camera is most adaptable to the real world, so pick a camera that fits all of your needs, not just your ghost life.

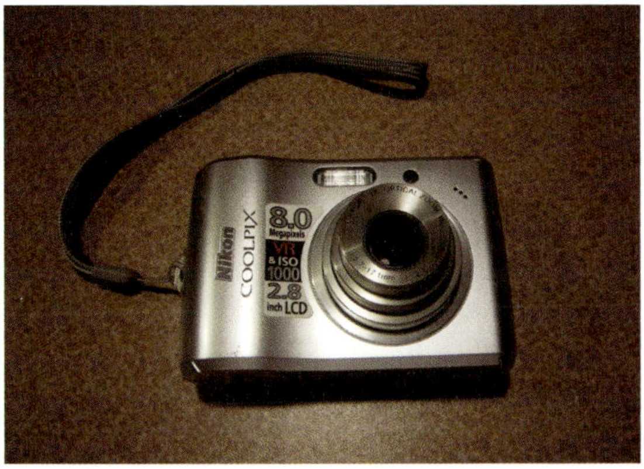

Figure 5.5
My new favorite, my Nikon Coolpix.

I had an old Kodak, which felt at times like the first digital camera made. I loved it, even though it did not have as many megapixels as some others. The reason was simple for me. It fit it my hand the right way and had a smaller preview screen and a larger viewfinder. Some would disagree, but when I look at the screen at night, I see darkness, and when I look through it during the day I see nothing but sunlight. It might sound unscientific, but it felt comfortable, which meant I did not have to think about it when out investigating.

Price is also a major concern. You can sacrifice based on the things we have talked about as being important and the features below, but you cannot forget how it fits into the larger toolbox you are trying to build. Do you need a strong Nightvision on a camera if you are going to invest in IR video cameras or can you cut price there? I suggest making a wish list of the equipment you want, including non-camera related pieces. Then do a little research and find the prices and put the whole thing on a sheet of paper listing the items by your wants and needs. How long would it take for you to be able to afford everything on the list? Are there things you can move up based on the price? When you know what you can afford, buy your camera. If you do not think you can afford something on the list for a while and you can upgrade an important feature, spend the extra $20 or $30 on the camera.

Or, just use what you already have.

Some Deciding Factors on Features

When people buy cameras, they are not looking to seek ghosts for the most part, so companies are not making cameras that intentionally see more ghosts. Go to your local electronic dealer and run your hands across the increasingly expensive cameras. What do you notice about each new level of camera? What makes them more expensive and does that make them better? When you are looking to invest in a new camera for the purposes of looking for spirits, there are some features that are worth the money and others that are a waste of your funds.

Think of those advertisements on television for cars. They say the car starts at $15,000, but by the time you add in the power windows, the leather seats, and the sound system, you are getting ready to spend $20,000. It's the same with cameras. The money is spent on the features, and the price can start to skyrocket when you factor in things you will never use. Think of a good camera purchase as a trip down the salad bar with a little compromise along the way. You might have to swallow the price for some things that are included that you don't need, but you will also be able to pick out things you like and don't.

LED Screen

The ability to review a picture is of primary concern for most commercial buyers of cameras. They take a picture and want to immediately look at it to see if it is worth putting in their album. They can delete it if Johnny has his eyes closed or the flash washes out everyone's face, and they know right away they need another picture to capture the moment. Newer cameras can even edit right on the camera, allowing people to bypass computer software to get the perfect image. This has led to the camera companies striving to make the largest and clearest view screen and to make that screen more interactive with touch technology that allows a user to access editing features and make changes to a camera's settings.

These are useless features for the paranormal investigator. To see in any detail you would need the resolution and screen size of an actual computer in the field. The price can jump dramatically because of this, with one camera increasing its price by more than $100 based on the size and pixels of the screen. It is of some use to be able to switch features on the fly and document settings; however, most of this can be done on a smaller surface with knowledge of the tool. If you are looking to save money or spend in a better place for investigating, avoid burning money on this feature.

Zoom

Just a few years ago a camera had to have additional equipment to improve its ability to zoom in on a subject. You had to invest in special lenses, often very expensive and bulky, to shoot from far away. There are still people who spend their money this way—a professional photographer or someone who has the funds to explore it as a hobby—but most cameras have the ability to do this without anything else needing to be purchased. Film cameras are lagging behind in this, but they too can get a close-up shot. Many ghostly anomalies are not seen with the human eye, so being able see what you want to focus in on is impossible in most cases anyway. There is some increase in price for an increased ability to zoom, although not as much as some other features. Besides, zooming in and out wastes your batteries

This is not needed for the majority of investigations you will go on, and picture-editing software makes it all but redundant. Most investigations are in an enclosed area, perhaps a house, or a building with limited visual range. There are outside investigations, but rarely are you looking to capture something off in the distance. There are some who say you will never know what you might come across in the supernatural world during an outside investigation, and there are reports of paranormal beings that hang around haunted sites that may be lingering a ways away, but a zoom is not needed for this. With simple, free software, you can take something in a picture, close up on it, and refocus the shot after it has been taken. If you find a camera is getting more expensive because of a sensitive or powerful zoom, put it down and keep looking.

Data Storage

Digital cameras have advanced in how much information they can store in their internal memory, with some going as far as to have their own hard drive. This is now true for both still and video, and as memory becomes less expensive, they keep adding more to it and upping the price of the camera. For some people this feature is useful because they want to take a lot of pictures of an event, or several events, and may not have time to download the photos. Nothing could be worse than being at your son's first birthday party and running out of room for a picture.

In Chapter 6, we will spend time talking about data storage and prepping for an investigation, but for now think of this. As the price goes down for storage inside the camera, it goes down for data storage you can put into the camera. If you can buy external memory for almost the same price as the increase for the camera you are buying, always go with the external. It has less of a chance of getting damaged and is easier to download and switch out.

Resolution and Power

A pixel is a single spec of information in a digital image. Think of it like pressing a fine-tipped marker on a piece of white paper. When you take your hand away, you strain to see it, but it is there. Now think of a digital camera as capturing an image and piecing it back together using this method. You have thousands of markers with different shades of color. You take each out and make a dot or two and then move on to another one until the picture is recreated.

A megapixel is one million of these little spots, so a picture becomes closer to the reality of the image. Try looking at a painting by Monet close up and notice how the image becomes a series of dots on the canvas. While this is what he was going for, it does not work in picture taking.

Here is where your money should be spent. You can sacrifice a bit of it on equipment you are using to document the investigation, like web-cams and stationary video cameras, but higher resolution can make the difference in the field. The higher the megapixel, the more dots you have, and the more dots you have, the more accurate the picture is to what was in the environment. You mix that with the additional range the lens sees over your own eyes, and you have a better picture of a ghost. The leap between 2 and 4 megapixels is huge, and the difference between 4 and 8 is the difference between the television we were watching ten years ago and a high resolution one of today.

This may be the one feature that contributes most to the price of a camera, but in the end the more expensive camera with higher resolution will serve you better in the field. Cut corners other places, and let this be one of the deciding factors of your purchase.

Flash

Technology has come a long way since people with flash pans would light a scene enough to get a good picture of something. Flash has come a long way, but for a paranormal investigator, a better flash might not equal a better picture. As we will discuss throughout this entire book, flash is the enemy of the paranormal investigator. It is great for lighting up a room, but reflects off of different surfaces to create false ghostly images. It may be needed in some environments, but try to avoid it. It then goes without saying that you should not be spending more money on a camera because of its special flash ability. This is usually more of a selling point than an added feature that makes the camera more expensive, but if it does have an effect on the price, pass on the camera.

Transitions and Effects

Being able to play with the images you capture and add them to a photo album is great for normal camera work, although somewhat unnecessary, but it does nothing for a paranormal investigator. I cannot think of a single reason to need a gentle fade or a star sweep between images, and if there is one, it can be done by software after the picture is downloaded. The same is true for making a picture black and white or making it look like an old west photo. Like the flash, the camera price does not depend on this, but a company might try to package it as editing software inside the camera and charge you a little more. There is no need to pay it.

Moving Pictures

THE PARANORMAL INVESTIGATOR of 30 years ago was at a slight disadvantage. While he may have been able to capture ghosts in a still picture or even voices on a tape, only those who had the funds could hope to go into the field looking to capture every moment on video. The technology was not new, but the quality of the camera and the resulting film made it little more than a running account of what happened. My parents have their wedding captured for all time on high 8 film, but the speed it replays at makes my mother's Twist on the dance floor give people headaches. Today the images we get can be filtered with technology that sees in the dark, and even someone on a limited budget can buy a decent camera that is more than satisfactory for what they need as a paranormal investigator.

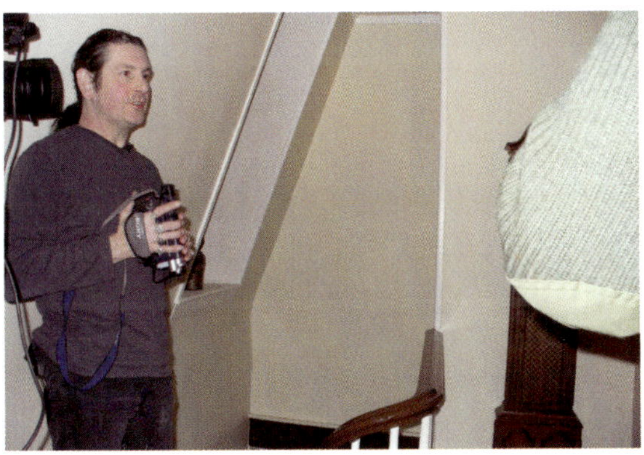

Figure 5.6
Tom D'Agostino taking moving pictures.

In fact, the video camera is somewhat obsolete, and the new cameras investigators use bring a whole new angle and approach that gives a full picture of evidence and documentation.

Video

For my bachelor party I went into the field to investigate a haunted cemetery. There were three or four of us, and by the time we were in the location, we only had enough power for our video camera and flashlights, not that we had brought much more. While we were there, we became surrounded by flashing orbs visible with the human eye and had a thick mist that followed us around everywhere we went. At the end of the investigation, a large dark object, somewhat like the outline of a human, rose from the ground, forcing us to leave. During the entire hunt, the scene was lit with nothing more than the light on top of the camera, which one person was filming with on his shoulder, and our flashlights. The resulting evidence was nothing more than a black screen with occasional flashes of light and a soundtrack of what we were experiencing.

I think of this whenever I take out my new camera, which is about the size of one of the smaller flashlights we used that night. With the cameras of today, and my video camera is probably five or six generations removed from the most sophisticated piece of equipment out there, an investigator can use one in the field, download the evidence, and share it easier than ever before.

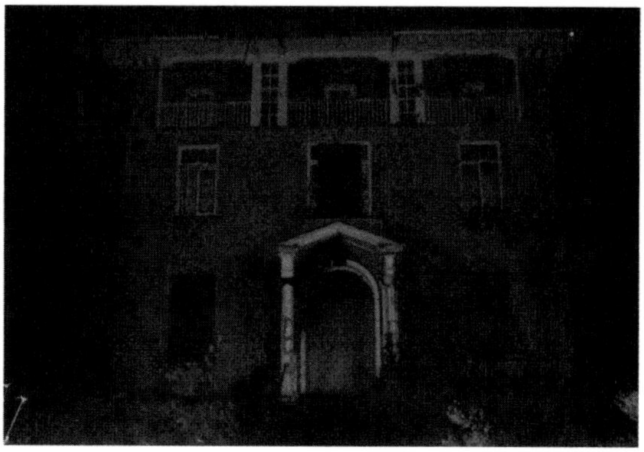

Figure 5.7
An image taken from a video camera.
This was one of the only useable shots.

An investigation without multiple cameras today is unheard of, and when choosing one there are several things to consider.

Film or Digital

While the debate may not be as heated when it comes to film or digital in the video world, there are still investigators that will only use one or the other. The same basic argument can be made for digital over film. I have never heard an argument for why film cameras are better, but some people stand by them. In the case of video cameras, going digital is an important step for an investigator to make. They may cost more, and the gap between the two types of cameras is shrinking, but here is a place where spending a bit can dramatically increase the quality of your evidence.

Digital is much easier to use in the field and can transfer a file easier to a computer for evaluation. Once in the computer, you can control the speed to slow it down and focus on something, zoom into certain areas, or even take a snapshot of a moment and evaluate it as a picture. You can do the same thing with video tape, but you lose something in the transfer. Also, metal tape technology, like you would find in an old VCR tape or a cassette tape, can be damaged or erased easily, especially in situations where you are dealing with magnetic fields. With digital, you do not need to buy tapes, and while you do not need to develop the film when you are done, the price of the cassettes can get expensive.

Unlike a traditional film camera, a film video camera does not produce a negative, so if you lose any information, it remains lost to the void forever. Switching tapes in and out can also become a hassle in the field, and the first part to break on the newer ones always seems to be the mechanism that loads the tape in.

Another argument people often do not consider is that you are transferring energy to energy with a digital camera. A film camera uses a photochemical reaction to get its image, whereas a digital camera uses energy and creates an energy file.

Looking into the Dark

The technology to see in the dark is standard issue now. While it used to mean a significant amount of money to get a Nightvision or infrared technology filter to use with a camera, most now have a switch on the side that makes it possible to record a darkened room.

While each company has its own cute name for the feature, like night shot, the reason for being able to capture the scene is the same. The images are gained by capturing any light coming from objects and amplifying it so it can be recorded.

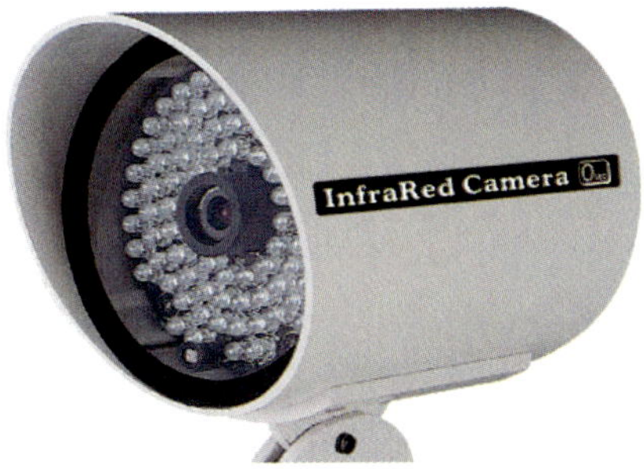

Figure 5.8
The Sony SuperHAD Color CCD DSP Night Vision Camera, which can be purchased at www.ghost-mart.com.
Picture courtesy of Ghost Mart.

Knowing the basics of how it works is one thing, but knowing how to use it in the field the right way, if you need it at all, requires turning off the television. Most paranormal shows seem to be shot mostly with Nightvision on, making the scene that much eerier for the viewer.

Security Cameras

These cameras are great if you can afford them because they are designed to be stationary. A nice handheld camera is useful for carrying and capturing things while you are on the move, but stationary security cameras, which can often be bought in packages of two or three, are made to be set up and left. There is also a certain ease to getting them into a recordable form, usually from a remote recorder, which may be able to handle several at one time. Again, the bidding starts close to $100 and they are not as adaptable to other situations. When you add an IR or Nightvision feature, which is standard on most of them, you up the price a bit, but they are the standard for investigating in the new millennium.

One negative aspect of these cameras is that for the most part they have no internal memory and do not record to tape. If something goes wrong with the recorder they are going into or the computer they are being fed to, you have lost any evidence you may have captured. One other note, if you can get one that has a motion sensor, avoid it. It is not known whether all ghosts can set them off.

Webcams

Webcams are one of the cheapest video cameras you can buy, but there is a balance to be struck. Many computers come with them built in, but you can get a fairly good one for $20 and an excellent one for a hair over $100. This means you may be able to invest in several that can be set up in different places. These are great for getting an overall picture of what is happening, and they are designed to plug straight into a computer, so it is easy to record with them. With multiple cameras, you can record the investigation from different angles, and some software allows you to review what is happening on all of them at the same time on a split screen. I am not a huge advocate of this feature, which we will talk about later in the chapter, but it does have its usefulness, mainly having an accurate record of what is happening in one room when something is occurring in another. You can also use the camera to communicate long distances with people when an investigation is over, so it is one of those tools that has a use outside of paranormal investigating.

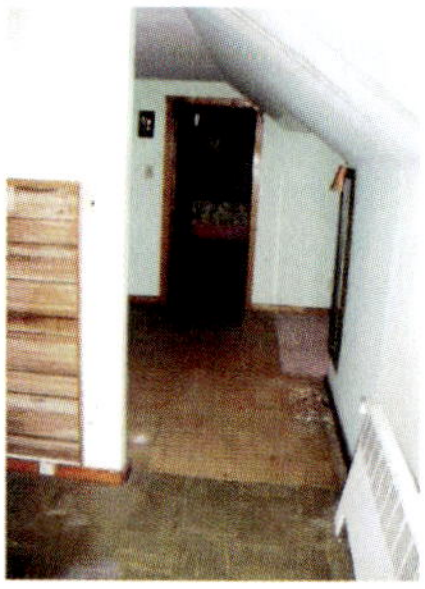

Figure 5.9
The shot from a webcam.

One of the issues you run into is the quality of the picture you get. Newer models with higher resolution have a better response time, but some have the feeling of those old shots of the astronauts in space. There is a delay of the information. Even on better cameras, you can get a great view of the bigger picture but the resolution gets worse as you zoom in.

IR Cameras and Nightvision

There are really two different types of cameras paranormal investigators talk about when they discuss IR cameras, which actually translates to hundreds of dollars from your wallet. The first is actual infrared cameras that take a heat measurement of an area and give you a thermal image. This falls more into the realm of the thermal imaging camera we will discuss later this chapter. These are very expensive and might not get you the best picture of a ghost.

The other IR camera really is just another term for a video camera that uses Nightvision or IR technology to generate useable light to help record things. As I already discussed, these are standard in the field today and well worth the investment. They work by amplifying all of the light in an area or by throwing invisible light on a scene that the camera can read but which does not disturb the environment you are in. Some claim that adding that light into a location may actually pick up a different wave of light and therefore see more, which will lead to recording more ghosts.

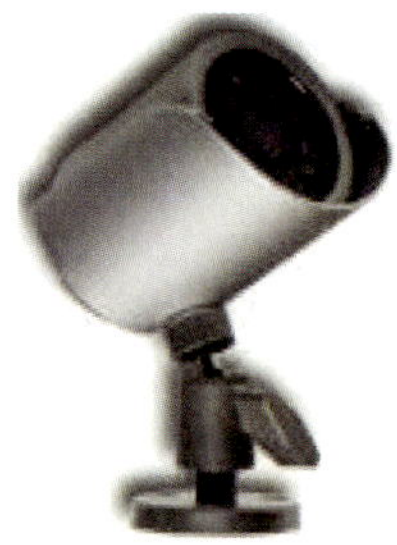

Figure 5.10
The Sony SuperHAD, which is one of the less expensive IR cameras at www.ghost-mart.com.
Picture courtesy of Ghost Mart.

When looking for the right camera, think about how you investigate. You should avoid making a large investment in them until you have seen what being in the field is like, but understand these cameras, or at least the kind that are mounted in a stationary position, are only good for investigating indoors.

Connecting It All Together

The trend in the paranormal world is to create a command center for investigating where one person stays behind and monitors everything that is going on. This seems to me like someone staying behind to watch security cameras at the mall. If you are out in the field, be out in the field. Every member of a team sitting looking at screens is another person who could be taking other readings or getting a still picture.

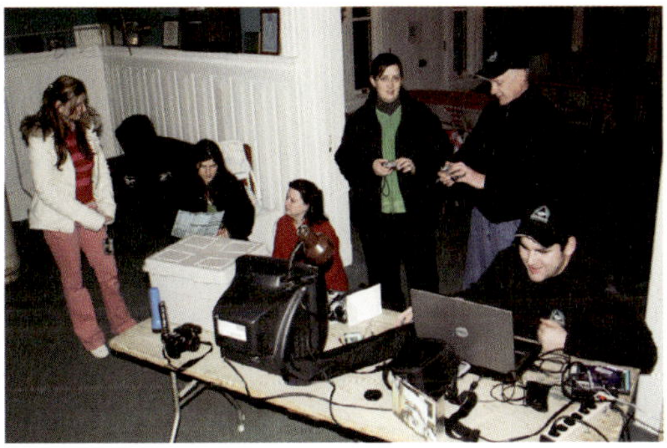

Figure 5.11
A command center for a paranormal investigation.
Picture courtesy of Josh Mantello.

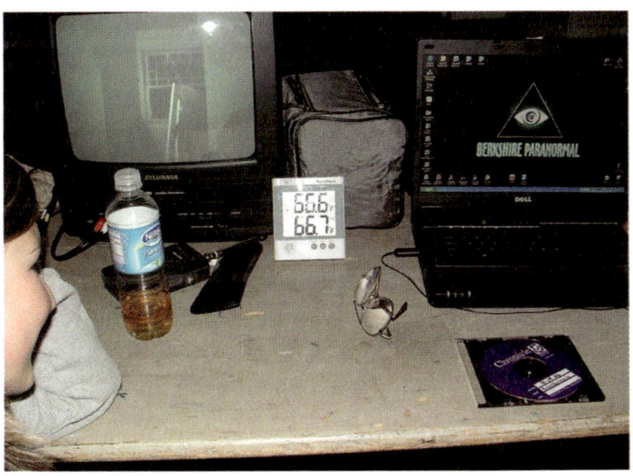

Figure 5.12
Behind the scenes of the command center.
Picture courtesy of Josh Mantello.

You should, however, have something set up to record from any cameras you have out in the field that do not have their own data storage. The easiest and least expensive method is to feed everything into a laptop. You can also feed them into old VCRs bought at yard sales, but then you are counting on metal tape technology and the resolution of those old VCR tapes leaves something to be desired. Creating still images off of them is also an issue.

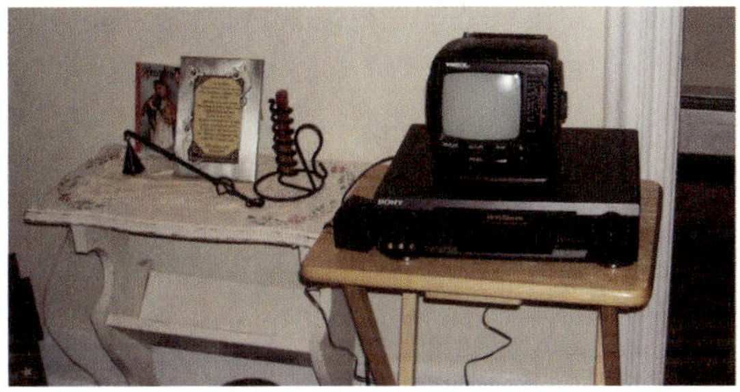

Figure 5.13
Going old school. The IR cameras here are hooked into an old VCR and television.

The newest idea in storage is the recordable DVR or digital video recorder. These work the same as a traditional VCR but they record to digital and not tape. This avoids the metal tape issue and creates a digital record you can manipulate, edit, and take snapshots of. The other advantage of the DVR is that you can hook multiple cameras into them and each has its own channel. You do not have to have multiple recorders or alternate cameras on the recording.

With DVRs, price does make the difference. You can purchase a less expensive one from a retailer or a paranormal marketplace like Ghost Mart (www.ghost-mart.com), for about $240, but people have complained about how those work in the field. The price goes up to $800 with additional features that are useful to investigators.

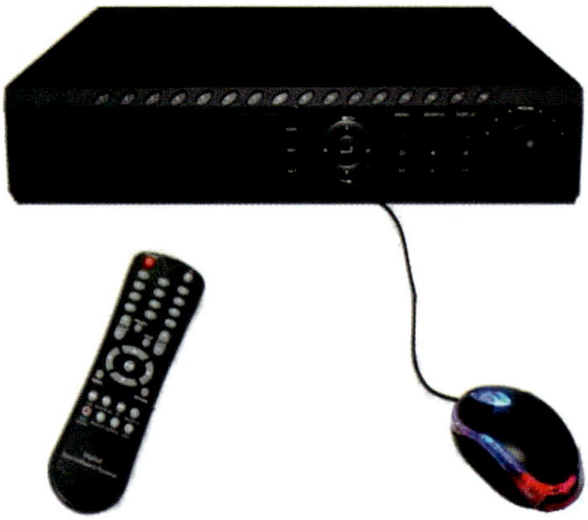

Figure 5.14
And new school. The 4 Channel SAMSUNG CPU MPEG4 Embedded LINUX Network Stand-Alone DVR which can be purchased at www.ghost-mart.com for under $800. Picture courtesy of Ghost Mart.

The average seems to be about $400, which is a large investment but one worth the price tag if you are serious about investigating.

Thermal Imaging

Let us return to basic high school science. Everything has a temperature to it, even inanimate objects that do not give off natural heat. Think of bringing an ice pack into a room and eventually it will lose its cold and become the same temperature as the rest of the room. Unless some chemical or mechanical reaction is going on, items in a room will roughly be the same temperature as the ambient temperature in the room. While living in Florida I learned the ambient temperature in a car parked in a parking lot for ten minutes is the same as outside, just hot enough to melt just about everything in the car. There is a give and take and then a balance reached.

Then you have the second important rule of heat. When there is a reaction going on, whether it be the biomechanical functions of a human or the lighting of a match, it will give off heat or take heat from the environment. This gives off radiation, which can be tracked and recorded. If ghosts are energy in some form they may give off heat or take heat in, which is the argument made by people who look to answer why cold and hot spots often occupy paranormal events. That change in heat can be seen using thermometers, but it can be recorded by using a thermal imager.

This high-tech piece of equipment measures the temperature in the room and shows increments on a screen by assigning each a color based on how much radiation it gives off. This type of seeing has been used for years by law enforcement, firefighters, and the military looking to find people who are otherwise hidden. This made it expensive and out of the reach of the everyday investigator. The most you could hope for was to get a firefighter on the team or to be part of a television show.

The price has come down somewhat, but it is still the most expensive item you will have in your toolbox. The low-end cameras run several thousand dollars and these would then need to be hooked up to some type of DVR to record any results you may get. The price scales up to over tens of thousands of dollars for a self-contained unit. This price tag takes it out of the hands of 99 percent of investigators, so do not be disappointed if you cannot get one. Some stores or companies offer to let people rent them, so it may be something you try out before investing anything for it.

In the Field

MY SON LOVES TO WATCH movies, but he gets bored of things like plot and storyline. At four he already knows that the best parts are the ones with action, and he also knows the remote control makes the boring parts go away. Hand him the remote, however, and he hasn't the slightest idea of what to do. The first time I was handed a tri-field meter, I did not have the slightest idea how it worked. I walked around the old military fort with it in front of me moving it from side to side and looking important. One of the investigators I was with asked me for a reading, but I did not know how to get one. I said, "Interesting. I want to see where this is going," which seemed to satisfy him. Then someone came along and turned it on for me with a laugh.

Having the right equipment is nothing without knowing why it is useful and how to use it. A simple idea like having extra film can keep an investigation from being a washout. Finding the right camera and equipment is the first step, and no matter how important of a step that is, the real work of capturing ghosts on film happens in your preparation and your work in the field. You have the right tool for the job. Now let's get ready for the job.

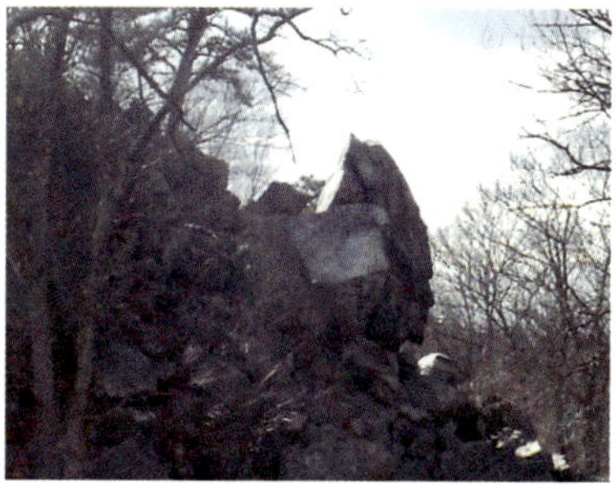

Figure 5.15
Does it matter? Three images of the same object from the same time period. This one is with a film camera.

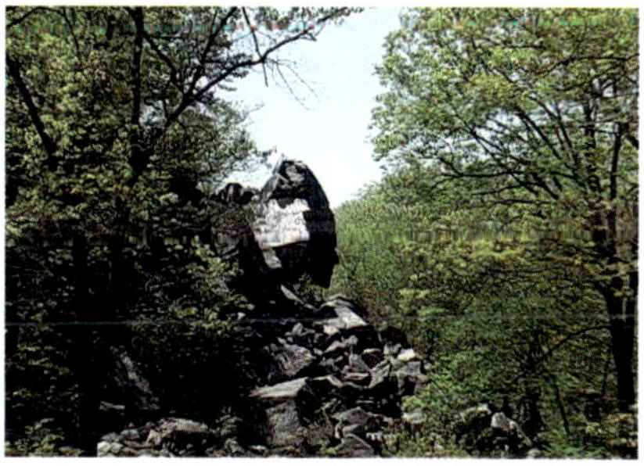

Figure 5.16
This one comes from a still on a video.

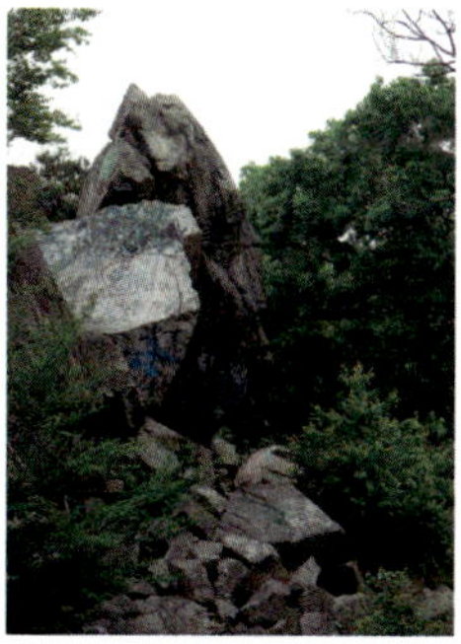

Figure 5.17
And this is the digital image. Judge and buy accordingly.

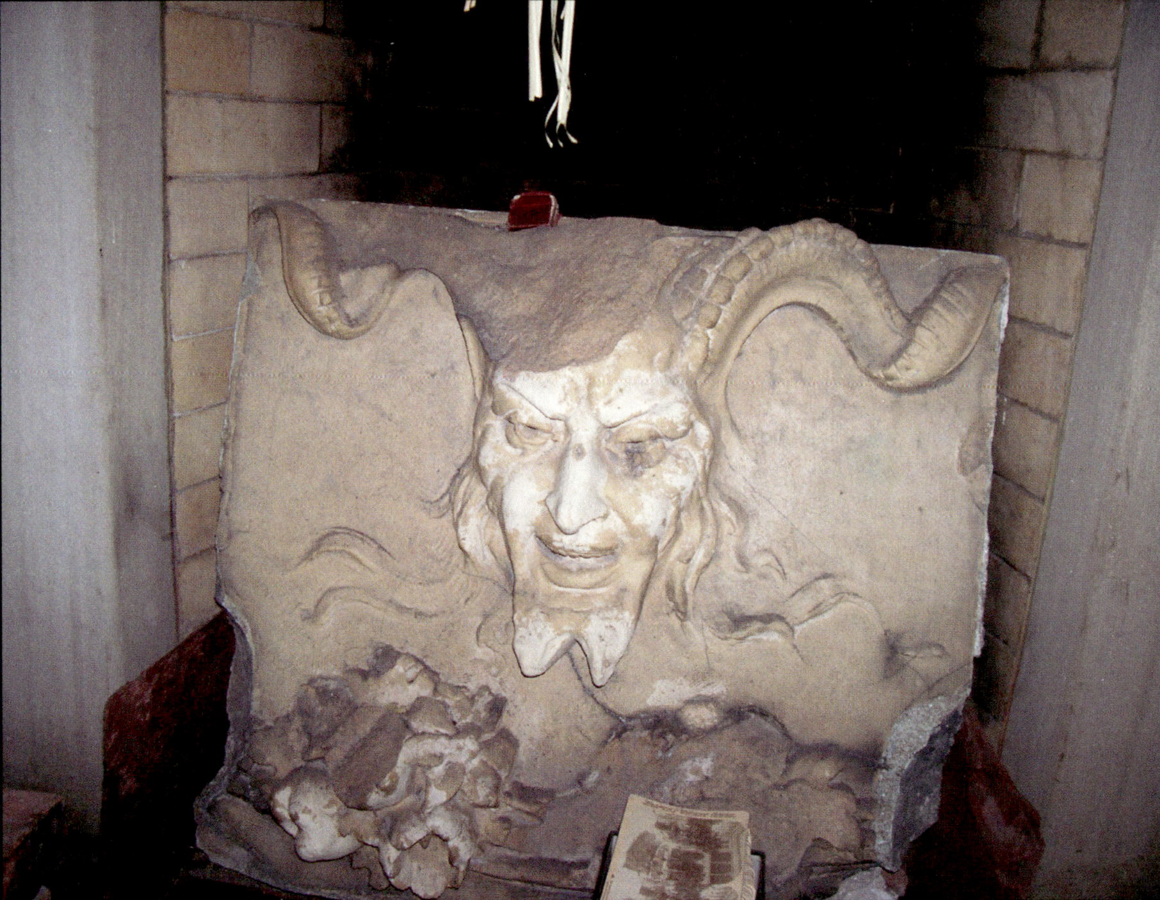

A picture in stone at a haunted location.
Picture courtesy of Tim Weisberg and Spooky Southcoast.

6

Before You Hit the Field

THERE IS A LINE FROM THE MOVIE *True Romance* that has always stuck with me and has set the tone for my investigative life. "If there is one thing I have learned this week is that it's better to have a gun and not need it than to need a gun and not have it." Assuming your ghost hunting does not involve actually carrying a gun, which I highly suggest it does not, the saying has more meaning for the equipment you bring into the field.

Investigating is equal parts preparation and observation. There were too many times during my early days in the field that I realized that I was ill equipped and needed something I didn't have. This feeling was always made worse when I knew I had the missing equipment and had left it at home. This chapter deals with picking the right equipment and then finding the best way to organize it so you don't lose your head, or your camera, in the heat of the moment.

I have always hated the phrase, "Failing to plan is planning to fail" and if you just throw your equipment together and go out on the investigation you may get very good results. It has been done before, and historically non-investigators have caught evidence by accident or in the heat of the moment, but a little planning and a little ritual will make it easier for you to transition from observer to photojournalist quickly in the field.

Good preparation for an investigation, at least as it pertains to getting visual evidence, can be broken down into three categories: equipment, date storage, and power and connection.

Equipment

THINK OF A PARANORMAL investigation like being the right fielder in a little league baseball game. Most of the players can't get the ball out to you, and you might spend more time playing with the butterflies than making the play. Investigating is long periods of boredom mixed with brief and sudden moments of excitement. Your adrenaline is pumping during those important moments, making you more likely to overlook something, and those chances are heightened by the fact you have been lulled to sleep during the down times. Think of running a sprint after your foot falls asleep. Better yet, think of it as having to win a cross-country skiing race after your foot falls asleep and you have to start by putting your skis on.

In *Picture Yourself Ghost Hunting*, I talked about my experiences at Fenway Park in Boston selling sausages. I placed my money in certain pockets so I would always know where my twenties and singles were. When investigating, if you know in which pocket a camera is or can robotically reach into a toolbox and pull out another roll of film, you will be able maximize your time and the amount of evidence you get. The more you are in the field, the more you will adopt the best place to put things so you can automatically, quick-draw your equipment. This all begins with knowing what you will need for any particular investigation.

The Equipment Equation

I like to think of things in mathematical terms sometimes. Even as a writing teacher, I find it useful to create a structure and then someone needs only fill in the template with their own information to create something. A while ago, I created this equation to help prepare myself for hitting the field.

Equipment = destination + manifestation − limitations

Think of it like this: your choice of equipment should be the balance of where you are going, what has been seen in the location or what witnesses have reported, and any issues you might have carrying all the equipment in your toolbox or on your person.

Destination

Where are you going and what time of day are you going? The classic investigation time is at night, but people who have been ghost hunting for long enough will tell you there is evidence to be gained during the daylight hours. More importantly, where are you going to be? For example, if you are going to be in a location where you will be moving, a tripod might not be the best use of your limited equipment space. Cameras that rely on a flash as their only source of lighting will be hard to use in small places where the flash will bounce off walls and reflect back, so keep them out of the catacombs below Paris and choose a different camera.

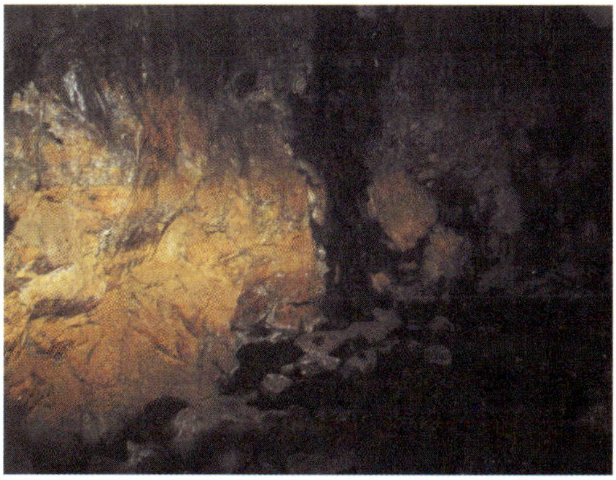

Figure 6.1
A haunted cave, not the best place for a tripod or a camera that needs a lot of setup.

Manifestation

If you are investigating with a whole team and have enough manpower and time, bring every tool you have. If there is limited time and only a few investigators, pay close attention to the background of the case and bring what will help you the most. For example, in a private residence people have heard an old man moan in their bedroom and a pounding on their wall every night for two weeks. They have never seen anything and the haunting does not seem to be intelligent. You may want to bring standard or baseline equipment, such as your EMF meter, but do not overload on cameras. You might catch something, but the general (a residual haunting is less likely to produce a picture because the energy present seems to be confined to one type of manifestation) and the specific (the people have never seen anything) tell you your time and space may be better spent focusing on other types of evidence.

Limitations

I remember the photographer at my sister's wedding had a beautiful young assistant whose sole job was to walk around with an elaborate flash setup on a stick. With the size of the church and the reception hall, this was necessary, and with the price Roger was charging for his services, he should have had a whole legion of assistants. If the wedding had occurred in a small cottage in the mountains, the flash stick lady would have had to be left at home. Every investigation has a certain variable, unpredictable element to it, and that is to be expected and embraced. You usually can go in knowing the terrain in which you will be asked to investigate, and you should prepare for it as specifically as possible. Don't bring a television monitor to an investigation in a cemetery and don't worry about the walkie-talkies in a two-room apartment.

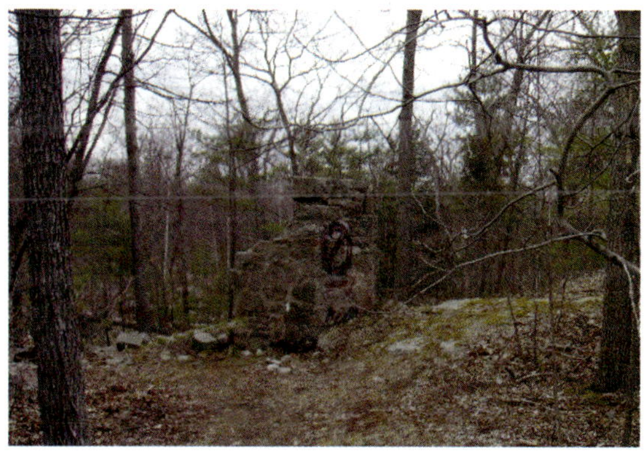

Figure 6.2
A marker on the mile hike through the woods to get to the cave. The limitations make this a hard place to investigate.
Picture courtesy of Bree Puliot.

Know Your Landscape: The Right Tool for the Right Setting

If you have a digital camera near you, hold it close. Look at the settings button, usually located on the top. Now, there may be some variation in this, but most will have this basic setup. There will be another knob with an abstract picture that you will be able to identify as a person. Then there is another usually representing a mountain, and maybe even another showing another person with a star shining behind her. We have discussed in earlier chapters the function of these buttons and what different settings mean, but for now think of it as a lesson in itself.

The camera company recognizes that not all pictures can be approached the same way, and one of the deciding factors in how to set your camera, or even what camera equipment to bring, is where you are going to shoot. Light, zoom, f/stop, aside from an experimentation you may be doing, all depend on where you are and what the conditions warrant. It is always good to be prepared for anything, but you also may have limited space and need to make decisions. Knowing your landscape will help to make some of those decisions.

Some of these suggestions may be common sense and others might seem like generalizations. The best piece of advice I can give you is to ignore everything I suggest if you think it might help, but think of these suggestions as the sound advice of several seasoned investigators who have searched for ghosts in all of these different environments.

A Smaller Residence

If you are in a situation where you are investigating a smaller residence, remember you cannot carry too much equipment in. Assuming you have some kind of video camera and a computer, whatever you need to shoot has to be on your person. Carry a more versatile camera that can shoot in low light without playing around with too many buttons. Chances are there will not be great lighting, and you also do not want to hit the location with too many tools. Even if the family is open to having you in to investigate, if you have more ghost hunting equipment than they have furniture, they may be intimidated by it.

A Larger Residence

This may be the ideal setting for an investigation. Although I have left equipment at an investigation before (maybe a subconscious attempt to be invited back), there is little chance of losing valuables, so bring all you can. Use both film and digital cameras, and bring plenty of video. With furniture and the right number of investigators, there are plenty of places to leave video cameras in a stable place. You may have the same lighting issues if you are snapping pictures at night and you will need to watch for reflective surfaces, but you will have time to evaluate each room, so you can document any potential bumps in the road.

Being in a larger location also means your equipment will be thin to cover all you need to see. Take advantage of a computer and a webcam in an area where there has been more activity reported and consider several tripods with video if your team has them. One of the common mistakes new investigators make is to have seven people in one room with their still and video cameras. If you have the numbers, spread out. Some will say there should be a buddy system in place, and I agree with this when you are investigating a large area. If you are in a residence or a confined area, to confirm things that were seen and done, a camera recording everything is as good as having a virtual buddy.

It has become very popular to "go dark" and shut off all the lights when investigating a house or indoor haunted landmark. I think this has more to do with ambiance than actual paranormal science. We will address the value of Nightvision in Chapter 7, but for now let me keep it simple. More light in the room means less of a need for a flash. Less flash means there is a smaller chance of having the flash bounce off anything from dust to a mirror on the wall. There is a time and place for darkness during an investigation, but think of it more as a complimentary part of the investigation.

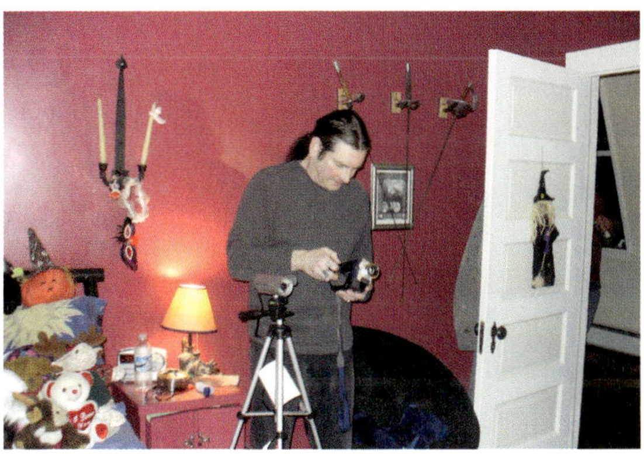

Figure 6.3
This larger house allowed investigator Tom D'Agostino to use multiple video cameras during the investigation.

An Abandoned Building (That You Have Permission to Be In, Of Course)

I am going to assume you have permission, so you will not need to run away from law enforcement. If you are investigating during the day, bring cameras that are geared towards shooting scenery and not portraits. Also, leave your $500 camera at home. There are a dozen things that can go wrong that have nothing to do with being chased out by a demon, and your camera will be the first thing you forget. If you plan on covering a large area in the building, break it down into workable segments, which we will cover in Chapter 7, and use all you can in one area before moving on to the next.

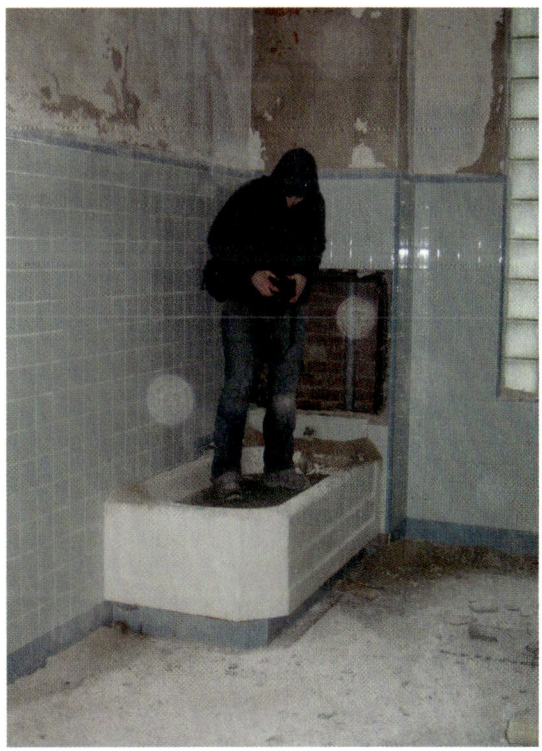

Figure 6.4
This shot was taken in summer at an abandoned asylum. Although the frozen water in the bathtub is unexplained, the orbs can be explained away easily.

If you are investigating at night, it is a different beast all together. Some will hate me for saying this, and I say it with some hesitation, but rely on video evidence and leave the camera at home. Okay, keep one with you, but there is very little need. There are too many variables in the setting for you to get any evidence that is beyond explanation. You will spend hours looking at dust orbs trying to figure out which are dust, which are water or bugs, and which are reflections of flashes from other investigators. If you use Nightvision you will be equally frustrated at how easily your ghosts can be dismissed. Why go through the aggravation? You can spend that time looking through the video for potential spirits.

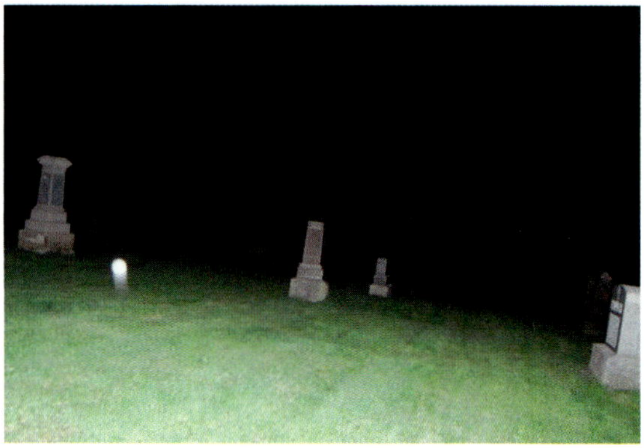

Figure 6.5
Cemetery orbs are a common occurrence.
Picture courtesy of Allen Dunski.

A Cemetery or Graveyard

Unless you are in a mausoleum or enclosed tomb of some kind (which most people will never enter and seems more the realm of treasure hunters than ghost hunters), any investigation in a cemetery is going to involve weather. A common preface to an outside picture someone sends me, usually from a cemetery, is that it was not raining when the picture was taken. That does not always matter. There is moisture in the air, and if it had rained earlier that day, you can even kick up a bit and get a great orb. This might be another time to leave the digital camera at home.

It is also important to remember you are surrounded by reflective surfaces. There is a great paranormal motif of the glowing headstone. People are drawn in to certain boneyards because they are known to have a headstone that glows an eerie color at night, usually accompanied by a glowing ghost of a woman. Trouble is, the stone they make most markers from will reflect any light near them, especially the light from celestial bodies. That is why the cemetery is lit during a full moon. This become worse when you use Nightvision on your camera because it works on the basic premise of intensifying existing light.

An Outside Location

This may be a bit better for taking pictures because you will not have as many glowing rocks, but depending on the area, you might have to think of yourself as a mobile unit. Chances are there will be no command center, so what you can reach on your person is what you can use. It might not be the best place to have a heavy toolbox full of equipment. Also, the chances of losing expensive gear is greater. You might want to stick with disposable cameras and make sure to note what you are shooting into.

Minimize the Old Mistakes

We will evaluate a picture taken of the ghost of Elvis in Chapter 8. The most common response for why it may not be the King is that the picture is most likely a camera strap. By taking a few steps with your camera equipment ahead of time, you will be able to have an answer for many of these issues. These suggestions can apply to digital and film cameras, as well as video cameras.

Remove the camera strap. **You can store the camera in a safe place, and you most likely use it throughout most of the investigation. You do not really need to have the strap dangling.**

Clean the camera before you leave. **It might seem like common sense to clean the lens, but there are other places dust and dirt can get into, especially where you load the film.**

Make sure there is nothing on the camera. **I was using a digital camera and got what I thought was a glimmer spirit. I looked at the screen and saw it clear as day, but when I looked at the camera, a piece of plastic from one of the disposable cameras I had with me had stuck to the lens.**

Go back to home. **Make sure all of your settings are at a basic place and adjust them in the field. You are more likely to forget to turn your Nightvision off than on, and a picture taken during the day with Nightvision may hurt your camera or just give you bad evidence.**

Know your cap. **Too many of the moments of my youth are lost because my dad clicked away before taking the lens cap off. Either go without one, or keep it in mind. Many newer cameras have a button that snaps it open or the lens opens when you turn the camera on, but if not, be mindful.**

The Forgotten Piece of Equipment

There are so many things you cannot predict in the field, and so many of the predicable elements are subject to being influenced by seen and unseen forces. There are settings on a camera that mean the slightest movement can create a smudged or false positive picture, and when something intense and unexplained happens, you are more prone to move your hands. If only there was something that could hold a camera in a stable environment and eliminate some of these variables that give investigators inaccurate results.

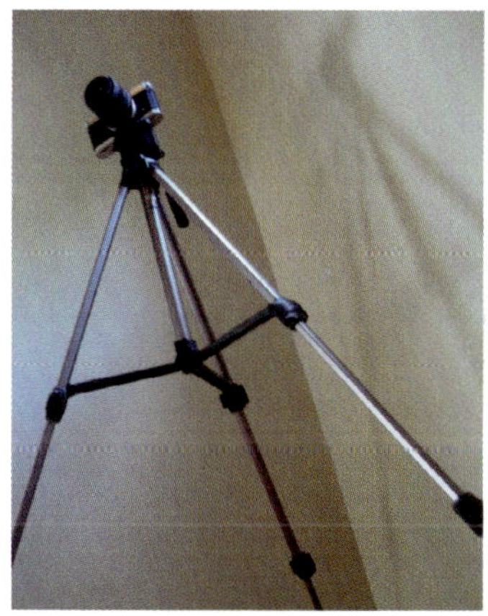

Figure 6.6
A basic tripod. Picture courtesy of Josh Mantello.

Many paranormal investigators use a tripod to keep a running diary of the investigation or to set up a video camera to monitor a room while they are in another room, but very few use a tripod to take still pictures. Almost none of the investigators who were surveyed used them, and none of them used them with a digital camera. The one who did use it gave this explanation for why he incorporated it with one of his cameras, "This camera is expensive, and I don't want to break it. It's better to keep it on the tripod so I don't drop it."

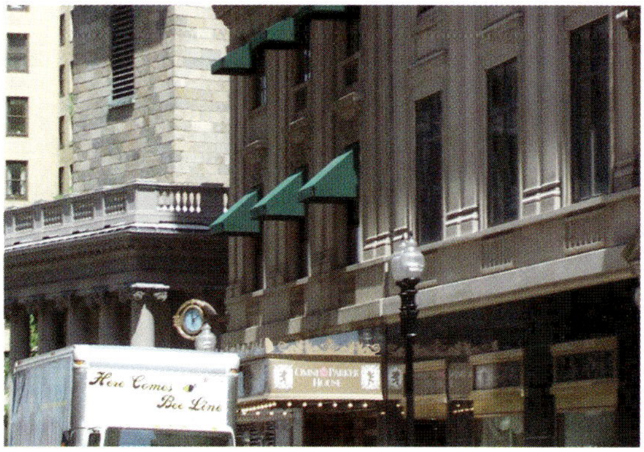

Figure 6.7
A picture taken of the famously haunted Omni Parker House in Boston. With no tripod and fighting car and foot traffic, this is the shot I got.

Investigation does not always equate to movement. There is a misconception because of the media attention and the need for motion on television, that there needs to be a high level of running during an investigation. I cannot remember an investigation I have been on that involved me running somewhere, although there were times in my early days I ran away from something. Being a responsible investigator usually means creating a grid and exploring each part of that grid, which we will talk about more in Chapter 7, which means the majority of your investigating is done while you are still. Why not take advantage of the stillness and set up a tripod?

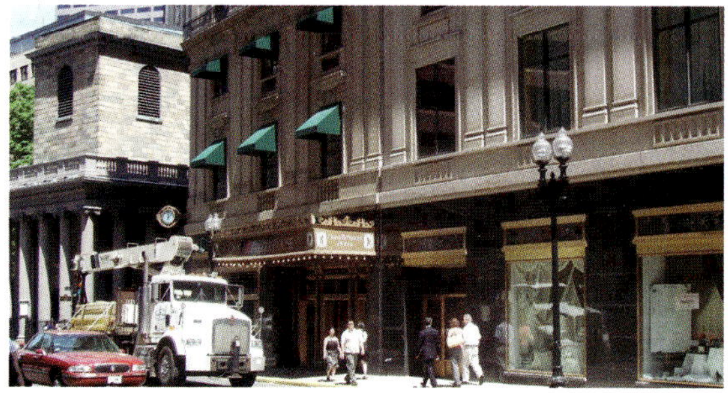

Figure 6.8
The same location the next day with a tripod.

Compared to some of the equipment that has been created or is now geared towards investigators, a tripod is a relatively cheap piece of equipment that can dramatically improve the quality of your pictures. The price of a tripod is usually based on how easily you can set it up and take it down, or the different ways you can manipulate it to increase or decrease its size and the angles you can shoot at. You can get a very serviceable one, and one that will give you everything you realistically need, for under $30.

It does take a while to master the use of a tripod. "I've always wanted to use them, but they're just too much work," says Jason Warrick of Tampa's Southern Ghost League. "It's hard enough to get evidence while you are out there. I can't take the time to get those legs unscrewed and adjusted. I can just hold my hand still or prop the camera on something and get the same result." Other investigators gave similar responses. Another investigator claimed, "a tripod restricts movement and fluidity."

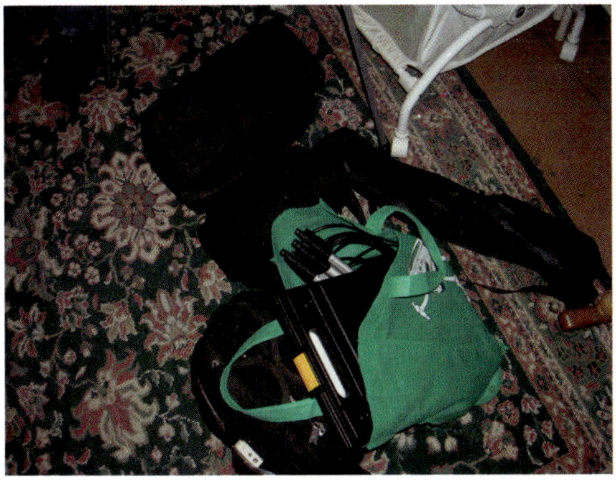

Figure 6.9
The easy to carry piece of equipment.
There are three tripod and three cameras pictured, all of which can be carried easily.

A tripod may only take two minutes to set up, yet many of the same investigators who do not use them spend much more time than that setting up elaborate audio equipment or unpacking EMF equipment and trying to get baseline information. Make the time and incorporate a tripod into your investigation. If you are looking into a residence where there is a room with more activity than the others, it is almost a necessity, and not just for video cameras.

For $7 I bought a tripod off a major retailer website. When in its case, it measures a little less than two feet and includes a bag that slings around my shoulder. When I take it out and stretch the legs out to their first level, meaning I would only have to make a few adjustments to place it on the ground, load a camera, and click away, it is slightly less than three feet. If you are going to be in the same place for more than 20 minutes, the carrying and assembling is a small investment.

Five Suggestions for Tripod Photography

- **Practice ahead of time.** Tripods are only logical to people who know how to use any particular one. There are little tricks to each one, so knowing how to use it ahead of time will make it much easier in the field.
- **Attach a camera to the head and keep it there.** You might want to get or recycle a camera and designate it as your tripod camera. Once you understand how to work your legs, you can save time by screwing a camera in and clicking it into place. Having it on during the whole investigation will allow you to put the tripod and camera into action quickly.
- **Don't get too cute.** There are dozens of adjustments you can make, but you don't need to make all of them for the perfect shot. The goal of using a tripod is to create a stable picture, so concentrate on keeping the camera still and not making the shot artistic.
- **Use your head.** Once you have set up legs, the main manipulation of a tripod should be from the head, not the body. On most you can get almost an unlimited frame just by using the arm attached to the head. For shots of the ground directly in front of the setup, you are on your own.
- **There is no setting where a tripod is completely out of the picture.** If you are scaling walls or swimming a long distance to get to your investigation, you may be left empty-handed, but other than that, it is not as hard as you think to sling the tripod bag over your shoulder.

Data Storage

ON MY VERY FIRST INVESTIGATION, I went deep into a haunted area in Massachusetts known as the Bridgewater Triangle. The town was so famously haunted, and we were so inexperienced as investigators, we were able to hit five locations during the seven hours we were there. It was a few years before the digital camera craze, so we all had film cameras with very few bells and whistles and no special film or add-ons. We snapped more than a dozen rolls of film, making sure to carefully store each used roll in those old black, plastic cases in the glove box of the car. There was a shadowy figure in an old burned down mill and an incident of hands being felt on our ankles in one cemetery we visited. We were snapping pictures as this was happening. The night ended when we were chased out of the largest cemetery in town by something stomping through the leaves alongside of us. We escaped from the town with our lives but no evidence. Every picture from every roll was gone. The glove compartment was empty, and all we had were our memories and a few pictures on the cameras we had in our hands.

Perhaps something sinister had removed the pictures, or perhaps we had just misplaced our hard work, but in the eyes of the outside world, our investigation may have been for nothing.

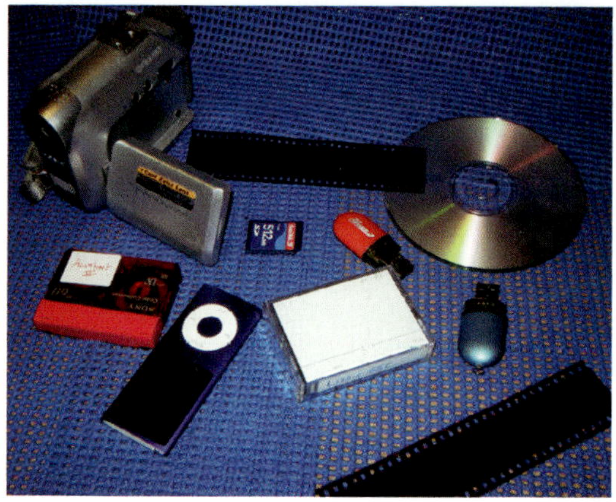

Figure 6.10
Some of the many ways we carry our pictures out of an investigation.

Regardless of the forces working against us, we were ill prepared for being out in the field. The issues are different nowadays, but the premise of preparedness is still the same. Unlike other equipment you may bring into the field that relies on human observation to work well, like checking a meter or thermometer, getting visual evidence during an investigation needs to have data storage to have a life after you get home. Many of the tools you use will have some kind of internal memory, but there is a very real need to have enough memory or enough film to record the events of the hunt, which means you need to have something to keep it on and some place to store it when you are done. Know what your equipment needs, feed the beast its favorite food, and be consistent when storing materials.

Snapshot

Be organized when you store your images and other evidence. Create organized digital files and make sure you know the path to get to them. Think about naming evidence based on the location and by date so you can travel back and forth between investigations and results, especially when you have been to the same place more than once.

Film

As we have already gotten into, never enter the field with only digital cameras. Depending on the quality of your camera and your needs, you may have only the most basic of film cameras, but it adds that dimension you may need for the best picture. If you have disposable cameras, unwrap them ahead of time and store them so you can toss one and grab the other. If you have film rolls, unwrap them as well and break the seal on the container. Think of the old photojournalist trying to get the perfect shot by hanging seven cameras around his neck. Rather than reload, he just grabbed another and never missed a step. You may not have to go to that extreme, but the idea is the same. The less time you spend loading film, the more time you have to get a good shot if something happens you want to record.

I am a heavy advocate of carrying a bag that stays over my shoulder on an investigation. For years I have used a small backpack I got at a sporting goods store. It is large enough, and has enough pockets for me to have all I need to be mobile during an investigation and small enough to not get in the way. The strap can be pulled tight against my shoulder, and when I am done with a roll of film, I can slide it into its container and toss it in the bag. I can do the same with disposable cameras. I place one or two in the pockets of the bag and toss them into it when I'm done.

The First Picture

Try to be beyond reproach with gathering evidence. When you open up a container ahead of time, there may be some exposure to the first picture on the negative. The chance is slim, but don't risk it. As soon as you load the film, snap off one shot of nothing or get a shot of one of the investigators you are with so you remember who you investigated with later. You may even be able to use it on your site so people can see how you investigate. Make note to think twice before using that picture for evaluation.

Snapshot

If you choose to use a film camera, keep one of those black or gray containers empty at all times. Go into the field with one empty and then your first roll just gets put into the empty and the one you are pulling out becomes the next empty one. Always think one function of the equipment ahead of time.

Digital

A digital camera is a different kind of beast, and there are some different challenges to getting your digital camera ready for the field. The main issue becomes one of power, which we will get into a little later in the chapter. Data storage can be a challenge as well, but with the size and memory of today's digital storage, this has become easier.

External or Internal, That Is the Question

Most digital cameras come with an internal memory, and the better cameras come with an entire hard drive. Ignore it. It should be used as a backup or even a quick fix if something happens while you switch storage, but it may unreliable. If something happens to your camera, including having it break, you may lose any evidence you have gotten. It may seem like a horrible waste when you consider the hard drive in some of them, but it can get confusing in the field. I have spent too much time waiting while someone made sure the right memory was being used during an investigation and had to weed through too many old pictures not relevant to the ghost hunt during the evaluation.

The price of high memory external drives makes them a viable option in the field. You can purchase a 2 GB memory card or stick from a retail store for under $20. You may go an entire investigation, if you are just taking pictures, and not need a second one. Remember, storage is like anything you buy in a store: it will cost you less to buy one twice as big than to buy two cards of equal size. Get a high numbered memory card and reduce your reloading time.

> **Snapshot**
>
> **Would you buy a pricey bucket over a cheap one to wash your car? There is some difference in the quality of external cards or sticks, but there really is no noticeable quality drop for going with a cheaper card. Companies will say name-brand equipment should be used together, but I have not seen the justification with the evidence. I have never said, "Wow, the memory on this Kodak card is just amazing." It may be a place to save a bit of money.**

Video and Recording Equipment

Much of the same rules apply to video cameras as digital cameras, but there are some differences. Most high-definition cameras have a large built-in memory that rivals some older computers. A digital picture will give you a better representation and allow the camera to make full use of its range. It will also make for a quicker transfer during the evaluation and you eliminate a conversion from digital to tape, which while it is not as dramatic as scanning an old photo, is still downgrading your evidence. If that is not available to you, try to get a camera that burns directly to CD or DVD.

I remember using and reusing old audio tapes. We would run a magnet over the tape and reset all of the information. Tape is the most unreliable data storage in the field, even harder to deal with than the film from a film camera.

While you are ghost hunting, you will potentially be coming into contact with ghosts and spirits that are known to produce or generate large fields of electromagnetic energy. That can run havoc on metal-based tape.

If you must use it, make sure you follow a similar process as with camera film. Load your first film and keep the empty case. Unwrap two or three tapes depending on the time you intend to be in the field and keep them in a place where you can access them. In getting ready, always assume pieces of equipment that run, like video, will be going during the entire investigation and prepare that much film. You probably will not keep it running the whole time, but it is good to have more than you need. An investigation might go long, or another recorder will go down and one will have to step up in its place.

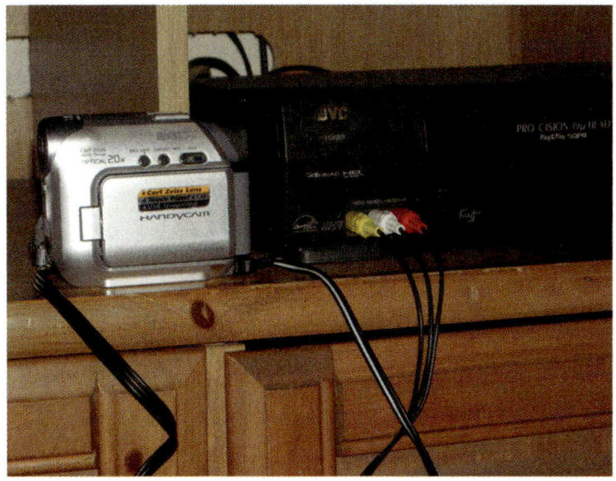

Figure 6.11
One example of a video camera plugged into an old VCR for monitoring and recording.

Monitoring Your Progress

Look behind your new television or stereo equipment and be prepared to need a degree from MIT to fully understand what is going on. Compatibility seems to be the desire of technology today, and examining any newer piece of audio or video equipment, even a computer, begs the user to try and connect things we used to not see working together. A few loose cords and I was able to plug my new baby monitor into my VCR and record my daughter sleeping.

In the field, these types of connections can be important. Many of the people I know who take video cameras in the field connect them to some device to allow another level of monitoring.

Personal DVD players and old television monitors can all be used to record the exact activity of a group in a haunted location. With the right knowledge and experimentation, three independent pieces of equipment can work together, and the versatility seems to go even beyond what the designers had in mind.

This can be a sticky situation with some investigators, and before designing a new recording system, think of its usefulness. Some investigators get so caught up in whether they can do something they forget to ask if it is useful. An investigator showed me a setup where he had a video camera hooked up to a DVD player; he had installed a remote, wireless connection to a monitor that could record the events the camera witnessed on a VCR tape. Although it works fairly well, he was dumbfounded when I asked him why he didn't just use the tape in the video camera. Don't get too cute. The simplest way to do things is often the best, and in a field where evidence is usually looked at by a third party, it is important to have your images be as explainable as possible.

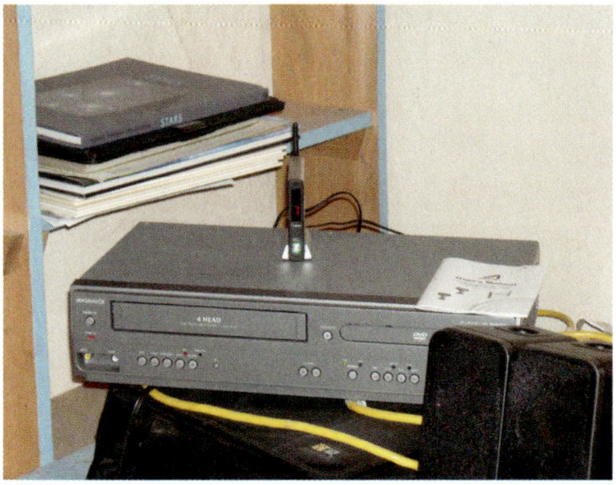

Figure 6.12
Another example of monitoring and recording. This VCR is linked to two Nightvision cameras like the one in Figure 6.13

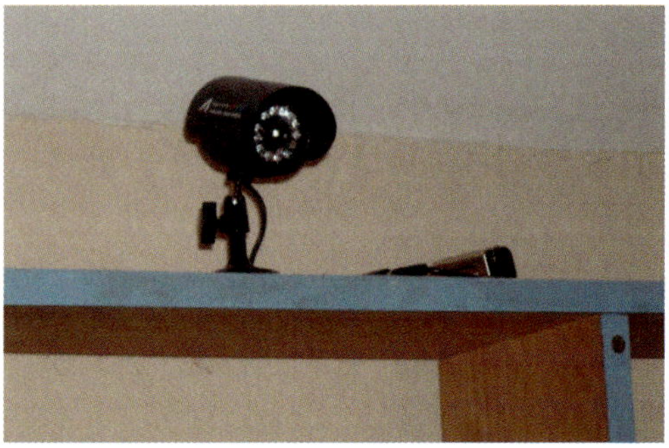

Figure 6.13
A Nightvision camera.

I am, however, a big fan of finding things at yard sales and converting them, and if you have the opportunity to get old video cameras, VCRs, and televisions, get them, even if there is an issue with the camera. I also like to find old baby video monitors at yard sales. For under $10 you might be able to produce a Nightvision camera that you can run into a VCR for recording.

It might not produce the best evidence, but it makes an excellent stationary monitoring system and provides a running account of the investigation.

Computers and Command Centers

I was impressed the first time I watched a television show do a paranormal investigation with a home base; in this case, a room within the house with television monitors and a computer set up with multiple cameras. The commitment to investigating of some groups, along with the dipping cost of video equipment, makes creating a computerized system with multiple cameras much easier, especially with groups pulling together money for equipment.

We discussed in Chapter 3 some of this equipment, but there is a need to prepare how to record what you are using. A balance has to be made between watching and recording. During an investigation, if the location is big enough, it might be important to have several cameras running and being run through a centralized recorder. At times the best arrangement is one that allows you to not have to think about it.

If your computer can handle it, get several webcams, which can be purchased for under $20, and run them to your computer. If you need USB extensions, it will still cost you less than expensive security cameras, and they need no batteries or power. They can also all be run through your computer and recorded. The downside is that the resolution and reaction time may be slower than conventional cameras, and many do not have Nightvision, but as technology gets better and cheaper, having a clearer picture becomes more realistic.

We Have Power

I HAD SET UP A STATIONARY camera in a room where people had reported hearing a man moan late at night. No one lived in the attic, so the people I was investigating with thought it was worth setting up a camera there for the duration of the investigation. We found the perfect corner of the attic that allowed us to see everything that was going on. I plugged the camera into an extension cord and looked around for the nearest outlet. I couldn't find one, so I got ready to reposition the camera by looking for a power source. Nothing. Eventually I gave up, reset the camera in the original position, and let it run for the life of the battery, Shortly after the battery ran out we heard a moan coming from the attic.

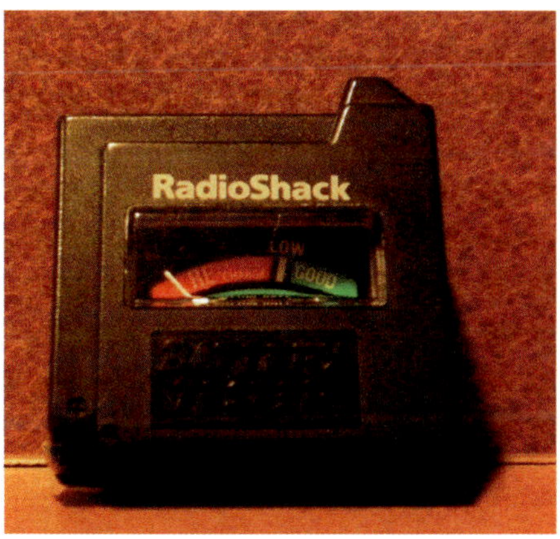

Figure 6.14
The battery tester, the paranormal lifesaver.

The first half hour of an investigation is often the time when people get the most evidence, but it is also a time when people can lose evidence because they have not prepared for the hunt in front of them. Power and connections need to be thought of ahead of time.

Batteries

Pictures may be a great way to prove to people you have experienced a ghost, but there are other common ways to report a ghostly presence. People often speak of a drop in temperature or a cold spot in the room. That is all well and good, but any investigator will tell you a better sign of paranormal activity, and one they often have to deal with, is the annoying practice of having to change out batteries when they mysteriously drain during an investigation.

Know this is going to happen and plan for it. Always have three or four layers of backup for your power supplies. This means if your camera takes three AA batteries, you should have nine to twelve AAs with you. They may be used for other reasons, but have them on hand. This is easy to say when you can go to your local store and buy a supply of Duracells. It becomes increasingly harder, and more of a hit to the wallet, the more expensive your equipment is.

The more expensive cameras have their own power sources, and replacements often start over $50. Using a video camera, especially one made in the last three years, means the price may be more into the $100 range.

Ask yourself these questions when you go to buy accessories and equipment. What do you need more and what are you out in the field for? Are you going to take the plunge and upgrade your EMF meter or get yourself a Geiger counter? These are legitimate things to add to your collection, but their results can be tainted and ignored by many of your peers who will throw around phrases like "false positive" and don't trust anything they didn't get themselves. A better investment might be in getting backup for your power supplies. It might feel like buying car insurance for something you never take out of the garage, but it is always the moment you don't have it that you need it.

Snapshot

Don't dip into your own power if you don't have to. Whenever possible, especially during a residential investigation, use the power already in the location. Plugging in a camera may help prevent power drain, but it will also make it easier to run your equipment for longer without having to switch power sources. If you have a stationary camera, plug it in. Keep in mind you never know what a house might have for outlets and where they may be. Part of your paranormal toolbox should be extension cords and adaptors.

Cords

When my grandfather passed away several years ago, we were left with the task of going through his workshop before selling the house. He was a bit of a packrat. He died at the age of 93, and some of the old radios and kitchen gadgets we found down there might have been older than he was. He had over 100 discs worth hundreds of thousands of hours of free Internet as promotions from different Internet providers, but he had no idea what they were and had no computer. He just didn't think anything should ever be thrown away.

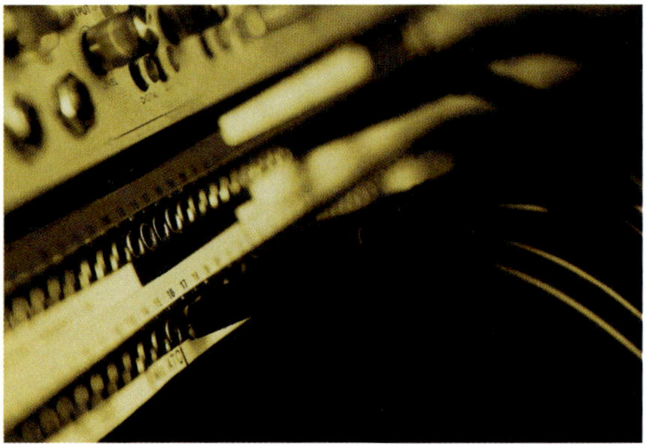

Figure 6.15
The back of a recorder.

One thing he kept, which I have incorporated into my life and my paranormal toolbox, is cords. You never know what kind of cord will be needed to bring two pieces of equipment together, so always have more than you'll need. This has served me well in my house as well as my investigations. This can get cumbersome, so I suggest having a separate toolbox just for cords. The ones that are needed for an investigation should be in a bag that can be stored out of the way until needed, while the wildcard cord can be left in your trunk.

Think of every wire you need to connect your equipment and have it handy, even if you will never use it. For example, if you have a digital camera with a USB connection, have that wire with you in case you want to view or save your pictures on site. If your video camera can be hooked up to a television with coaxial cables, have them in a safe and easy to get to place.

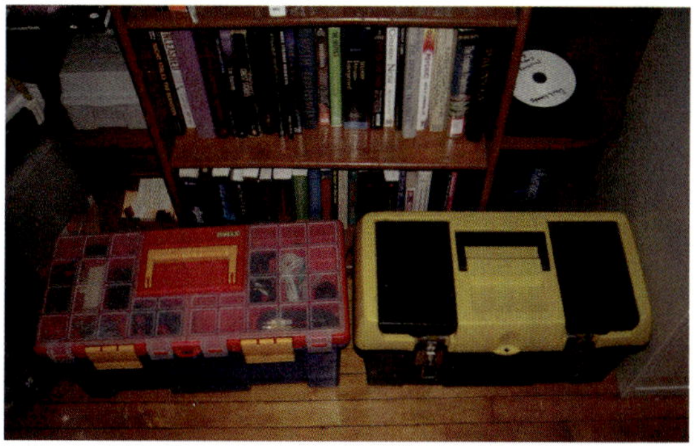

Figure 6.16
My paranormal setup with one toolbox for equipment and another just for cords and additional power supplies.

Save all your cords, even if you get rid of the equipment. I had two old cell phone chargers for my car that could not connect to my phone. I kept the chargers and the old phone, and when my battery got drained during an investigation, I plugged my old phone in and charged the battery before putting it back in my new phone. These cords are meant to connect two or more devices, and they have a way of being able to take on new life, even if you have no experience with electronics. There are a limited number of types of connections, so a little mixing and matching and you can find a use for almost any one. At some point, all good investigators have had to become MacGyver in a haunted house.

Wrap Up

IT'S SAID THAT TOP ATHLETES visualize the game long before it ever happens and see themselves making the plays over and over. Science has proven this process actually helps to cement behavior patterns more than practicing the play in real time, although it does not prepare their bodies as well. So much of an investigation happens before a ghost hunter hits the field. This has to do with understanding what might happen in the field, but also with visualizing what equipment might be needed and the trouble that might come with it. Now that the equipment is ready to go, it is time to investigate and begin to see how the visual aspect of your investigation completes the right paranormal approach.

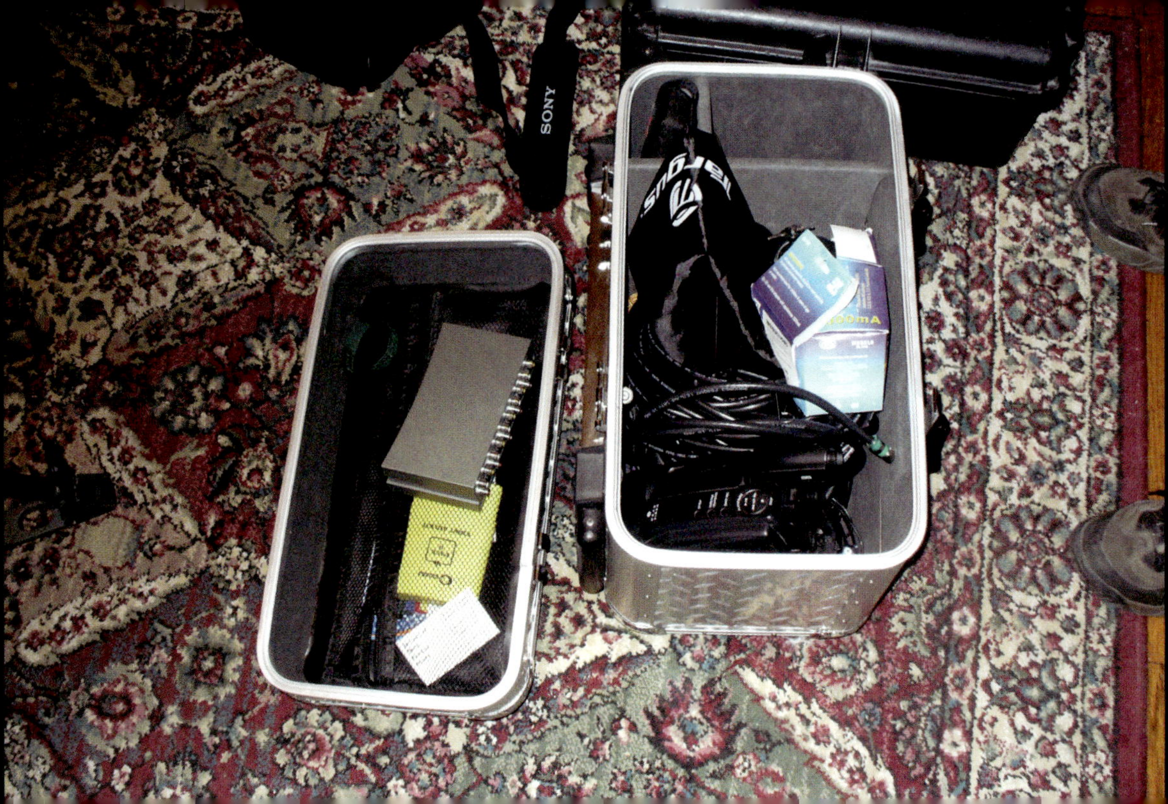
SONY

7

The Afterlife in the Field

Compelling to me means there is absolutely no doubt as to what you are looking at. We have captured some black mist and ectoplasm that we could not debunk. This would be compelling visual evidence to us.

—Alan Dunski

Ideally a full apparition. Orbs just don't do it for me. I want to see something physically there that could not have possibly been there when the picture was taken.

—Jessica Stone

Photos that match up with history, energy, or psychic readings. Quality shots that show faces or body forms.

—Robyne Marie

I would say that I have never seen compelling visual evidence, but I have a lot of interesting pictures and video that make me think that we are not alone.

—Louis Antonucci

It all comes down to this. You have documented the haunting as told to you by other people who have had experiences. You have packed your toolbox and have a basic idea how you are going to attack the location. You placed batteries in every spare pocket you could find just in case.

It is time to go out there and try to find some ghosts, and when it comes to using cameras, you are ready to capture some on film. Unlike some other types of evidence gathered during an investigation, your images can be stored and scrutinized, so pick up your toolbox, run through a few more things in your head, and go get some ghosts.

You're Halfway Out the Door

THERE IS SOMETHING YOU are forgetting; it will not make your investigation a complete loss, but it may be the difference between just going out and ghost hunting and getting evidence that may make the time more than worth it. Think of this section as your parent annoying you as you are about to head out to school as a middle school student. Did you remember your homework and your lunch? What are you doing after school today? I will spare you the kiss on the forehead and telling you I love you, but I will ask you to take inventory of some things before you start to investigate.

What Are You Trying to Do?

Gaining evidence, or more accurately, your motivation in getting evidence, is a balance between what you think constitutes compelling or strong proof of a ghost and what you can do in a setting during the limited time you have there.

By adding cameras to your investigation, which is often thought of as the first level of the paranormal toolbox, you are committing yourself to spending time taking pictures. Video that runs during the entire investigation aside, this means you will spend less time taking readings of temperature or electromagnetic waves or any other number of ghost hunting methods. Is it worth it?

You can handle doing a little bit of everything, and the more investigators you have on site, the better you can manage it, but a few decisions need to be made. Included in your reasoning should be how much weight you put into the science of the other activities you could be doing during the investigation and how important you think those things are. If you do not buy into temperature as an accurate measure of paranormal activity, or if it is enough for you to just note you felt the temperature drop, then you should not spend too much time running around with a digital thermometer. Maybe an ambient one set in the area you are investigating is enough.

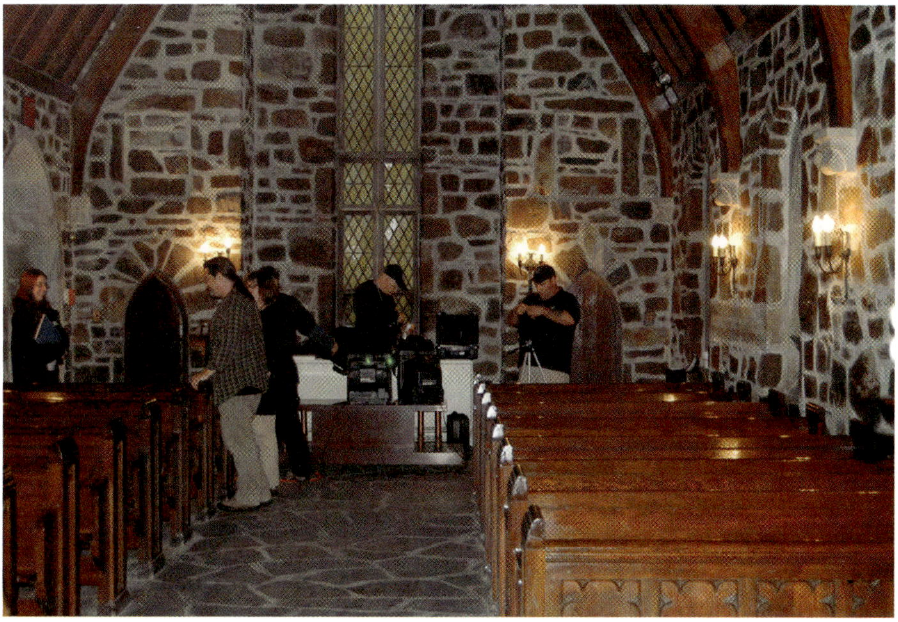

Figure 7.1
When planning how to hit a certain location, map it out ahead of time or when you first get to the location.
Picture courtesy of Josh Mantello.

Go through this evaluation before you and the team you are working with leave for the investigation. Think about the type of activity that has been documented and what the environment is like. This kind of balancing was discussed in the previous chapter, but now you have to make a commitment to it as the investigation begins. You brought equipment for a specific reason; remember that as you move forward.

Documentation vs. Evidence

There are two different ideas behind the major function of visual equipment during an investigation, but a good investigator needs to pick a bit from column A and a bit from column B. I have the argument with people all the time about the role of equipment, but hitting a haunting from both levels will produce a full account of the moment as well as act as a scalpel.

As we have already discussed, cameras pick up things our eyes are not able to. Their range and speed allow the investigator to look at an environment in a completely new way; however, there are some old-fashioned ideas you need to embrace. Cameras and video can be used to get evidence you may not capture with your human eye, and you should lean on this equipment to do that. Also, remember this equipment needs to be used to document what you are doing. You need a running record of what you did, the setting you did it in, and the things that were done to you while you were there. As you read the rest of this chapter, and as you investigate, try to have enough camera coverage to do both successfully.

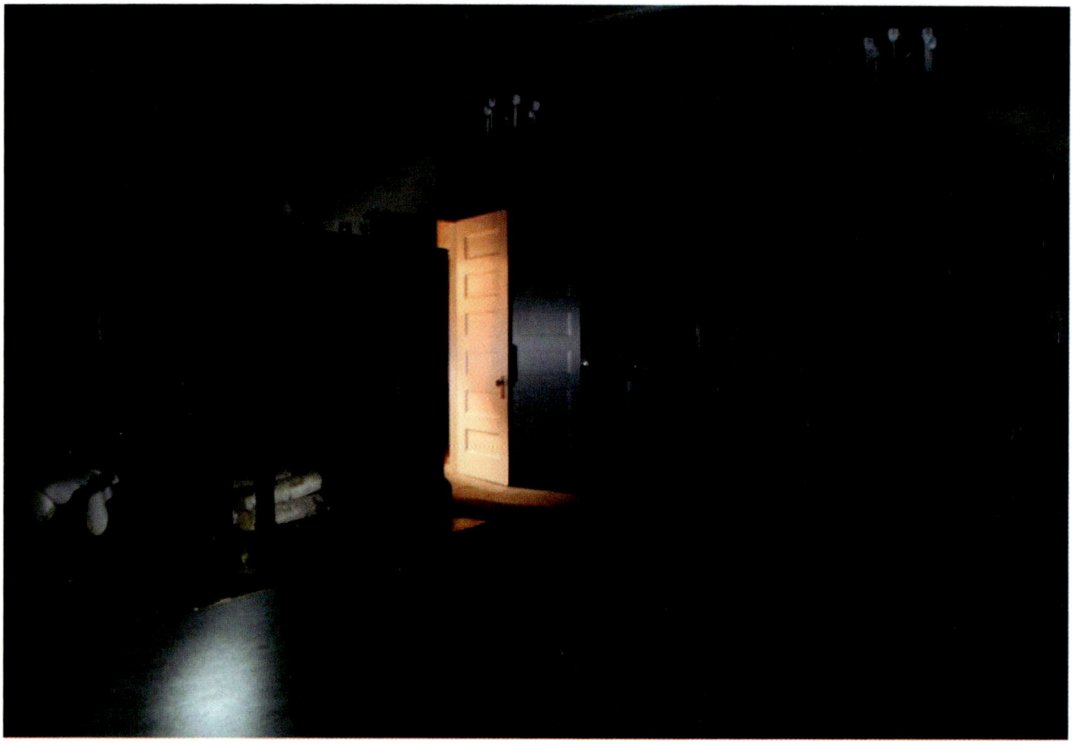

Figure 7.2
An example of an establishing shot that helps to see the whole room.
Picture courtesy of Josh Mantello.

A security guard walks into a darkened room and runs the beam of his flashlight through the room. There is nothing there so he moves to the next room, confident his job has been done. His job is to make sure the building is safe and to keep people out when the place is supposed to be empty. Just because he did not find anyone in the room and tackle them does not mean he did not do his job.

Your purpose in the field is to search and document, not just to gather evidence. Not taking a picture of a ghost is almost as much of a success as finding something. It might not be as useful to the community, but it is to you and whatever the reason is you are there investigating. While there is no definitive way to say a place where you cannot get evidence is not haunted, and beware of any group that claims their hour investigation proves it is not active, no evidence does say something about the haunting. It was not a failure.

Getting in the Mindset

Some of the most frightening and important stories that have been told to me have been lost forever. It is a lesson learned, but when I began documenting the paranormal, even before I had that much experience in the field, I relied on my sharp mind to remember everything. All of the details of what someone told me about their experiences or an exact quote that was worth adding into one of my stories could be remembered so there was no need to get it down in the moment. No such luck. I'd get to a place where I thought I had a story down and then forgot everything except the basics of the story, making it more like a rumor than a true story.

I learned to keep a tape recorder with me at all times and to maintain a level of preparedness for transitioning from normal guy to ghost reporter. There are times that I know I am meeting a person at 3:45 PM to speak, but most of the time it happens at a moment's notice. Paranormal investigators learn to keep cameras with them at all times and have EMF meters in their glove compartments because an investigation can happen at any time. There are such things as spontaneous investigations, but most have a level of preplanning about them. You know where you are going, have an estimated time you are going to spend there, and maybe even an idea of what kind of ghost you may encounter. This kind of foreknowledge can be beneficial, especially if you do not have a long time to be in the location.

The Importance of the Back-Story

In the last chapter, I talked about understanding the back-story of a haunting to prepare for the right equipment to bring into the situation. The same can be said for how the back-story tells you what to look for when you get there and how to shoot the haunting. The most obvious benefit is having a map of where to look when you get there. If someone keeps hearing banging in the kitchen late at night when everyone is supposed to be asleep, then you might spend extra time in that room. That may not be the only place to look, but it is worth revisiting that room time and again, establishing vigils, which we will talk about later in the chapter, and establishing a stationary investigation post there.

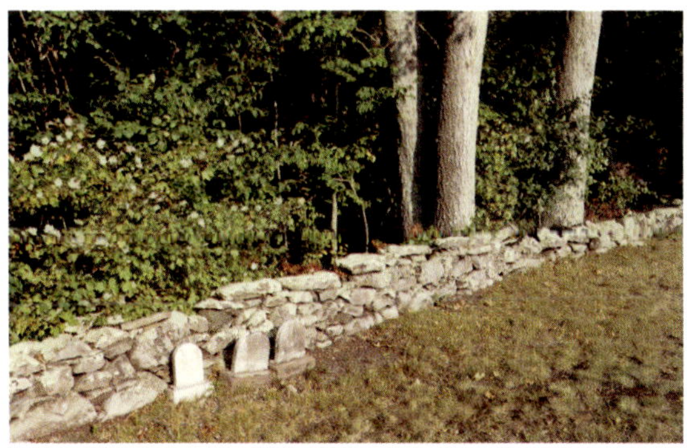

Figure 7.3
The back-story of this haunting revolves around three graves and an old man visiting early in the morning.

You also want to keep this back-story in mind as you investigate to determine the settings on your equipment and how you use it. If people have reported hauntings during the day and you happen to be investigating at night, keep the lights on and reduce the amount of flash that you use. If the ghost is seen walking down the stairs, set a stationary camera near the stairs and do not keep a handheld on it while you walk up and down the stairs. Most of the paranormal occurrences residential people discuss can best be documented by standing still, but if there are reports of activity all over the location, imagine having to rely on handheld equipment to get things in the moment.

Be aware of how precursors work in the back-story and think of them as alarms. If the reports tell of smelling an awful stench and then witnessing mist coming from across the third floor of a building, be ready to get to the third floor if you smell something dreadful. If there is a loud crash and then three knocks on a bedroom door, get your camera on that door if you hear a boom. Remember the paranormal is happening in several different ways at the same time and not all of it is being received by all of the senses. If people who report the haunting say one noise is accompanied by another, do not just try to get audio evidence. Try to take a picture as well.

The Paranormal Storyboard

If you were going to be a film director, which kind would you be? There are some who have no script, but rather a general idea of the story and a situation, maybe even some basic dialogue. They go out and shoot and hope the magic happens. There are others who have the whole script finished, although they are open, and they plan seven or eight different ways for the camera to record the story. They go out and set the cameras up, run a scene, and then leave it to editing to sort it out.

There are others, and many of the most successful directors in Hollywood use this method, where every shot is blocked out. The story exists in his mind and he's only looking for people to say the lines and bring that story to life. He's open to those surprise moments, but he has the movie detailed on storyboards down to the last shot. These are usually the directors that finish their movies on time and within their budget.

With very few exceptions, you will have a limited time in any given haunted location. You might be able to go there several times, but you are not spending three days snapping shots and taking readings. Instead, be prepared to have a bit of a fire under you, even if you are there for hours. There is much to get done, and if you go in unprepared just running around looking for the perfect piece of evidence, you reduce your potential to trap lightning in a bottle. If you are in a private residence, you might also lose the confidence of the people who own the house.

If you know the history of the location, and I am obviously a big fan of being informed before I enter, imagine the investigation like a movie. Your investigative techniques, whether it is trying to get visual evidence or some of the other ghost hunting staples, are shooting that movie and getting your sound. Before you go, block out what you are going to do. In *Picture Yourself Ghost Hunting,* I advocated investigating in a location several times before making any conclusions, and one of the reasons is to get the layout of the place. Knowing the way the rooms connect or how many rows are in the cemetery, makes being in the field more about getting results than groping in the dark hoping for the best.

Investigation List

Private residence
3-26-09

Front hall-laughing and shadow
–video and still

Stairs-footsteps
–set stat. camera for whole inv
–vigil at top

Upstairs bedroom-shadow (tv incident)
–set stat. camera for whole inv
–tv exper.

Son's room-old man, lights, cold spots
–vigil, video

Hit stairs twice before and after

Keep camera stl. on top and bottom

Figure 7.4
My plan of attack for a private residence.

Three Phases of Investigating

An investigation should never be thought of as predictable, and when they are it is usually due to the investigators involved. There are variables and moments of surprise, but through the years investigators have noticed moments of activity take on a personality through their investigations. Whether this has to do with the intent and approach of the investigator or some special paranormal timing, an investigation can be broken up into three parts.

I call it the three phases of investigating, and when I lay out the experiences I've had and the evidence I have gotten, I can see this pattern come out. Each has its own time, especially when given the different times you will spend at any given location, and own characteristics, and therefore a different approach. It's at least worth looking at it as we move forward with how to get good evidence.

Think of it as the beginning, middle, and the end.

Hit the Ground Running

I hear the same argument all the time. "If there is such a thing as ghosts, why don't they just make themselves known? Why do they never just stand up and say hello?" I think the question is fair and the answers, if we could ever discover them, might shed some light on what ghosts are and what they tell us about who we are after we die. There might be physical and metaphysical reasons, but one of the characteristics of spirits investigators encounter often is that ghosts like to run.

There may be paranormal rationales about spirits wanting to communicate to move on or that they are just looking for someone to pay attention to them, but ghosts are famous for leaving an area very quickly when investigators come to see them.

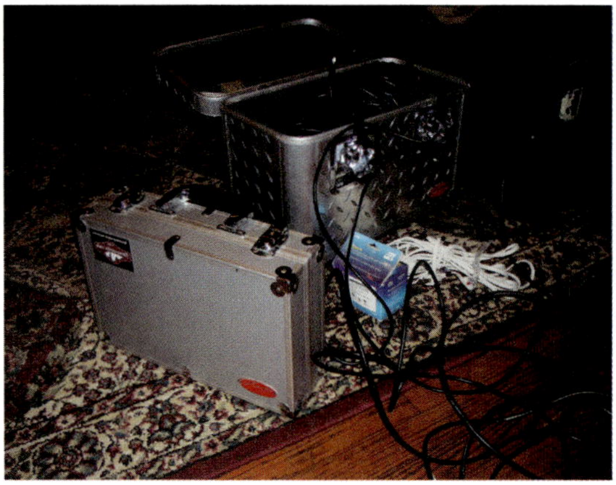

Figure 7.5
Another paranormal set up. Two cameras were already running when this picture was taken.

Investigators have even gotten audio evidence of ghosts telling each other to stop making noise or saying they need to leave so investigators do not see them. Some locations are famous for the timid nature of their spirits and the speed at which they can leave the room. It is important to enter a location already filming to take advantage of this. Set up where the activity has been reported, but film yourself doing everything from setup to cleaning up.

Some investigators tell of ghosts that are the exact opposite. The spirits are curious about the equipment investigators come in with, especially if the soul might have died a long time ago. Ghosts might also be offended by your presence and stand there defiantly, letting you know you are not welcome. EVPs are loaded with communications during this time. I have recorded a spirit saying, "What is that?" or "You're not going to record me," upon entering a haunted location. "I even suggest telling them about the equipment you bring to an investigation," says Matt Moniz, paranormal investigator and real-world scientist. "It might be a way to get them to talk, or it may help them if they have some apprehension about you coming in. If they died a hundred years ago or are a small child, they don't know what this stuff is."

An investigation begins the moment you get out of your car, if not before. I suggest starting long before you arrive by telling people you are investigating with the story of the haunting and all of the information you know about it, formulating a plan of attack when the team arrives, and by asking them what their expectations are of the investigation. The camera runs the whole time. Everyone gets on the same page while documentation is already being started. Then when you arrive, you do not miss those first few moments that might be the most productive for getting results.

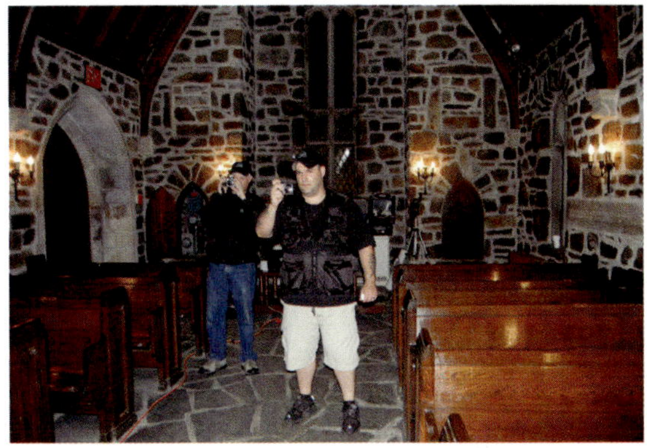

Figure 7.6
Video and photography being used together.
Picture courtesy of Josh Mantello.

Parallel Lives

I was leading some high school students of mine on an investigation and we were running pretty thin on evidence. They were checking their cameras after every shot, and other than a few spikes on some of the equipment, we believed we were empty handed. When we returned to the classroom, we began running through some of the evidence and saw an odd light, like a bright mist, when we looked closer at the pictures, but what I also noticed was that one of the student's EMF meters was showing a hit. We decided to check the video, and when we broke it down, we also had an EVP on the audio track of the camera saying, "Hello. I'm here," at the exact same moment.

Proof of the paranormal takes a step forward if you can get evidence that can be verified. That proof becomes even tighter when something happens on more than one medium. Some groups will tell you it is good to get a picture on film and digital and even video mediums at the same time, while others tell you it is proof of something natural, not supernatural. You often see investigators click pictures or take a temperature reading when they hear a noise to try to get further evidence something is there. The more layers you can use to back up evidence, the better. If you get the same red orb on digital and film, you might be able to see its cause more clearly on one or at least have two angles of the same manifestation.

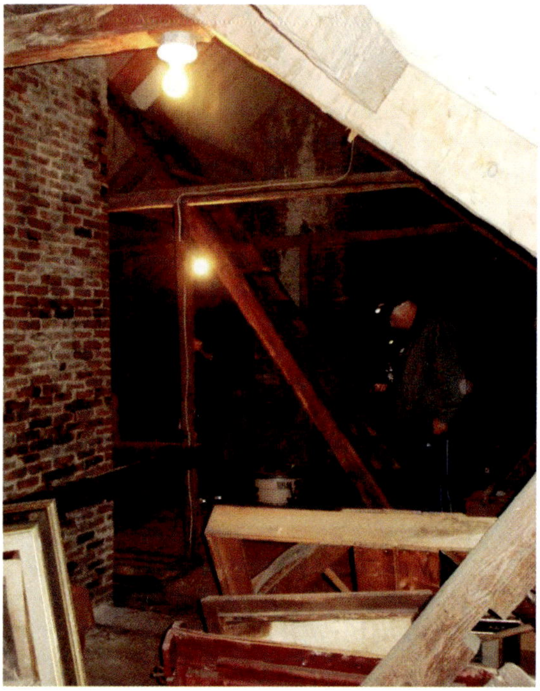

Figure 7.7
Another parallel situation. Notice the light in background could be mistaken for something paranormal if the one in the foreground did not help to establish what the light looked like on camera.
Picture courtesy of Matt Moniz.

Strive to maintain parallel documentation of your investigation. Always have a video camera rolling and then use your cameras to try to gather evidence. In a perfect world, you will get something on both, but in the worst-case scenario, you have proof of how you gathered the evidence. Of course, most times you will live somewhere in the middle. You might have to try to explain why a rod exists in one shot and not the other, but the running video will allow you to see what might have caused it, any other conditions that may have occurred at the same time, and a wider shot of the environment at the time.

I have seen investigators not notice a temperature drop, but the camera captures something unexplained in a picture and looking more closely at the image shows the ambient thermometer in the background with a dipping temperature.

Establishing Shot

If you really want to learn how to set up a haunted area for an investigation, do not watch television shows about the paranormal. Instead, watch a good movie. If you can imagine the paranormal activity as the main action of any scene, watch how good directors set up a scene and then allow the action to unfold. One of the ways they do this is to gain an establishing shot to allow the audience to see the whole environment and then use other techniques to express emotion or let the story unfold. It is this establishing shot we can use in our paranormal investigations. It also gives context that might be lost when you zoom in on an object in later pictures.

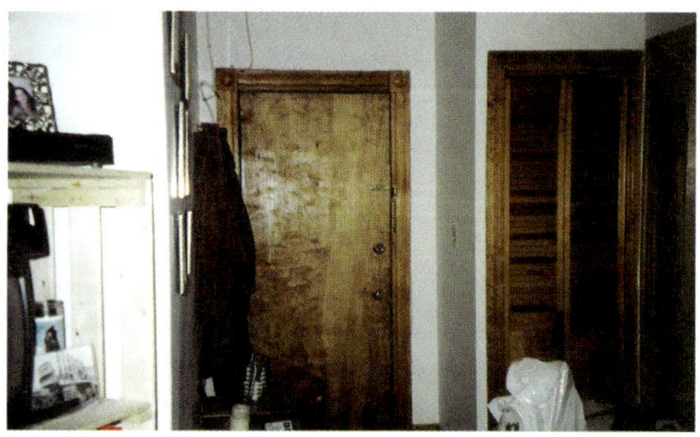

Figure 7.8
The establishing shot of a doorway with heavy activity.

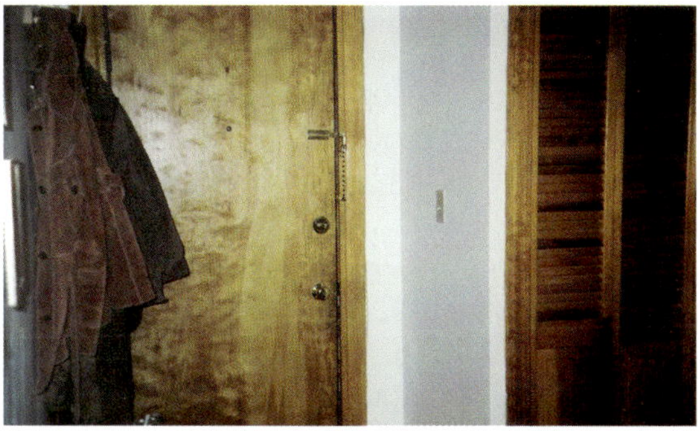

Figure 7.9
Then closer to try to focus on the corner where the shadow was seen.

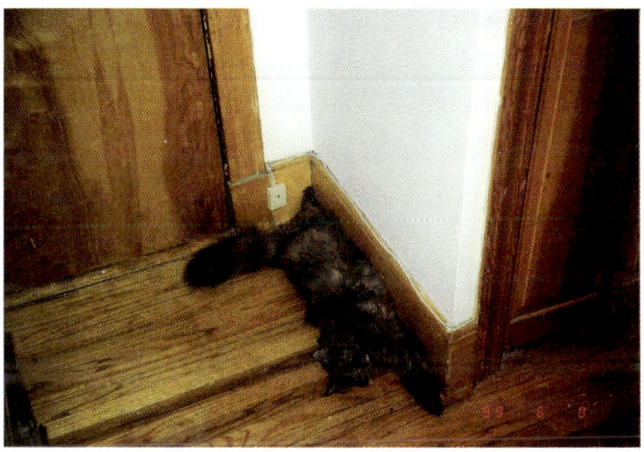

Figure 7.10
The cat, who would respond to the ghost, joined in the investigation.

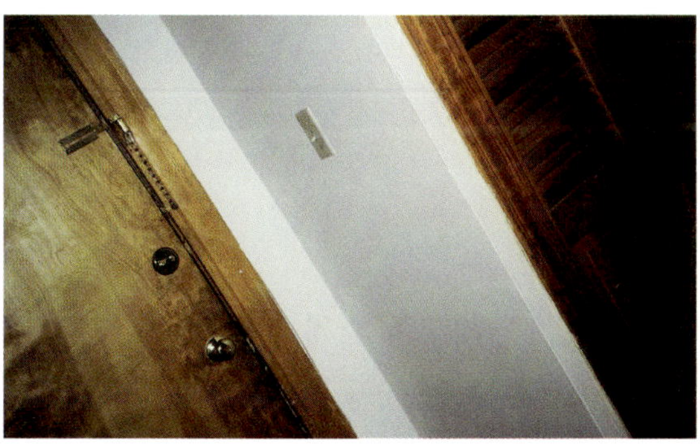

Figure 7.11
And one askew.

An establishing shot is when a camera, still or video, is set up in a corner or entrance of a room so it can take in what is going on in the entire room or environment. The best way to get this done is to use your tripods. You can see everything, including what you are doing in that environment. Think of paranormal investigating as putting out a fire. You have a main hose that is being used to hit the flaming building as a whole and then you have individual firefighters who use their hose to get the flare ups they see and believe are the most dangerous. Your establishing shot gets the big picture, literally, while your handheld cameras are the ones in the thick of things getting the dirty work done.

If you have the resources, allow a webcam attached to a computer be your establishing shot, along with some still camera you can return to periodically to take a picture or place on a timer. This allows a constant power source that it may need and does not take up film with what may be something you only use afterwards to confirm something or remember aspects of the investigation. This is somewhat difficult, and not suggested, in an outside investigation or where you might lose your computer, but if you are in a house, plug it in and just keep it running.

Snapshot

Speaking of good directors, try to avoid being Steven Spielberg when you attempt to take pictures. The Academy Award winning director has a distinct look, especially in his early work. One of the things he is famous for is lighting a character from behind and then having the actor move out of the light so it shines over his shoulder. It is great when it comes to creating a dramatic moment in a film, but I have seen too many lights glowing behind investigators, creating all types of ghosts on the film afterwards.

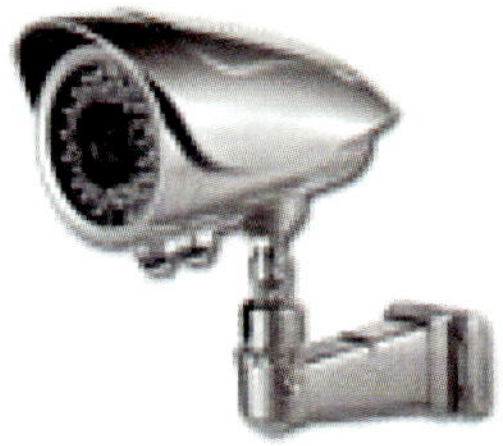

Figure 7.12
The 530TVL Super Hi Resolution camera, perfect for setting the perimeter. Picture courtesy of Ghost Mart.

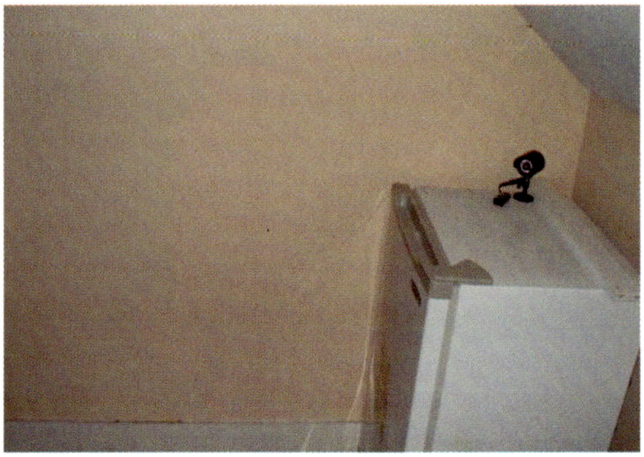

Figure 7.13
And one being used in the field.

Setting the Perimeter

The best way to get the full picture, and to get the most out of your establishing shot, is to set up several cameras in the areas you are going to focus on. In your storyboard, you decided where you were going to focus your investigation. Now you set up your cameras to capture activity in that frame. Many investigators like to do this with smaller Nightvision or infrared cameras, which can then be fed into a monitor, recorder, or computer. These may break the bank; Ghost Mart advertises models ranging from $100 to $300 a camera, and then you still need to run them into something. Instead, sweep garage and yard sales for old video cameras and make a setup of your own.

If you are investigating a larger area or you are outside or in a place where you might run across the general public, be careful where you set up this perimeter equipment. If you know of a haunted area, other people might as well. In the Spring of 2009 there was a news report out of Rhode Island where teenagers were hiding out in an abandoned school known to be haunted. When investigators would come in, they would rob them and sell their equipment. Try to use common sense in any investigation when you put your cameras down and remember you have more to fear from the living than the dead.

The Paranormal Tourist and the Paranormal Jumper

There are two typical negative methods of getting moving video used by inexperienced investigators in the field, and some people on television and the movies, that make it hard to get accurate evidence and continue to corrupt the minds of people investigating. They are both born of the idea that you need to be moving, and your cameras need to be moving, to be an active, effective investigator.

The first is the paranormal tourist method. This is where the video camera is used as the eyes of the investigator. Instead of holding the camera still or holding it in a position and trusting it is capturing things, the person shooting holds the camera to his eyes and does not take it away. The result is a series of shots of directly in front of him, then a quick cut to the side, then his own feet and then back to the other side and then to a random place when someone hears something. The effect is much like a first-person video game or a scene from the *Blair Witch Project*. There is nothing valuable gained because nothing can really be seen. It also makes one wonder what the investigator is missing by not being aware of his environment.

The second is the paranormal jumper, also known as the attention deficit disorder ghost hunter. This usually happens when an investigator is outside and feels the need to video everything that is going on, but it can also be seen in hunts involving a large area. The person with the camera shows one area, focuses on it for 15 seconds, and then moves on to another area for a few seconds. There is something to be said for patience. You may not get anything by keeping your camera still for five minutes on one area, but you will definitely not get anything by switching so quickly. This is why many of those same investigators often have five stationary cameras that keep their film running instead of going between them, but they still do it when they have the camera in their hands.

Second Phase

LOOKING FOR GHOSTS and trying to capture ghosts on film is really a series of cycles of movement and waiting, meaning the transition between the first and second phases will happen several times over the course of an investigation. Plan and practice how to do this well, and maintain some separation between the two, knowing the paranormal likes to make itself known in the bookends. The second phase should be all about observation and triggering the trap you set in the first.

Going Dark

Once the cameras are all set and running, it is time to move to the next phase. To many investigators this means turning off the lights and relying on Nightvision to get their evidence.

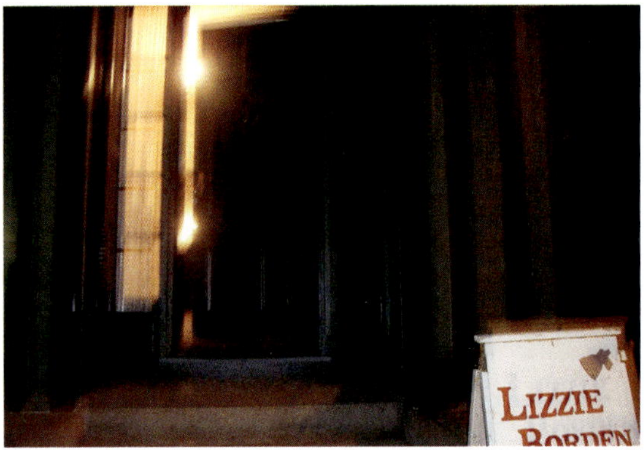

Figure 7.14
The effect of this picture is a result of Nightvision being used with sufficient light in the area.

This should be done in moderation and only when you are trying to use Nightvision to expand the way a camera sees, but an entire investigation done in the dark is only half the picture. It may be impossible to avoid in some locations, but if possible, spend some time utilizing the natural light and artificial light that exists in an area. The two methods are in conflict with each other because any technology that amplifies light hates a bright environment, so try investigating a little both ways.

Here's a method that might work: If you are in a house and you have stationary cameras with Nightvision, leave them in that room and go to another to conduct investigations in the light. When you have completed the sweep of that area, switch approaches and place a stationary camera where you just were using light. It might mean a little more time setting up each portion of the ghost hunt, but that dual approach may get better results.

Introduce Yourself

You never get a second chance to make a first impression, and an intelligent haunting will have one of three attitudes about you. It will either want to make contact, want to avoid you, or not care. There are paranormal motifs about the motion of the spirit world; for example, a suicide victim cannot leave the room he killed himself in.

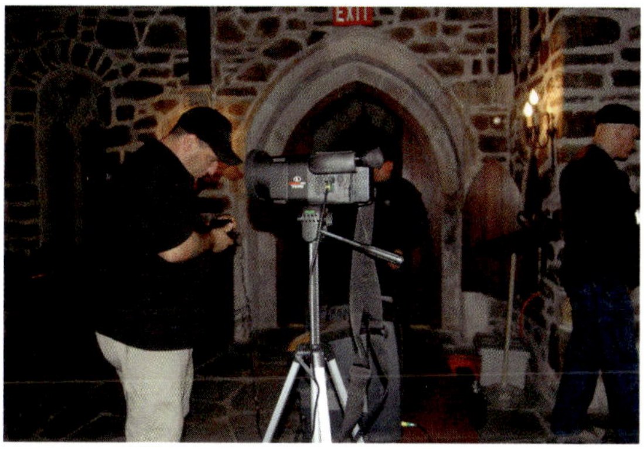

Figure 7.15
Getting to know the environment while getting into the Second Phase.

These are not hard and fast rules but are based on limited observation. The energy in a room, or some other kind of environmental condition, may mean a spirit is drawn to a certain area or can make itself known better in that area, but do not assume the ghost stays where it is.

Say hello and ask the spirit to present himself or offer proof he is there. Although many investigators and almost all television shows about investigating advocate getting the ghost mad, this does not have to be part of what you do. Simply say your name and explain why you are there.

If there is a motivation behind the investigation, for example, a family that is being bothered by the spirit in their house, tell them that. Do not enter a house and start yelling for the ghost to go back to the void from which it came, but explain the situation. One of the motifs I agree with is that many spirits may be confused about what is going on or even that they are dead. Just explain the situation to them.

Walk the Grid

Investigating should never be done alone. One reason is because it may pose a danger from the living and the dead, but another reason is to provide multiple evidence attacks during the investigative sweep. Allow one investigator to sweep the area using some kind of measurement device, such as a Geiger counter or EMF meter, while the second takes pictures of everything. The photographer should alternate between pictures of the whole scene, pictures of the other investigator's immediate area, and then places where the other investigator is not.

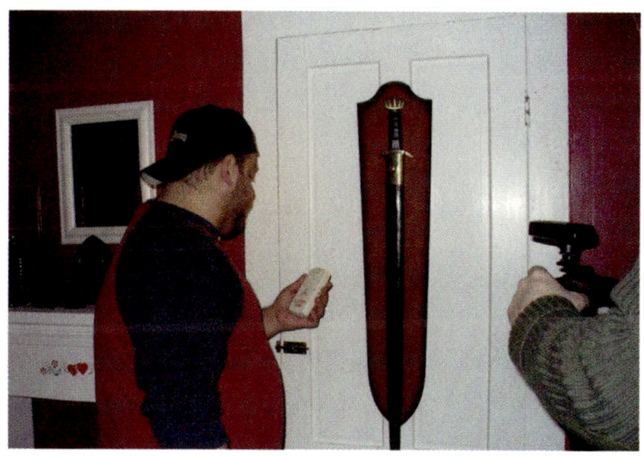

Figure 7.16
Walking the grid.

Think of it like filming a television show and you are cutting from camera one to camera two to camera three. You may want to set a rate of two pictures every minute, and if something happens in between those times, you have the ability to set and click. Have a stationary camera running the entire time to catch moments you may miss.

During your time in a single location you should be trying to communicate with the sprits there or trying to encourage them to make themselves known. Taking pictures is one aspect of the investigation, and as you spend more time looking for ghosts, you will develop methods you like and incorporate them into your work. You might find you are a meter person or that you like to sit still. You might like to press the buttons of the spirits that might be present in the location by making fun of them, which I am not an advocate of. Whatever you do as an investigator, it should work side by side with taking pictures of the methods you are using and the environment you are in.

It is hard to tell how much time to spend in one spot before moving on, especially because the amount of time you have to investigate varies. Do not spend too much time in one area, even if it is the only place where activity has been recorded. Move on to another point in the location, telling the spirits you are moving on, and reset your investigation. Depending on time, you can come back later and try the same spot twice, but it is better to go several places with small lulls than to try to spend the entire investigation in one room.

Engage the Other Side

A vigil is a quiet moment during an investigation when one member conducts some kind of experiment or tries to communicate with the spirit while the others document what happens. For example, one investigator has an EVP session where she asks questions and tries to get a response while the others film it. Some investigators do not like the idea, but it might be the best chance to get evidence. It acts as a direct calling to the other side, and if there is a spirit that wants to make contact, they might take that chance to do it. You might be able to get a picture of them trying to do that. It also helps to divide the investigation so the hunt does not consist of three hours of five people moving around a one-bedroom apartment.

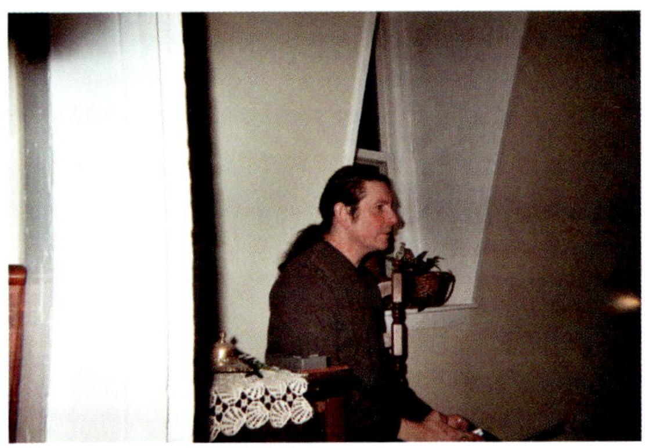

Figure 7.17
Writer and investigator Tom D'Agostino in the middle of a vigil. The yellow light on the right is from a second camera on Tom, but the shadow in the upper left might be something.

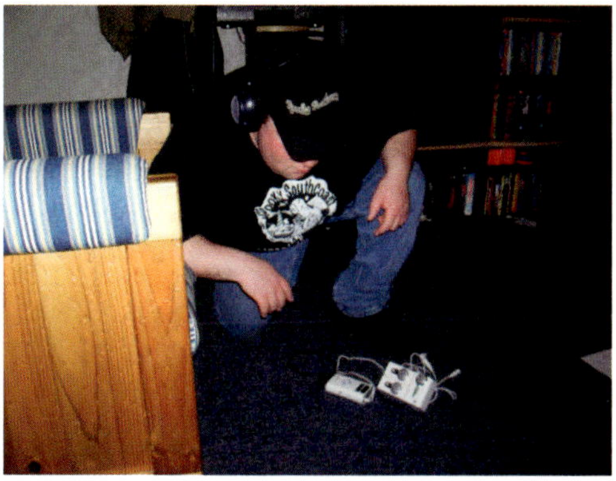

Figure 7.18
Radio host and investigator Tim Weisberg experimenting with the Shack Hack, a method of trying to talk to the dead, during an investigation.
Picture courtesy of Tim Weisberg.

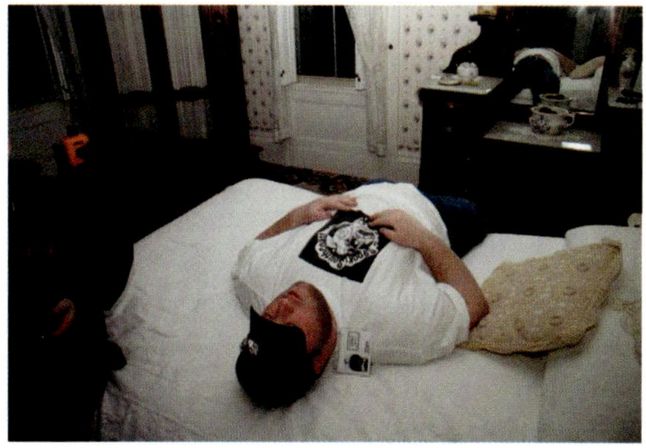

Figure 7.19
Weisberg experimenting at the Lizzie Borden Bed and Breakfast trying to recreate a moment where something unseen lifted his feet.
Picture courtesy of Matt Moniz.

The other side of the vigil is a moment where an investigator tries an experiment; for example, playing with a toy the ghost keeps turning on. This may also be a moment of reliving an event that will spark the spirit to talk, like sitting in a rocking chair that has been found to move by itself. Whenever I am at the Lizzie Borden Bed and Breakfast someone always wants to place themselves where the murdered bodies were found, and when I go there with Tim Weisberg of Spooky Southcoast, he tries to recreate a moment where unseen hands lifted his legs while he was sitting on the bed. These should be documented and filmed and other evidence should be experimented with while this is going on.

Investigators do not need to overcrowd the experiment. If you have five people investigating, one can be running a camera of some kind while another might monitor other equipment. You may be surprised how you can juggle equipment when you are sitting still. The other investigators should be in other places trying to get pictures of other activity or trying to capture that stray ghost who may be coming or going from where the vigil is happening. Work it the best you can; just remember, too many people in one place is a bad use of your resources.

Best Methods

There really is no downtime during an investigation. Television shows portray investigations as if they were all ten-round fights with the other side. People in the field know that is not true and that the majority of the time you are setting up or waiting for something to happen. That is not really idle time, however. We think the paranormal comes at us head on, or at least out of the corner of your eye, but true paranormal experiences are often little rustles or peeks around the corner. Do not think because the walls are not bleeding blood that you are not in the presence of a spirit.

Too Much Time on Your Hands

You should be taking pictures while sitting still or during calm times. In the worst-case scenario, you are creating pictures to use as a baseline to compare when you get something. At best, you catch something with you. Follow the same methods as with "active" investigating, continuing to take random pictures, a series of pictures, and a full-scene picture. You might just catch something watching you.

> **Rest, Relax, and Reload**
>
> **When there is a moment of stillness, check your film. Use that time to load if you need to, or to check the settings on your cameras. Check your batteries to make sure they are charged and that your extras are easily accessible. Organize the evidence you already have and make notes.**

Talk It Up

The first time I spoke at a conference, I joined in with the investigation sponsored by the organizers. I was known for my writing on urban legends and the paranormal and had spent time investigating the old way: with a flashlight, a tape recorder, and a camera. I was introduced to Derek Bartlett of the Cape and Islands Paranormal Research Society who had a trunk full of the latest equipment. He shoved an EMF meter in my hands and told me to watch the readings. I said okay, although I did not have the slightest idea what EMF was, and as we walked through a haunted cemetery, I tried to watch what he was doing. I actually learned quite a bit that night about investigating, but one thing really sticks with me.

Although it now seems like common sense, I was impressed by the fact that he always notified people when he took a picture. There are many things that can contribute to bad paranormal pictures, but one of the most common is fellow investigator error. The flash of a camera can impact another investigator's picture in several ways. Whether you pick up the flash as a blur or orb or you see the reflection of the flash in your shot, it is important to know where everyone is and what they are doing.

As a practice, always tell people when you take a picture. Think of a simple buzzword, like "flash" or "picture," and say it whenever you take a picture of something. This tells people you have just snapped, but it also tells the general time when you have taken it. Many ghost hunters use this method, but they forget the precursor to flashes. Many cameras have a red light they throw out that tells the camera how to adjust the shutter and how much flash to use. Remember to look for those when you evaluate your pictures. You match up the picture with the running video camera or a tape recorder.

> **The Notebook**
>
> **If you have not gotten the idea before, I will say it one more time. Carry around a notebook and take down as much as you can about the situation you are in. You do not need to document every picture you take, but when you switch settings or conduct a vigil, make note of the time. When things happen you cannot explain, write it down. As much as the running video, this gives you an unchanging account of the investigation.**

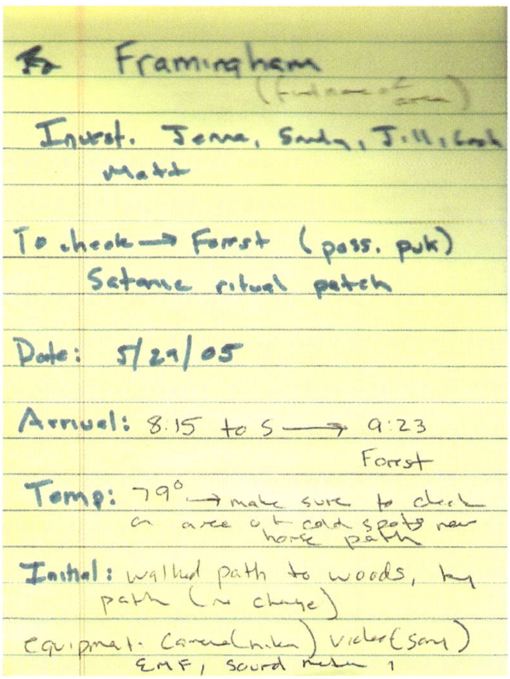

Figure 7.20
One of my journal entries from a haunted forest.

Follow Your Stomach

Taking pictures may be thought of as part of the scientific side of the paranormal, and the way we have discussed it touches upon some basic principles of science, but there is another side that always comes into play when investigating the paranormal. Whether it is based on a different, more primal part of science or more of the spiritual, psychic side, there is something to be said for the little tickle in your stomach when you investigate the paranormal. While science-based groups try to ignore the urge, your own senses may be as good of a ghost detector as any equipment you can buy. Your body is in tune with your environment, and listening to those signals and responding may give you another tool in the field.

On one side you have evolutionary science. Back in the day it was crucial for your body to be in step with your surroundings, so evolution instilled basic fight or flight reflexes. When something was unusual, it would trigger and heighten your senses to evaluate the situation and make a decision. The paranormal may trigger that response still part of your DNA.

The psychic side tells us that we all have some level of connection to the other side. We might refuse to engage it, or we may work to develop it and make it stronger, but it is always there, talking to people and getting messages like a radio not tuned to the exact right channel. During times when there is more psychic energy, the static gets louder, even though the station is still not coming in.

Either way, listen to your stomach. You do not have to believe in it for it to work. If you enter a room and feel something, go with it. Snap a few shots and make note of why you did so. If the feeling pulls you somewhere else, go there and take a few more. With digital technology all you will lose is a few pictures you can compress and store away, never to look at them again.

In the same vein, if you hear a voice inside your head that tells you to take a picture, take it and ask questions later. If you could interview a ghost, he might tell you the thing that gets them the most is that they are always talking and no one listens.

A View Askew

Do not look for your evidence head on. I can't say it more simply than that, although some people have become upset when I advocate this. If you look at the majority of pictures with some kind of evidence, you will see the paranormal hiding in the corners of the picture. There are orbs in the corners of the room and a shadow off to the side. It sometimes feels as if they are hiding on you, playing around in your periphery. When we try to capture these images, we shoot straight on, as if the spirit is getting ready to smile and say "cheese." Instead, shoot doorways and rooms at angles or randomly, without working to make the picture look good.

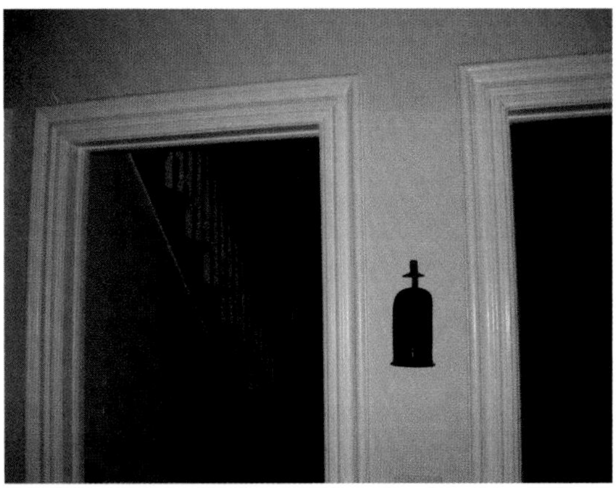

Figure 7.21
A picture of a doorway with reported activity taken on an angle.

Click a few off without focusing by holding your camera to the side and not looking at what you are shooting at, especially if something happens and everyone else is looking forward. Shoot behind you for the same reason. You may not be able to post it as a nice picture on your website, but it may get more evidence.

Take a Few

If you have the ability to take a few pictures at one time with your camera, and you have a steady hand, use that setting often during an investigation. Having more than one picture of the same moment will establish anything that changes during the duration of those shots as well as increase your chances of catching something that appears for only a moment. If you do not have this feature, merely take two or three shots every time you take a picture. This is easier with a digital camera, or at least less expensive, and you might be surprised at how much the picture moves, showing you how much your hand actually does move without you realizing it. This helps to show the before and after of a picture with evidence.

For example, I was investigating and got a bright glow when shooting alongside a white wall. That might be easy to explain, but I took three pictures with only one showing the glare. In the same location, another investigator took two pictures with the same result, one picture with something paranormal and the other without.

This method also reveals problems with a picture and can be used to explain away something. If you continue to get a dark blur in the same spot, it's probably something occurring in the camera and not paranormal.

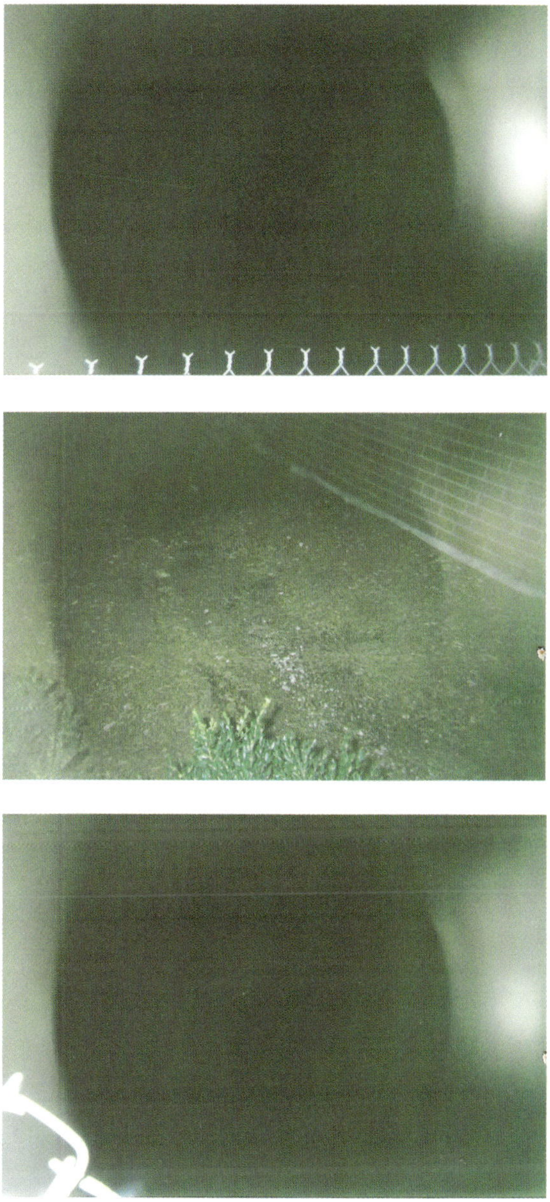

Figure 7.22
These three pictures were taken within moments of each other. Notice the same tunnel effect on each. Alone it might be considered a vortex, but together it establishes a camera malfunction.

Looking as You Go

I went to my son's Easter egg hunt last year and found myself running around with three-year olds looking for colored eggs filled with candy and pennies. My goal was to get more pictures than treasures, and as my son moved from place to place, I snapped as many pictures as possible. A camera has a strange effect on children, and all his friends demanded I take their picture. Then, as a sign of the times, they all begged to see the pictures, and I had to tell them I was using a disposable camera because my digital camera was at home.

Many investigators will stop during an investigation to check their evidence. This may satisfy a momentary urge, but I have seen some ghost hunters spend the whole night basking in the orb they got in the first ten minutes of the investigation. I never look at a picture until the end of the night, or when we are switching equipment over during a lull. Imagine what you are missing by looking at what you have instead of observing more. If you are investigating the right way, you will have many pictures and may be able to document the movement of the spirit, but if you snap and look, you will lose out on getting a second shot in a non-paranormal follow-up picture that reinforces the spirit in the first.

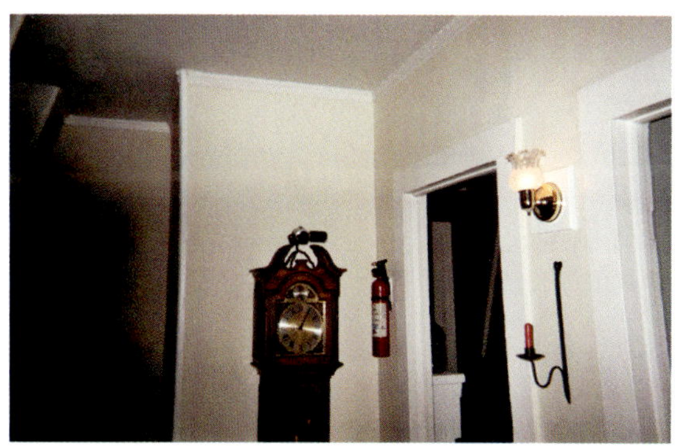

Figure 7.23
The shadow here is the result of two cameras in different rooms shining into a third.

The Seven Deadly Sins

Your time in the field is crucial and often limited. There are many bumps and distractions in the process, so understand the value of actually being in a haunted location.

Sloth—Load, reload, and store your equipment in an organized way. You may taint anything you get, or even lose it, if you cannot keep track of it. You may also not be able to get a camera out and set up in time if you have it stored haphazardly.

Envy—Have an idea of everyone's responsibilities during an investigation, although you do not need to be militant about it. Some run when activity happens to one investigator, leaving what they are doing to snap off ten pictures that five other investigators are also taking. Ghosts have a habit of moving through a haunted location, meaning if someone feels a cold breeze go by them, it is moving out of the way and to somewhere else. Instead of being envious of them having something happen, try to get the spirit moving to you.

Pride—If you are part of a team, you may be part of a power struggle in the field. It is a very real part of investigating that needs to be known, and if you can't find the bossy, overbearing lead investigator, it may be you. You may also just be intent on what you think will happen during the hunt. Do not sacrifice good evidence because you are stubborn and think something needs to be done.

Greed—This may also fall under the title of lust or envy, but there are times when you want to have unlimited time in one place to continue to get evidence or refuse to leave an area because another investigator gets a good picture there. That is the place you want to be, and nothing can change your mind. Remember, there are haunted areas all around a location where you may find fresh, unique evidence.

Wrath—I am not a fan of antagonizing spirits or calling them out, but I can see the benefit of it during some investigations. I have also seen investigators get genuinely mad when something does not happen when they want it to during an investigation. Try to keep your emotions intact. Most people are more likely to miss something when they are overly emotional. In a metaphysical sense, negativity might allow or attract negative spirits to where you are.

Gluttony—Spending five hours investigating the bedroom of a haunted inn may be a good way to concentrate your efforts on a single location, but you have to ask yourself if you are getting too much of the same four walls. Investigate, spend a little time, and then move on to another angle or another location. Think of a haunting as the engine of a car. If the engine is not running right, it may be because of an issue somewhere else. Try to see a haunting as both a cause and effect of the paranormal.

Lust—Don't fall in love with any piece of equipment, especially the seductive nature of some of the new forms of ghost hunting tools. It is part of the reason I am opposed to specialization in the field, or one person being responsible for gathering just one form of evidence. Think about what you might not be taking a picture of because you cannot take your eyes off a thermal imaging camera. If you want to focus on one form, pair up with someone during an investigation who is getting an alternate form.

Third Phase

DO NOT WEAR OUT YOUR welcome for the benefit of the living and the dead. Do what you went there to do and then go home. Don't worry, the investigation will continue on after you leave as you look at the evidence. Tie up your loose ends, say your goodbyes to all involved, and leave the location the way you found it. You are a representative of all paranormal investigators when you are conducting an investigation, and a misstep gets the word out quickly to a community about the negative side of ghost hunters. Looking at the paranormal newswire it is clear the everyday news is more likely to cover something bad done by an investigator and ignore most of their good work.

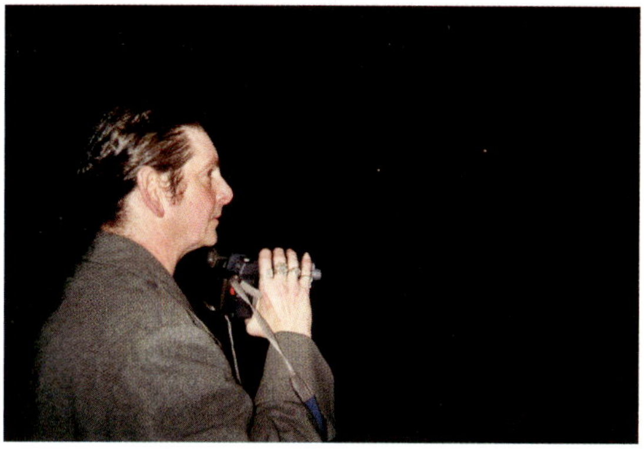

Figure 7.24
The lights in the background are not paranormal, but evidence was gained on video as we said goodbye right after this.

One Last Picture, Please

When you have decided to leave, make sure to tell the spirits you are going. You may feel foolish, but if they are there, it is just polite to say goodbye. More importantly, it is a way of telling them this is their last chance to make themselves known. Some have even said this closure will help make sure they do not come home with you. I prefer to think of it in terms of proof. There has been just as much evidence gathered in the last ten minutes of a hunt as there has been during the second phase, and much of that has been in the form of pictures. It also allows the ghosts to know you are leaving, which may set that whole paranormal migration discussed earlier.

Snap a few as you leave, taking pictures in the area of every setup you established as you take the equipment down.

Packing Up the Equipment

Think of packing up your equipment as the opposite of setting it up. The first thing you put away should be your meters and paranormal extras. Then you should put away your recording equipment and take down your stationary cameras before packing away your handheld cameras. Always leave out one recorder and one video camera to record everything about taking the scene down and leave a camera handy in case you need to get some quick evidence. Oftentimes, even when they are shy, the spirits do not want you to leave and will do something to keep you there.

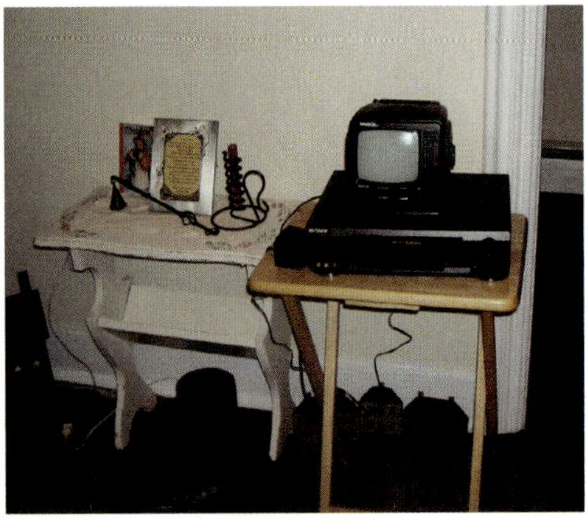

Figure 7.25
One monitor and a camera still going as we got ready to leave an investigation.

During the filming of the DVD for *Picture Yourself Ghost Hunting* we caught a shot of Maureen Wood getting psychically attacked. This actually happened as we were taking down the equipment, and I had to call out to cameraman Andrew Lake to come back and start running the camera. If we had not been outside and needing to pack everything away to make the journey back to our cars, the entire incident would have been captured, but because the video camera was the last thing packed, we were able to get some of it on film.

Saying Farewell to the Living

STOP INVESTIGATING THE paranormal at private residences if you ever hear yourself telling the owner of the location that you just investigated that you can say without doubt the place is not haunted or that you know for a fact they share their house with ghosts. Investigating tells you very little. It is when you look at the pictures and evaluate the other evidence afterwards that the whole situation become clearer. It might not be that clear even after that, which is why I think any location worth investigating is probably worth investigating more than once before you present any results.

The people who live in the haunted location will be very anxious to hear what has happened. Chances are they have been living with the activity for a while and they contacted you because they need some explanation of what is going on. They are putting their psychological well being in your hands, and some investigators are not known for their tact in dealing with the living. You do not know the context of any evidence you may have gotten yet, so do not get too excited or disappointed about your time there.

I always tell the people I am not quite sure what I have gotten and I will get back to them in the next couple of days. Thank them for allowing you in their house and eat their brownies if they offer them. Tell them you will try to discover what is happening. Then make sure you pick up after yourself.

Snapshot

According to my own experiences, these are the five most popular activities investigation groups engage in after ghost hunting

- **Coffee drinking**
- **Going to a bar**
- **Eating Chinese food**
- **Going for pizza**
- **Going to a cemetery**

It seems investigators don't want to go home after an investigation.

Go for Some Coffee

EVEN IF NOTHING HAPPENED during an investigation, there has been a release of adrenaline and you may be coming down from that when you leave. Whether you are running hot or running out of gas, you are in no condition to look at the evidence in a critical way. The investigation is over, so let it be over.

I suggest meeting with your fellow investigators afterwards to discuss things you noticed while you were ghost hunting, perhaps over coffee, while things are fresh in your mind. You do not need to record these conversations, although I often do, but try taking notes on everyone's impressions so they are not lost.

Then go home and go to bed. The evidence will be there waiting for you.

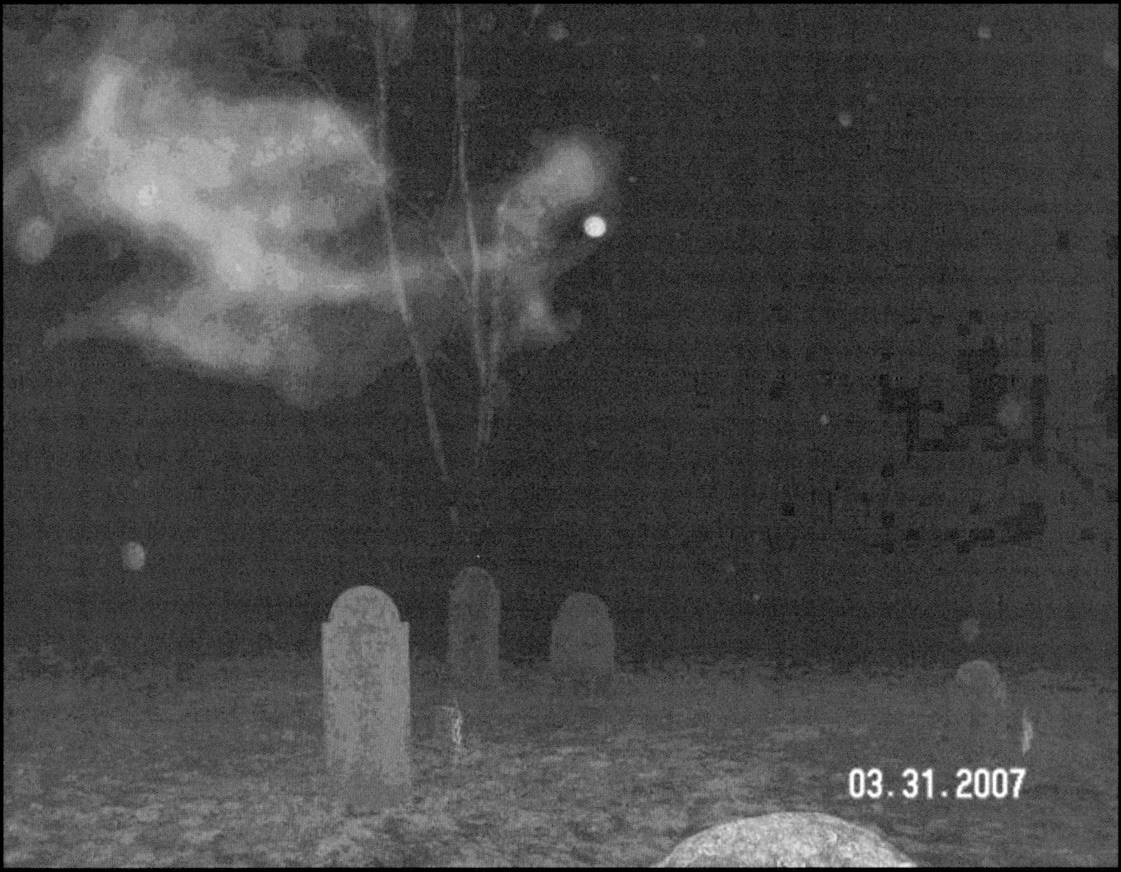

Picture courtesy of Louis Antonucci.

8

Evaluating the Evidence

WHEN PEOPLE OUTSIDE OF THE PARANORMAL community think of a ghost hunter or a paranormal investigator, they envision a group of people, probably dressed in black, marching through an old insane asylum or cemetery snapping pictures while all their bells and whistles go off. It is the kind of vision gained by stopping in on paranormal television shows, and the scene often becomes what investigators themselves see as their role as well.

That is really only half the picture. Time out in the field is usually long moments of waiting broken up by occasional moments of heightened activity. If ghost hunting were a sport, it would be baseball not basketball. The highs and lows of evaluating the evidence afterward are much the same, but the lull in activity is much lower and the high is more reserved because you can never be sure if what you think you have is real or not.

I remember a story by EVP expert Mike Markowicz. He was recalling the first time he found a ghost voice in a recording he had made. He was alone in his room, surrounded by recording equipment and computers. He listened closely to all of the buzzing and pops and was almost hypnotized by the boredom of it. Then a voice came through clear, as if the person was whispering in his ear, and said, "I'll be talking to you later." His mouth dropped open as he listened to it again, and at that moment, he knew what he was destined to do.

That moment might not be as dramatic for everyone, but it illustrates the essence of evaluating your visual evidence. You'll have plenty of pictures that have nothing in them, and you'll file them away as failures. You'll have some with dramatic anomalies in them, and then in a moment of clarity you'll see your buddy in the corner taking a picture and know there is a natural reason for your supposed ghost.

Then, just when you have reached the moment where you are ready to file them all away, something comes up you cannot explain. It is that one percent, and it makes all of the work worth it.

Six Basic Rules for Evaluating Pictures

These simple rules apply to evaluating all kinds of visual evidence, from a quick shot taken by a Polaroid to recorded thermal imaging. As everything in this book, think of these as true only as long as there is not something that makes them untrue.

1. **Rule 1—Balance:** As a teacher, I am often asked to administer standardized testing. Reading the instructions means having to say the same things repeatedly. "Do your best, but do not spend too much time on any one question." This holds true for ghost photos. Do not spend too much time on any one picture, but look at and evaluate each of them.

2. **Rule 2—Context:** When you were in the field, you were keeping notes of moments when something happened or when an outside element may have tainted your evidence. Refer to these notes, and if you manipulate the evidence, make notes of your changes.

3. **Rule 3—Control:** There are highs and lows when looking at evidence, but try to be somewhat level. Do not take yourself too seriously.

4. **Rule 4—Distraction:** A friend once asked me to look at a picture she believed was clear proof of the paranormal. I agreed that the shadow looked like a foot dashing behind a corner, not wanting to be seen. It was worth taking the time to see what might have caused it. She asked what I was talking about. She was referring to the orb in the middle of the picture. Do not fall in love with one element of a picture and ignore whatever else might be there. One might be able to be explained away and the other one cannot, or the two images might relate to each other or explain each other. Too many times, I have seen people throw away a picture because they did not see the ghost they were looking for only to miss something else.

5. **Rule 5—Logic:** Everything has a potential natural reason. By its very nature, a picture is a moment in time, so there is no way to document all of the other things that may be playing in that moment. Even video has blind spots. Don't make leaps just because you worship at the altar of debunking. Even your natural reasons for a picture need to have a limit. At some point, a reason can become as ridiculous as some people believe the existence of ghosts is.

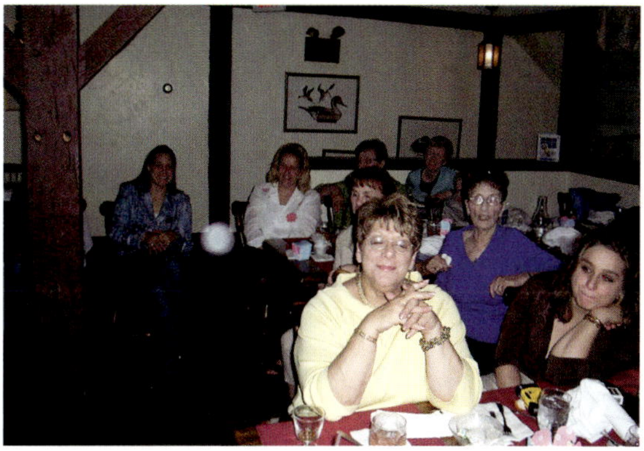

Figure 8.1
The full picture.

6. **Rule 6—Reflect:** Reflective surfaces can be the tip of the sword in the paranormal world. You may be surprised by the things out there light can reflect off of, and that should always be in the back of your mind, but keep an eye on the main offenders. Metal objects, mirrors, and windows will make wraths out of flashes and nightlights. Play it the other way as well. Spend extra time looking at mirrors and windows when looking at your pictures. When I began investigating, we used spirit boards often, a practice many people now preach against. While others were fixed on the planchette, I always watched the shadows, the mirrors, and the windows. People who do not rely entirely on science in their investigations often subscribe to the use of mirrors in their work. There really is no reason why they should show ghosts, but many of the best spirit photos I have involve them.

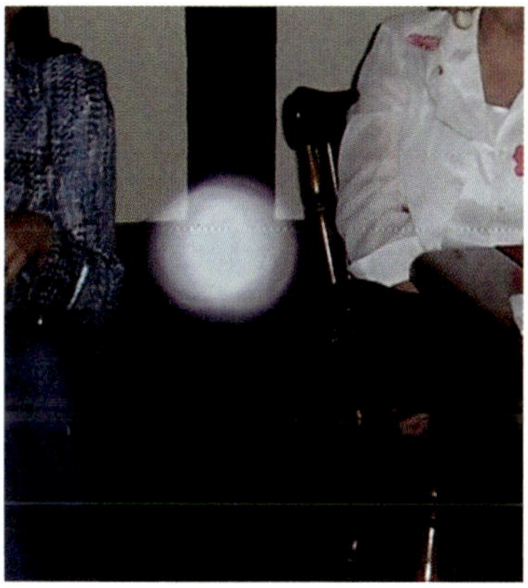

Figure 8.2
A close up of the anomaly

The last, and perhaps most important rule has no number because it is used in the other six. Follow the bouncing ball. Whenever you see light in a picture, whether it may be from the flash or a ghost running through your shot, always try to follow the light to its source, even if that source is off camera. In our physical world, light has to follow certain rules and it cannot break these just because there may be a spirit nearby. It cannot turn corners or shift directions unless something lets it.

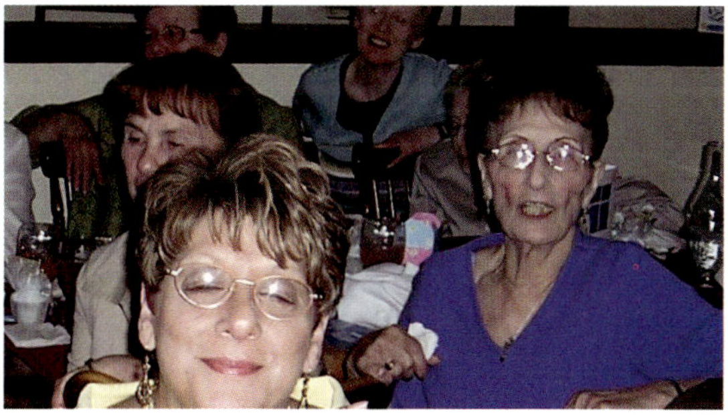

Figure 8.3
The direction of the flash.

Let's forget the back-story of the picture and the haunting, which alone would cause you to see this as a picture of a real ghost. Follow the light. In the full shot, Figure 8.1, you see the picture seems to have two different sources of light hitting it. Maybe you think one is the flash of the camera. A close up of the image, Figure 8.2, shows the two angles, but a close up of one of the people posing, Figure 8.3, for the shot shows the flash is coming from a different angle. By following the flash, we can see it did not cause the light on whatever may be floating in the room or any other light source or reflection. More importantly, by not having a source for the lights on the ball, we can classify it as unexplained.

Snapshot

If you belong to a group, or even if you investigate and evaluate alone, you should have some standard for how you look at evidence. Doing the same thing time after time makes all of your evidence have the same baseline. Also, as you start to experiment, you can remember where you started and how you veered off.

Those Old School Pictures

AS WE HAVE DISCUSSED, most respectable investigators will recommend using both digital and film, but many ignore good old film. Many more use it as a baseline for looking at their digital pictures, holding fast to the belief that a newer digital camera picks up more because of its range. The evidence you gather from a film camera, whether it is a disposable or a high-end camera, should go through the same workout you put your digital pictures through. The process is just different.

Get Out Your Magnifying Glass

All evidence should first be looked at in its entirety. Take the picture, get under a good source of light, and see if you can find anything. Then look at it again. I am a firm believer in looking at things a new way, so I always physically flip the photo and look at it from a new perspective. When you are looking for something out of the norm, you sometimes have to look at it in an unconventional way, just be careful not to find something that is not there.

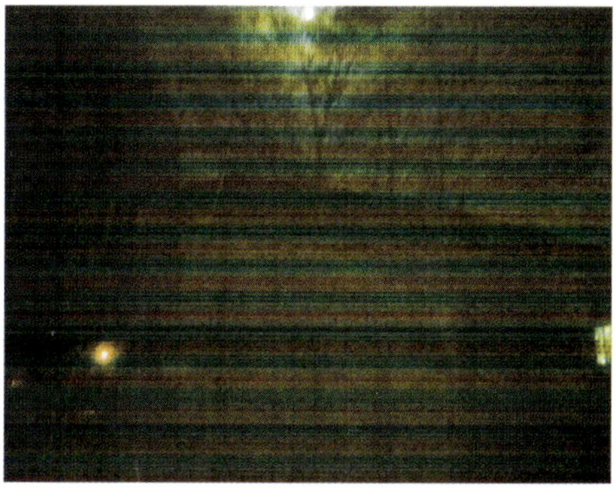

Figure 8.4
A bad example of a film picture that has been scanned. Untouched, the picture is grainy and unusable, and the original, before the scan, was not much better.

Assuming you have a normal size picture, the image is fairly small. Get out a magnifying glass. You may feel silly, like Sherlock Holmes, but it is the only way to enlarge old pictures in their purest form. Start in the lower-left section of the picture and work your way around the edge of the picture. Then move back to the middle, where your eye naturally went when you began, and put the picture down. If you have discovered something, focus on it the moment you spot it and then start the process over when you have determined if you have captured something.

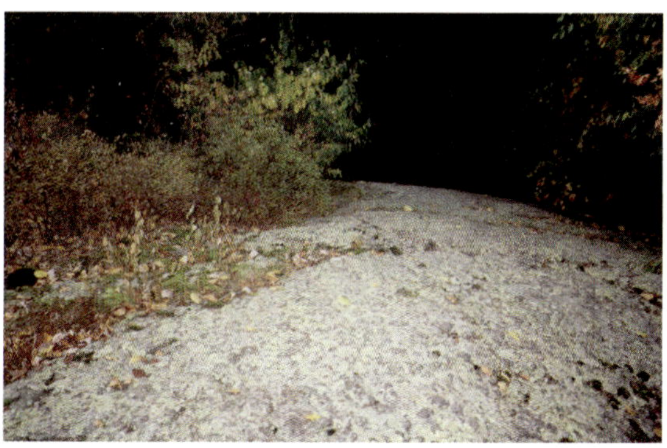

Figure 8.5
A better film shot and because it is clear to begin with, you can start looking for something paranormal.

Depending on the time you have, it is always a good idea to go back to the picture later. A fresh perspective might pick up something. Never throw away a picture because you did not find anything. I was investigating a famously haunted place and had seven pictures with nothing in them. I came to the eighth one and found an unexplained glow. All of them had been taken over the course of less than a minute, and in only one was there something there. The other seven gave some context to the last, making it all that more mysterious. The odd thing about that set of pictures was that the glow could be explained away if not for the others.

Sometimes It's Good to Be Negative

Before the days of digital, a few of the real photographers developed their own pictures. For most of us, the process looked really good in movies, creating a dramatic feel, but to actually do it meant more money and more time. If photography was your hobby it was worth it, but the rest of us just wanted to freeze our memories of our vacation. If you use film during an investigation, it might be worth it to learn to develop your own film, but most of us do not have the money or time or a space to turn into a dark room.

Even if you do not, you will still get the negatives of the pictures you have taken. The same attention might not be given to your pictures that once was, but there is still a process that turns the negative into a picture. Toner and developer are added, and machines now try to make sense of an image, a process often left to digital equipment.

The negative is the most direct representation of what the camera saw. While you may not be able to see the detail you have with the finished product, it is worth it to look at the negative and see if anything shows up. Again, do not take too much time, but a few minutes might bring something else to the evaluation, even if there is something you did not see the first time around.

Scanning

"We don't review scanned photos either. Even with higher quality scanners these days, there is still plenty that can go wrong and corrupt evidence. If we review anything, it is straight off the memory card and onto the computer."

—Allen Dunski Jr., Equipment Manager/Lead Investigator, Wisconsin Paranormal Investigators

There is a debate going on in the paranormal community about whether a scanner should be used to evaluate a picture. As we will discuss later this chapter, a digital version of a picture can be run through programs and analyzed, but the hard copy of a photo has to be taken at face value. It is a pure representation of what the camera picked up, or as pure as possible, but you cannot get a closer look or play with the brightness to bring out elements that draw your eye.

The only way to get to that next analytical level is to scan it and save it in a digital format. Many people, like Allen Dunski of Wisconsin Paranormal Investigators, feels any change to the picture makes it useless as evidence because the image has been changed somehow. You are basically taking a picture of a picture, and some of the newer scanners will analyze the picture before reproducing it, making the image what the computer thinks it is. In a field where everything is in question, that makes a tremendous difference.

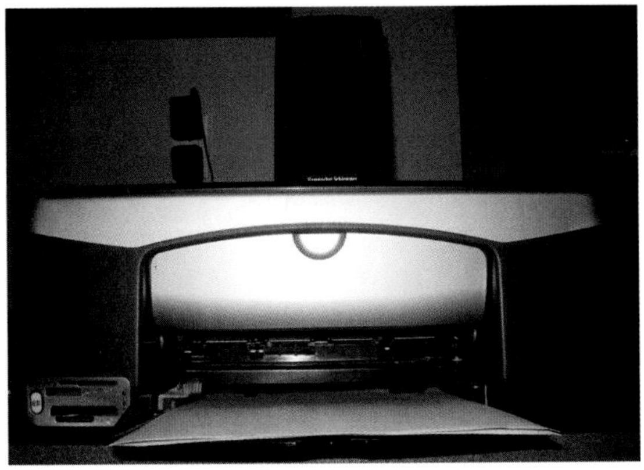

Figure 8.6
A scanner and a negative scanner.

The fact is no picture goes through real life, capture, and format of any kind without there being some form of corruption. Some might even say this corruption leaves the image open to that "intent argument" we discussed in Chapter 1. Film images should be scanned, if for no other reason than to format it so independent people can give an opinion on it, and as long as you document the machine you used to scan it, as well as the settings you had it on, the picture can stand as another element. Maybe it's just not the best proof.

When you scan the picture, use a color setting, even if the picture is in color, and use the highest resolution and size option you can. Most scanners will offer you several different settings, and the higher-end scanners will even bring out things your eyes see cannot because of the way it analyzes the picture. Keep it as large and powerful as possible and reduce elements of the picture when you apply features in your software picture program to it.

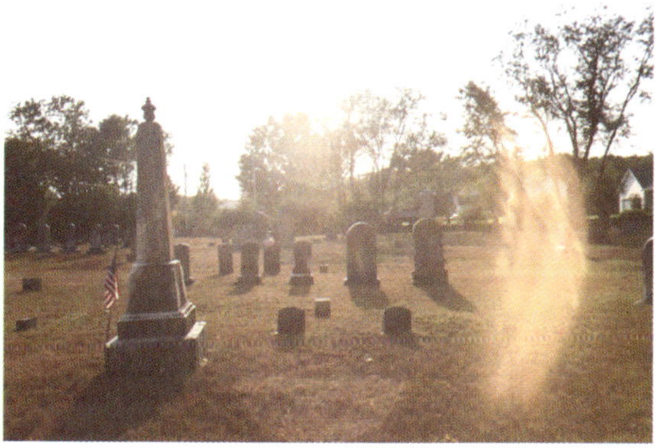

Figure 8.7
A picture scanned.

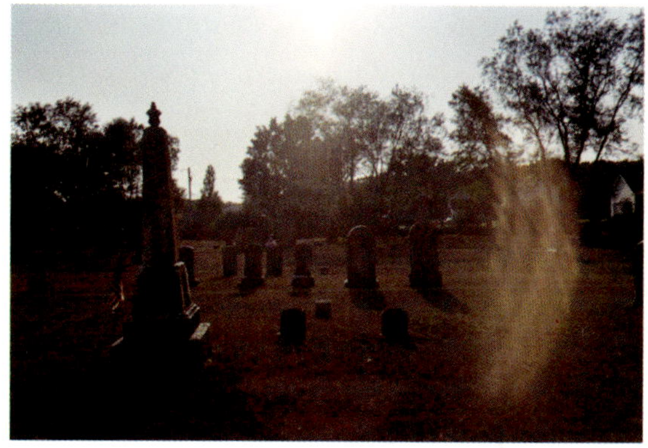

Figure 8.8
The same picture run through the negative scanner. The second image is a bit better.

I recently was even given a slide and negative to digital picture converter. I originally had planned for it to be used to sift through my grandfather's yellowing slides of the old country, but it can also be used to take negatives and create new digital images. The same problems apply as with other scanned pictures, but it opens up a whole new world of potential evidence.

> ### Snapshot
>
> **The ghosts of the past may be lurking in those old family albums. If you are looking to improve your ability to find spirits in film pictures, bring out those old albums. If you remember any old rumors about a relative's house, or even have pictures of things that deceased relatives might have been drawn to, scan them through and take a look. At worst, you sharpen your ghost eye, using available pictures, and maybe even rediscover a love of your past. At best, you find a full-bodied apparition standing over your grandmother at her retirement party.**

Going Digital

We download all pictures to PC and burn original photos to CD. The evaluation begins when we place the pictures on a large high-definition display one at a time and examine every inch, one inch at a time. We manipulate color, contrast, tint, and brightness to try to examine the photo's full spectrum. During this evaluation, we document the photo number and any anomalies and what program settings if any were being used when the anomaly was documented.

—Ericka and Rick Benson, Blue Spirits Paranormal Investigators

In general, pictures are first examined using Adobe Lightroom. Here I look at the content of the photo for mist, orbs, figures, etc. The next step is enhancing the photo by brightening the image. This usually brings out objects that were hiding in the darkness. This inspection usually results in finding one picture out of ten that warrants future investigation. These pictures are then examined using Adobe Photoshop.

—Louis Antonucci

While there are some standards most investigators agree on, looking at digital evidence depends solely on the investigator, and can be as varied as the investigators out there. Most feel a digital level of evaluation is needed, but some feel pictures should be left alone. Others feel an image should be run through every program you can download to bring out any possible unexplained speck.

Again, all methods are on the board, especially as you develop your own methods and discover what kind of investigator you are. The most important thing to remember is to document what you do.

Robyne views as a clairvoyant and goes into remote viewing. This is done separately, as to not influence the other members. The case manager makes note of findings. Members blow up photos and spend roughly four hours or longer on analyzing each still.

Areas are circled and questioned. All photos are passed onto each member for cross-check. All opinions are noted by case manager and compared after she reveals what the medium found.

—Lights Out Radio Show Investigations

It's All About the Equipment

The tool may make the ghost hunter. There are a variety of programs out there for looking at your images, and most investigators hold to their favorite like a little baby holds his blanket. When I asked investigators what they like to use, they all had a quick response, although none were able to tell me what they actually liked about them.

- **Adobe Photoshop Creative Suite**
- **Irfanview**
- **Windows Picture Viewer**
- **Adobe Lightroom**
- **Gimp**
- **Microsoft Picture Manager**

In addition, many specific cameras, and even film processing products, have their own software they may ask you to install when you purchase it. These stay on your computer and will try to sneak their way into your daily life as your default camera editor.

Which is best? I always apply the same logic to all aspects of paranormal equipment. Whatever is the best quality product that fits into your budget is the one you should select. Remember, Photoshop is both a proper noun and a verb these days, and by the responses, it seems to be the program of choice. You can download free versions of it, and the more features you want the more that you pay after that.

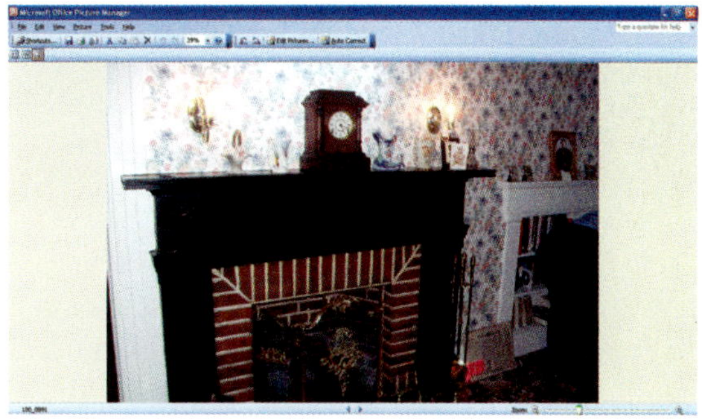

Figure 8.9
Evidence being looked at with Microsoft Picture Manager.

Prior to and during the investigation, all weather and climate conditions are recorded in order to eliminate anomalies such as breath and water orbs. Pictures are then examined on a computer screen for shadows, fingertips, camera straps, and other naturally occurring phenomena. Colors are inverted to help rule out human error. All remaining pictures are then printed out to an 8x10 size where they are examined even closer for explainable reasons for the anomalies. If no natural explanations are found, the photograph is then considered to be evidence.

—Clarissa Vazquez, CCPI

There is a fine line between them, but you must always manipulate and evaluate a picture. Once you get into editing a picture, you are changing it too much and the integrity of it as evidence is compromised. Creative Suite may be good for making your group's new logo, but it may entice you into too much editing. Gimp is great for making a newsletter, but too complicated at times. The best combination of functionality, price, and results may just be the free Microsoft Picture Editor that comes standard on most newer PCs.

Take a Closer Look

Once you have opened a picture with your favorite software, the best way to look at the picture is to blow it up. Perhaps the best feature of any digital picture software is its ability to easily enlarge the image to a size that lets you focus in on one area. Take the same process we discussed with the old-fashioned magnifying glass and apply it to your digital image. Scan the entire picture and do not just look at the obvious things. Enlarge anything you think warrants closer scrutiny, just remember when you enlarge the picture the larger pixels lose their properties. This may lead to seeing things that are not there and losing the context of the situation.

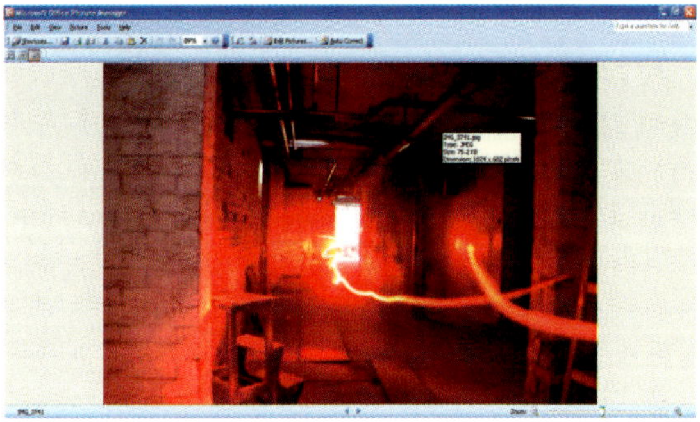

Figure 8.10
A picture of a light streak.
Picture courtesy of Josh Mantello.

You can also use your software to flip the picture in 90-degree increments, allowing you to look at it from a different perspective. One of the limitations of Picture Editor is that this is the only degree of movement. Other software makes it possible to rotate the picture as much as you want. Doing this and confusing your eye may help you see things in a whole new light and make an element in the picture new to you.

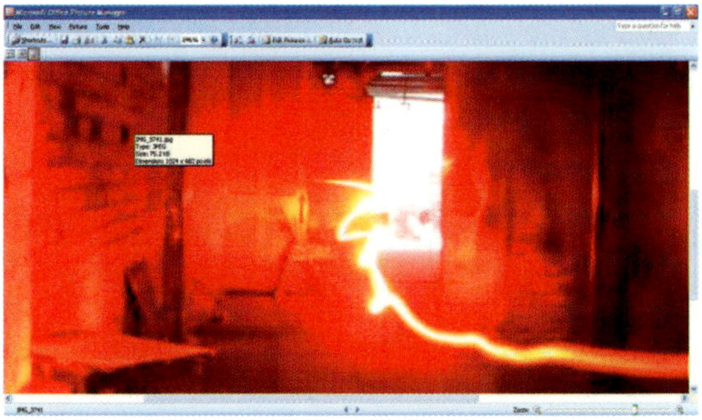

Figure 8.11
The same picture zoomed in to try to detail the figure in the middle.

Do not zoom in too much. The computer will adjust and refocus an image the best it can when you zoom, but everything looks eerie when you look at it close up. Think of those old Saturday cartoon puzzles where they would focus in on a picture and the more they panned back, the more you could recognize it. Anything is otherworldly when you get too close.

Contrast

A picture does not know what it is, just like a camera does not know what it is taking a picture of. A digital image is not what really happened; it is merely the camera's interpretation of the contrast in light and dark and color and texture of a scene. No matter how smart a camera is, it cannot look for a ghost, or a ghostly element. It just captures what is there. Sometimes the energy a ghost gives off or uses to manifest may be taken in, but the camera does not know what to do with it. It might be so subtle it does not register enough to make a big splash.

Figure 8.12
A picture taken in a hallway.
Picture courtesy of Luann Joly.

Playing with the light and brightness of a picture changes the image, but it may apply a new contrast that brings something up. This is not editing the photo as much as it is going back to the virtual darkroom and adding different amounts of chemicals to the negative to add new life into the photo. Same picture, different package.

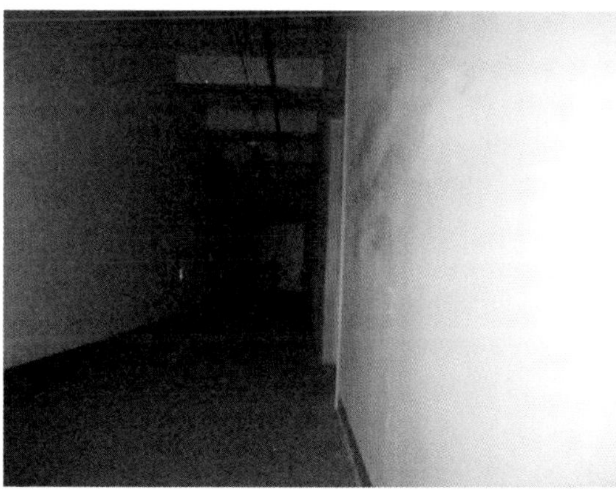

Figure 8.13
The same picture, with the brightness changed, shows a ghostly figure at the end of the hall.
Picture courtesy of Luann Joly.

The first change I suggest is adjusting brightness. There are some in the paranormal world who would disagree with me, but I feel good evidence can be gained by shooting with less flash and then making the picture brighter in the evaluation. I do this, as I explained in Chapter 6, by changing the flash exposure compensation and then upping the light after the fact. This reduces the chances of the flash creating more ghosts than it helps to capture.

Brightness can be your friend. Just by making a picture darker or lighter, it shifts the way your eye sees certain things. The contrast between the two elements remains the same, but the standard is different and some things become clear.

You can move the brightness, contrast, and midtone to change the lighting of the image. All start at 0 and can go up and down into the negative and positive ranges. If you go to the extremes of any of these, your picture will be all dark or all light, like looking into the light at the end of the tunnel. Instead, try to move the numbers in small increments to affect change. There is usually a line where the image is its best, and it might take a few minutes to find it on each setting. Always record what you have done to the picture so others know where it moved from, but think of any finished picture as a natural extension of the investigation, not something you created.

Color

One of the more interesting ideas I heard from a paranormal group involved color. They suggested flooding a room with filtered light and then taking pictures to try to capture a ghost. For example, take a green gel from a theater lighting system, run a bright light behind it, and then conduct an investigation. The resulting pictures might bring out more ghosts, and depending on what color brought them out, an investigator might gain more insight into the nature of spirits.

Figure 8.14
A fuzzy, dark picture taken at a haunted location.
Picture courtesy of Jason Lorfice and Paranormal Investigators of New England.

What insight and why this would work was never fully explained to me, nor do I fully embrace it now, but it was something new. Then I realized I had been trying to do that after the fact for years. I had been injecting my pictures with extra color using picture software trying to find a small change, and while it tells me nothing about the nature of the ghost itself, it sometimes helps me to see it better.

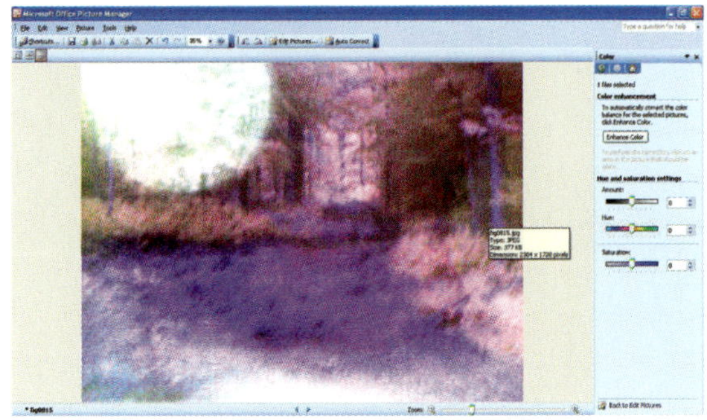

Figure 8.15
The same picture with only the "enhance color" feature used.

To manipulate the color in the picture, you need to change the amount of certain colors in the picture using the hue and saturation features. All pictures are created by a balance of primary colors. In other words, a deep red is formed by combining red with another color. The scales are typically RGB, or red, green, blue; or CMYK, cyan, magenta, yellow, and black. Think of a hardware store mixing colors at certain levels to produce that Cappuccino Cream color you used in your bedroom. Better yet, think of a printer with these three or four color cartridges. You can do the same thing by manipulating color and contrast features. This is more of a trial and error process than a science because it is impossible to know how the image will respond to change, but it is worth it to bring out a potential spirit. Just make sure you document the changes you made and keep the original picture.

There needs to be color in the picture to begin with for this kind of manipulation to work. If you have a picture that is too dark, like Figure 8.14, you have no color to change. The "enhance color" feature might be a better tool, which changes the overall color of the picture based on what in the picture is supposed to be white.

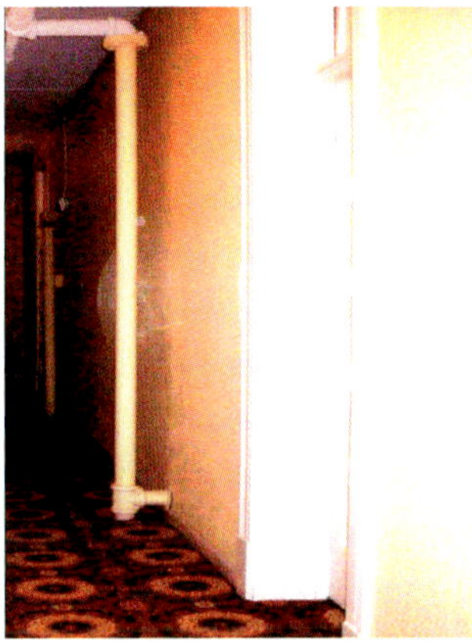

Figure 8.16
A shot of a potential spirit in the hallway.
Picture courtesy of Clarissa Vazquez.

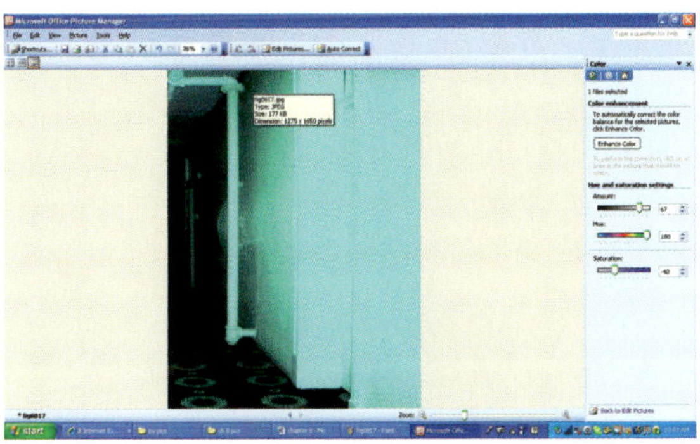

Figure 8.17
The same picture with some of the color features changed. The mixture of saturation and green washed out the color of the walls and made the object in the middle stand out.

The Matrix Is Not Just a Movie

I remember an old episode of the *Twilight Zone* where a woman was in an asylum because she was convinced demons were trying to get her. She believed they talked to her, and tried to attack her, through faces in the cracks of a normally smooth surface. As she looked at the imperfections, they began to look like noses and mouths and eyes. I think of that episode whenever I am looking at the pattern on my mother's bathroom wall, and I try to fight it when I am looking at evidence after an investigation.

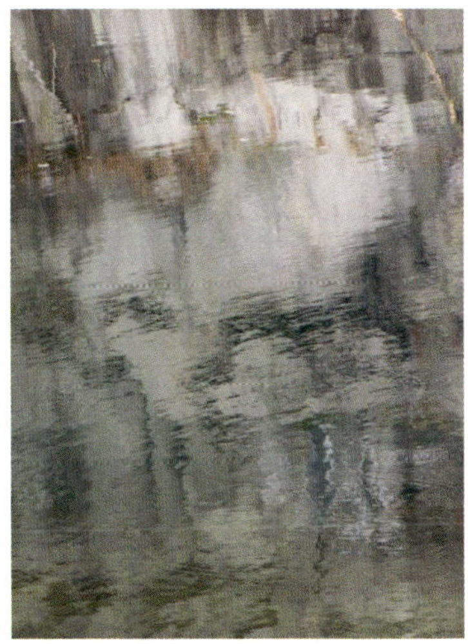

Figure 8.18
The face of a monster seen in the water of a haunted location.
Picture courtesy of Spryng Benjamin.

Matrixing is the process, or the condition, where the human brain tries to make sense and create order from anything that is seen through the human eye. Ever see someone and think they look just like your best friend from camp when you were ten? The closer they get, the more they become an individual, and you usually cannot even see how you thought the two were connected.

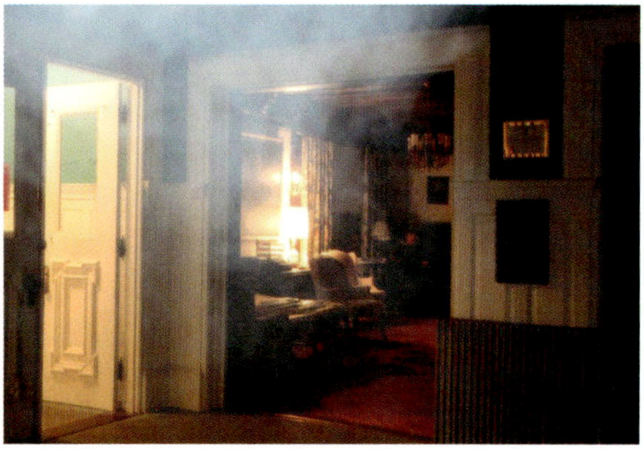

Figure 8.19
Smoke is famous for its matrix factor.
Picture courtesy of Josh Mantello.

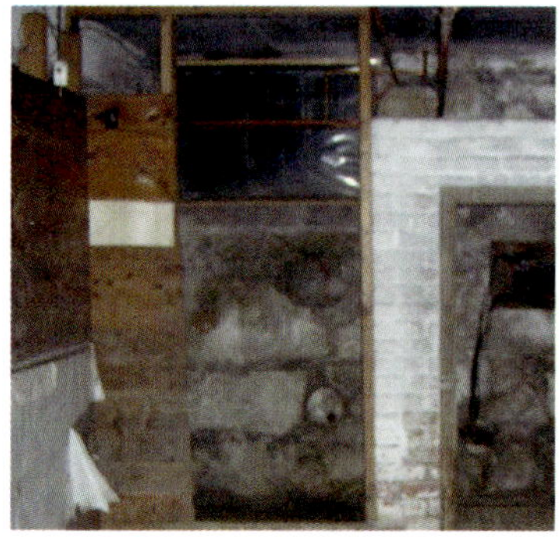

Figure 8.20
Notice the screaming child?
Picture courtesy of Jessica Stone.

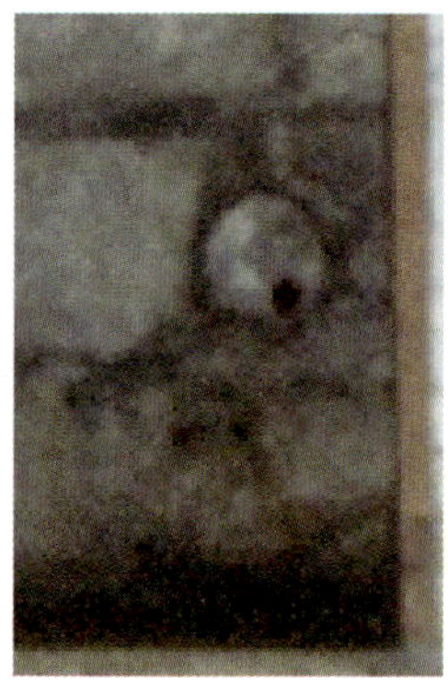

Figure 8.21
How about closer up?
Picture courtesy of Jessica Stone.

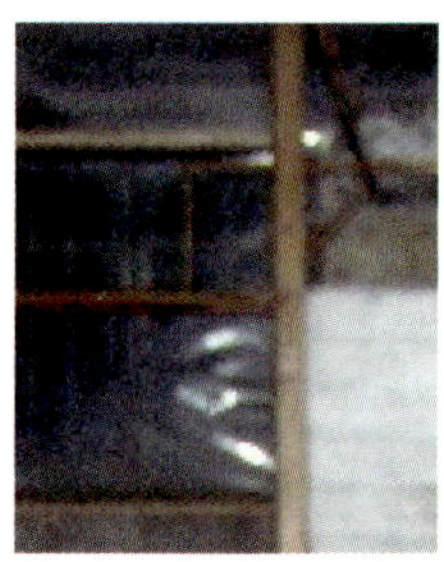

Figure 8.22
Or is this the potential ghost in the picture?
Picture courtesy of Jessica Stone.

Your brain is designed to recognize patterns and familiar rudiments, and when it sees something, it runs it through everything you have ever witnessed, even if you do not know you witnessed it, and determines the closest natural match. This came in handy ten thousand years ago when you came in contact with a vicious animal. Your memory matched it up with the animal you saw eat the hunters last rainy reason, and before your waking mind made a decision, your feet were taking you far away.

The downside of this evolutionary tool is that your mind is constantly putting things in order, even things you do not want to put in order. It is the reason there is a face on the surface of the moon, and why I keep seeing faces staring back at me in marble. One form of spirit communication we will talk about in Chapter 11 relies on using visual white noise, such as television static, to create a blank palette for spirits to use. Some feel matrixing accounts for the sighting of some of the spirits seen during these sessions.

The Suggestion Experiment

Matrixing becomes an even bigger issue in spirit photography when you are told what to look for. Most paranormal investigators do not ask other ghost hunters if they see what they see. They just ask what the other person might see in a picture. I received an e-mail last week where a man asked, "Do you think the two red spots behind the drummer are the eyes of something? There is even a bit of smoke that comes down around him. That looks like an arm. Do you agree?" It is the "don't look down" concept. I opened up the file containing the picture and immediately began looking for the eyes and the arm.

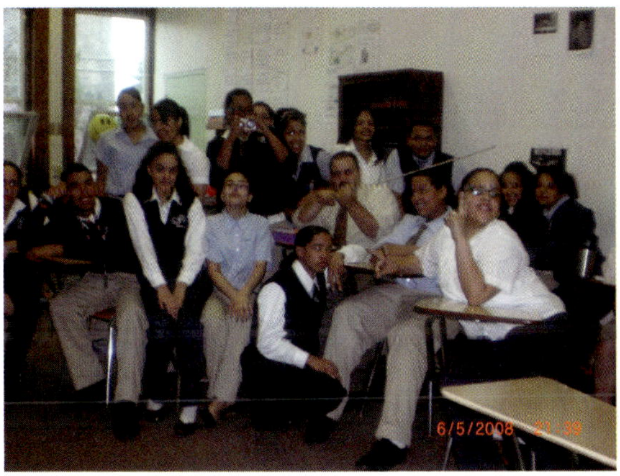

Figure 8.23
An end of the year picture and the root of the Suggestion Experiment.

People who approach paranormal investigators looking for answers often do so with a description of the picture. With the added map supplied, matrixing will find it, even if there is nothing to find. I recently sent out Figure 8.24 to 20 investigators I had never spoken to or worked with. I asked them if they believed the figure in the mirror was something paranormal. I told them the school had been in existence since 1810 (a lie) and several people had died there over the years (another lie).

There are several small anomalies seen in the windows of the picture. If you wanted to focus on something, there is a stain in the shape of a woman with a Victorian hat. I did not tell them what window to focus on or what I saw. My only map to the matrix was to look in the windows and the age.

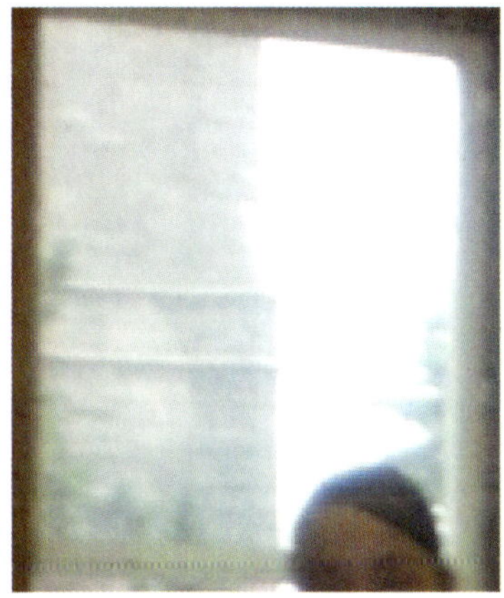

Figure 8.24
A close-up of the window where people have seen a woman in Victorian dress.

The responses I received back were telling. Of the 20 people I approached, all but two saw something in the window they believed warranted further investigation. Ten asked if they could come and conduct a ghost hunt. Three asked me if there was a history of a demonic activity in the building. Thirteen saw, in addition to several other figures, the Victorian woman, although one investigator, probably taking a cue from the fact the students are in Catholic uniforms, suggested the woman was a nun.

Beware when you evaluate pictures to keep other people's ideas separate until you have formed your opinion. More importantly, identify when you have been briefed on a picture, especially if it becomes evidence.

The paranormal field can take its biggest steps forward with some form of standardization. If investigators could look at the same picture, untouched and unedited, and have a common way to classify it, it would make talking about them easier. For some time now, Josh Mantello of the Berkshire Paranormal Group has been working on the issue. His work on a classification system for pictures has been adopted by other groups and continues to be a point of debate and argument, but it offers a jumping off point for the discussion.

Photographic Classification

by Josh Mantello

The Issue Addressed

Over the past few years, the people in the electronic voice phenomena field have been placing their recordings into classifications based on the clarity and the ease of understanding. It ranges from Class A to C with very little explanation of what lies in between the headings. This system has worked well for them, but I wondered why other aspects of paranormal investigating had not adopted a similar grading system. Recently, I was preparing a presentation based on photographs and the paranormal that would show a series of pictures ranging from fakes to pictures that I thought truly had a ghost in them. I wanted an easier way to explain and categorize the pictures for the attendees and why I thought they were ghost pictures or why I thought they were fake and misleading based on known, naturally caused anomalies.

I developed a grading system not unlike what the people in the EVP field use, putting the pictures in a class ranging from A to C. I had the idea to use these on all future investigations and other possible evidence pictures and offer it up to other investigators to possibly help document their photographs.

The System

CLASS C: Natural causes can immediately be contributed as the cause of the anomaly in the photograph. Through an understanding of the environment or other cues in the picture, those natural elements can be determined and are applied to the picture. In other words, not a ghost picture.

Examples:

- **Orbs in a picture that was taken in a dusty room or when raining.**
- **Fogs, mists, and ecto in pictures when someone was smoking nearby or it is foggy outside.**
- **Apparition in window when someone was standing behind window with sheet over their head.**

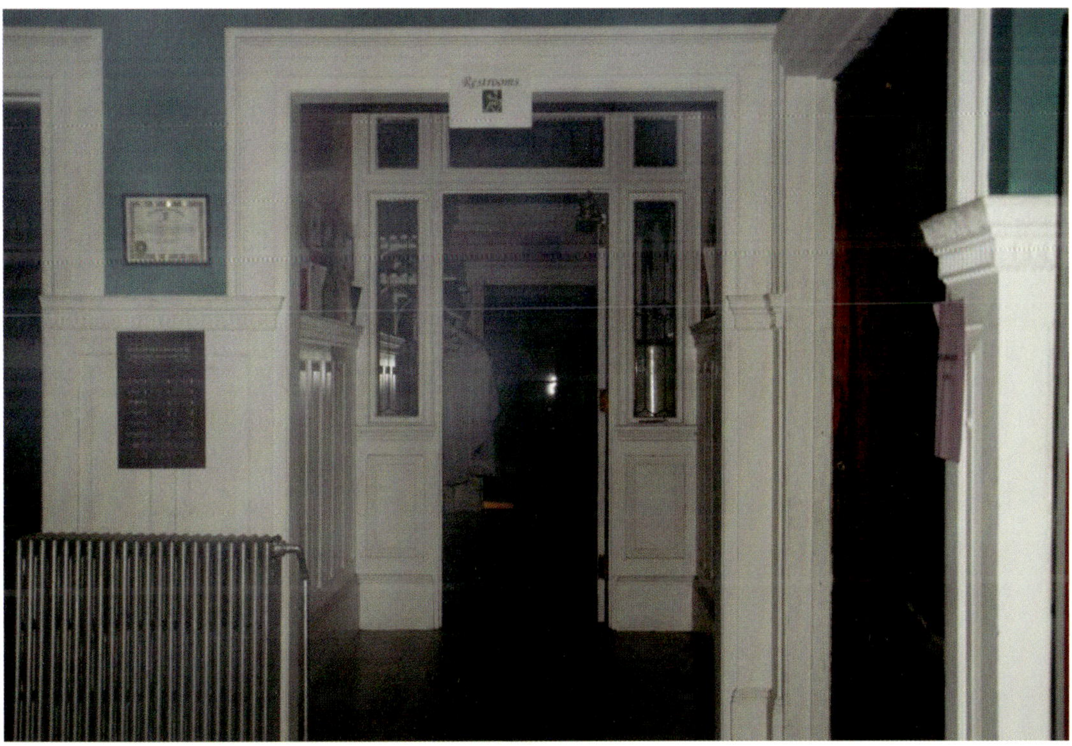

Figure 8.25
A smoke picture that falls into Class C. Picture courtesy of Josh Mantello.

CLASS B: Natural causes cannot be ruled out as the cause of the anomaly in picture, but other documented paranormal activity was occurring at the time the picture was taken. In other words, the picture may be dismissed on its own merit, but it has more weight because of the context the picture was taken in.

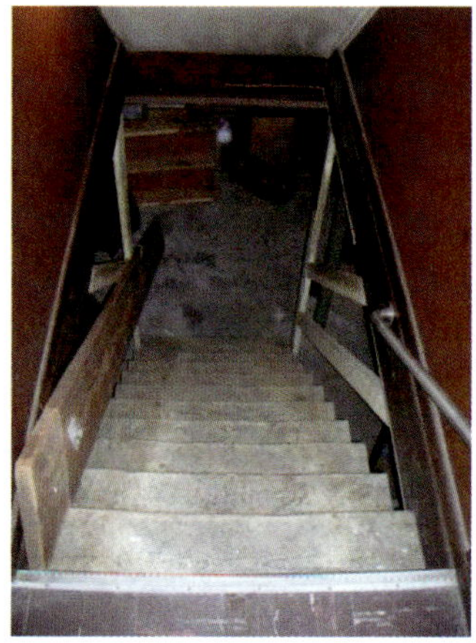

Figure 8.26
An orb taken at a haunted location. The picture was taken after we heard footsteps on the stairs when no one else was in the building.

Examples:

- **An orb that looks similar to dust orbs but its placement coincides with someone's personal experience or high EMF reading and/or temperature variations**
- **Matrixing cannot be ruled out as the cause of an apparition, but someone else present during the picture taking might have seen or experienced something**

CLASS A: Natural causes cannot be found as the cause of the anomaly in the photograph. All of the standard reasons for a bad picture have been exhausted and the picture must now be evaluated on what it might represent in the paranormal world.

Examples:

- **A smoke or mist in the pictures when it is known that no one was smoking at the time of the picture taking and it was too warm for breath to show up.**
- **Light streaks when the shutter speed on the camera was set to a fast speed or tripod was used.**

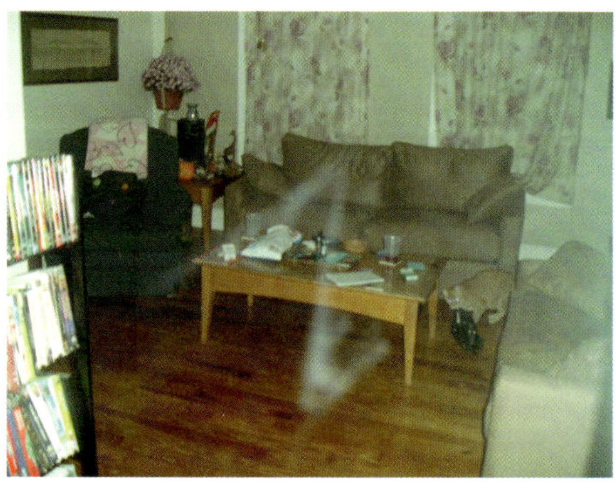

Figure 8.27
A strong Class A picture.
Picture courtesy of Katie Zahner.

Upon Further Review

It is possible to mix these using a + / – along with each classification. This classification system wasn't made to be complicated to learn or put into use. I also made it simple so that it can be adapted to fit each investigator's needs. These classifications can come in handy and work well when we, as investigators, start trying to present our pictures as evidence to other investigators or the public. Obviously, we won't be showing our class C pictures to either the public or other investigators as evidence. They are most likely best used within your own group to help demonstrate to new investigators what some of the naturally causing anomalies in pictures look like. Another aspect of a class C picture is that you may go back to your client after an investigation and show them how what you got in their location could be natural. In most cases, when a group is approached for an investigation, the client usually has some sort of picture with what they feel is ghost or ghostly related phenomena in it and want you to perform an investigation in their house. If you can re-create the picture they supplied as a Class C anomaly during your investigation and actually explain why it is there and how you created it, it may actually help put your client's mind to rest.

A Class B might be something worth showing to other investigators as they will respect and understand the personal experiences and paranormal-related events surrounding the pictures, whereas the general public may not. These pictures may also be shown to your client if you're investigating someone's private residence. Just be careful when explaining to them that though you feel the picture may be paranormally related there is still a strong chance something natural caused what they are looking at. The key to this is being able to back up your personal experience or other paranormal evidence at the time of the picture. Anyone can get a picture with some sort of evidence in it and then make up a story behind it. Obviously a Class A is what you want to show to the public and let the skeptics and naysayers try to pick it apart. Maybe a good Class B+ picture would still be suitable for the public with good explanations and documentation as to why you think the anomaly isn't naturally caused. Offer up these pictures knowing that you can't find a logical and reasonable explanation for the anomalies but someone else with more knowledge and background in photography may. Even if you do choose to use all the classes of pictures as presentable evidence, at least putting them into a class for the public to see will help them understand the picture and what they may be looking at better.

Just because we give the label of Class A to a picture doesn't necessarily mean it is the final proof of the paranormal. I would only say that this may fall under being 70-to-90-percent proof of documentation of a haunting. I surely wouldn't say a house is haunted based on one Class A picture. There are so many possible natural causes and environmental effects that even the most scientifically controlled investigation can't control or document all of them.

We have the classification system down and its basics covered, but let's look into what will help us show what makes each picture fall into its different classification system. A lot of what we need to show and prove for the picture to lend its creditability can simply be found in some good quality documentation. A good example of this is a picture showing a mist or fog. This anomaly can be ruled out very easily due to many different natural causes such as your breath on a cold night or even cigarette smoke. But what if it was 80 degrees at the location you were investigating and a strict no smoking policy is followed by you and your investigators? Well then, that picture with the mist suddenly goes from a Class C to a Class A. Now we don't need to be meticulous with our documentation but a simple note of what the general temperature was during the investigation will cover it. I like to have someone document the temperature at the investigation site every 15 to 20 minutes.

The documentation does not have to go as far as writing down every single detail at the time of each and every picture. But try to document what was going on during particular blocks or groups of pictures. For example, write down the different camera settings, environmental conditions, and any other relevant information, including paranormal activity, for pictures 1 though 10 and then the same for pictures 11 through 20. Another great way to document what was going on while each picture was being taken is something you very well might already be doing and that is videotaping your investigation. Your video of the investigation might show you taking the picture in question that has some sort of anomaly in it and it might very well show something that the camera did not see that is causing whatever is in the still picture.

When you have an anomaly in a picture, you can go back to your notes and determine any possible explanation for the anomaly. If in your documentation you find that something naturally caused the phenomena in the picture, you may have just turned a Class A picture into a Class B or C and maybe saved yourself some later embarrassment of passing of faulty evidence as true. For example, a week later I am looking at my pictures and I notice a light streak or shooting orb through picture number 42. I can simply look at the notes and see that it was caused by one of my own investigators. Just as I can say that if I have a lot of orbs in pictures 30 through 33 it is most likely due to bugs flying around my camera.

Picture #	Temp	Weather	Shutter Speed	Flash	Tripod	Paranormal Activity & Notes
1–12	72	Clear	1 Sec.	Off	Yes	None
12–24	68	Inside	Auto	On	No	EMF spikes
25–29	32	Snow	Auto	On	No	Could see breath
30–33	80	Clear	0.5 Sec.	On	Yes	Buggy
34–39	70	Inside	Auto	On	No	Large amount of windows
40–44	66	Inside	8 Sec.	Off	Yes	Someone walked through frame on picture 42 with light

Figure 8.28
An example of Mantello's documentation system.

The King of Evaluation

EARLY IN 1996, A FRIEND OF MINE was scheduled to start classes at the satellite school of our college in Hollywood. With a little time to spare and an adventurous spirit, she decided to drive across the country to get there. She left Boston with a friend of hers and drove to North Carolina to visit the friend's family. They spent a few days and began the trip west to California, and because they both were such fans, they planned a trip to Graceland to visit the home of Elvis.

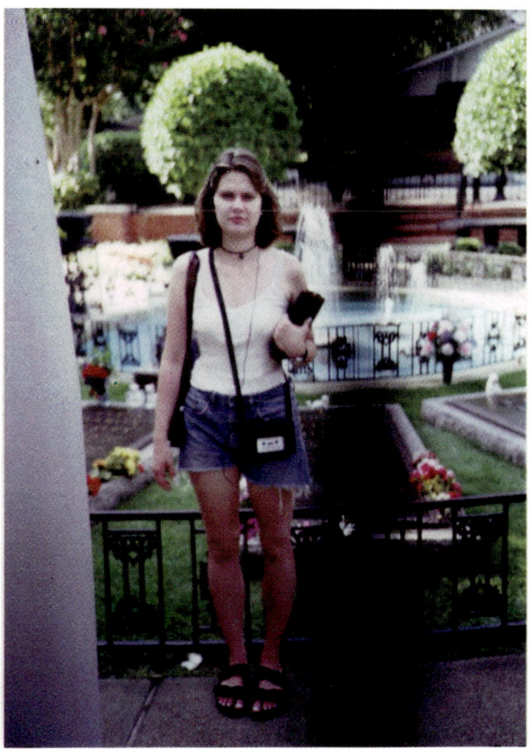

Figure 8.29
The original scanned picture.

This picture was taken of my friend in front of the grave of the man who changed Rock and Roll forever. Although she did not originally notice it when she developed the film, I immediately saw the figure when she showed me pictures of the trip.

I submitted the picture to several investigators to see what they thought and to present to you how different people see the same picture. I told each investigator when I sent them the picture:

I am sending through a harmless ghost photo, and I'd love to have everyone's opinion on it. It has not been altered in any way, although it is a scan of the original, which I know some of you may have issue with. It was taken with a standard film camera with no special adjustments other than autofocus. It was also taken during the day, sometime before dusk, so no flash was used. It is a picture of a friend of mine taken around 1997 or so at Graceland. The marker behind whatever is there is the grave of Elvis.

There is no right or wrong answer. I am looking to see what you think and why, so please explain what you think it might be and how you came to that conclusion. It is not a trick or set-up picture, just an unexplained one.

When I received some responses back, and always when asked about specific details, I added the following information:

- **The young lady in the picture has been on paranormal investigations, but none before the picture was taken.**
- **The young lady did have an interest in the paranormal before the picture was taken.**
- **The young lady considers herself slightly psychic, but she felt nothing when the picture was taken.**
- **The young lady and the person who took the picture got into a serious, life-threatening car accident only a few days after the picture was taken.**
- **That accident may have damaged the film, although the camera made it through with no damage. I am unsure if the film was out of the camera at the time of the accident.**
- **The young lady had lost someone close to her less than a year before the trip.**

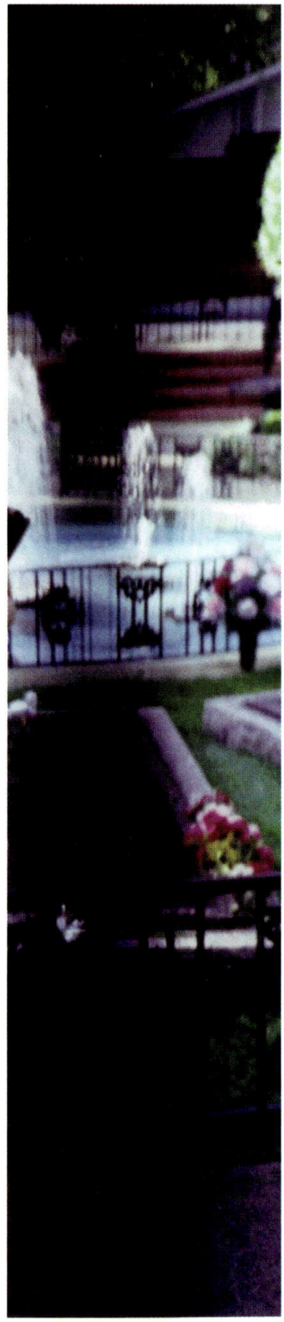

Figure 8.30
A close-up of the band of black.

Here are the responses I received:

1. The photograph you sent brought about some questions. The first question being camera position. The photograph appears to be vertical. I'm curious to know if there was also a horizontal picture taken as well, since that is usually the case with vertical pictures. If a horizontal picture was taken immediately prior to or following the picture in question, then discrepancies like film integrity and camera strap can be eliminated.

   I can almost completely eliminate structural shadows, simply because the anomaly appears to dissipate in the middle, which I found to be both fascinating and strange.

   I cannot rule out the possibility of a stray hair though. Particularly a hair that has been colored or even has some curl to it. Both of those could account for the dissipation in the middle.

   —Clarissa Vazquez

   Note: There was no horizontal picture taken, but the person who took the picture had both dyed and curly hair.

2. After viewing your photograph, I personally don't think there is anything paranormal going on here. I believe this could be a printing error. In order to rule that out, I would ask to see the negative of that picture.

   Also, without knowing time of day, conditions of the weather and surrounding objects, it is almost impossible for me to say that it is paranormal.

   —Allen Dunski

   Note: The negative no longer exists.

3. I looked at the photo and to me it looks like a standard camera strap.
   - It goes all the way across the image.
   - The picture is not '"sharp" so there had to be a longer than normal shutter speed. With the longer shutter speed it would allow the strap to move enough to look transparent and to capture the details behind it. It also looks like she is standing in the shadows and I don't see evidence of a flash bounce anyplace. Once again leads me to think no flash was used, which equals a *slow shutter speed.*
   - The streak looks to be wider at the bottom. This would happen because the strap would swing from the top, pivot point, and the bottom would swing further.
   - If you look closely at the streak you will see the left and right edges allow more of the background to show through while the center is harder to see through. This also lends to the theory that if the camera strap is swinging in front of the lens, it passes twice through the center (example: once when it swings left, once again when it swings right), which makes the center darker.

   —Gene Lafferty

4. The photo looks like it has a strap of some kind going across the lens to me. But I think the clear portion of the middle is unexplained unless the strap was twisted at that point making it appear edge on. That would give the out of focus black portion the widest part of the strap.

   —Mike Markowicz

5. Of course, my specialty is doing spirit readings off photos. This is an older, short woman. She is actually facing the grave and looking down onto it. She is praying. She has light hair, and I want to say white. When I do my spirit readings, the spirit shows animated as if they are alive today. It is their energy that comes through and I can communicate with them this way. But this is my style blending psychometry and remote viewing. This lady is very sad and a feeling of missing in her heart. I can feel the emotions.

   Scientifically, of course, there is a significant shadow showing vertically—it almost looks as if there is something tall behind the photographer that may be casting this shadow across the lawn and water. It looks as if it shadows the staircase in the far background (my skeptical side). If there was nothing tall casting this shadow, then I would have to say there is a shadow person standing directly in front of the photographer, practically beside your friend.

   —Robyne Marie, Lights Out Paranormal Investigators

What They Saw

Each investigator took an approach based on their own belief system and their own experience, and what was similar and different about their responses tell much about who they are as investigators and gives a well rounded picture of how to look at evidence.

As we discussed in Chapter 3, one of the most obvious explanations for a ghostly figure like this is a camera strap. Given the age of the picture and the fact it is a film camera, that is a legitimate reason for a column of black next to a figure in a picture. The gray figure on the left side of the photo is unexplained, and would even point to the fact the photographer would be more likely to make a mistake and have something not desired come into the frame. All of the investigators who responded asked the right follow-up questions and noted the picture's limitations. The time of day is unknown and would have an impact on shadow and light, which can also be said for the weather conditions at the time. Clarissa asked about camera position and a contrast picture, which we discussed in this chapter and in Chapter 7, and her opinion was echoed by other investigators who viewed the pictures. Allen asks for the negative, which is a step that should always be taken if it can be.

The differences are what keep the field of paranormal investigating moving forward. Many people out there ghost hunting take the approach that nothing is paranormal and something has to be proven supernatural before it can be held up as evidence, and the debunking culture fostered by many of the paranormal shows have made this the dominant approach. Allen, for example, is more comfortable saying the picture is not paranormal because he can come up with a reason for it to be there and cannot know everything there is to know about it. Mike, by contrast, seems to come from a place where you must evaluate everything as potentially being paranormal, and his response talks about what may be explained and then leaves open the possibility for other elements to be unexplained.

The biggest point of contention is over the narrow part of the shadow in the middle. Some feel there is an explanation, a twist of the strap or a swinging motion, while others hail it as a reason for a second look.

Robyne is the most obvious deviation from the other responders. As a trained psychic, she takes her evaluation to another level, and her group relies on her to see things in the picture a software program would never see. She connects with the subjects of the picture, but she also offers a more scientific slant as well. This is a crucial aspect of all paranormal investigating. There is no way to be a complete investigator without bringing in other ideas, but many psychics will not embrace science and science-based investigators will not use psychics. By using both, you may be able to get some answers that would be overlooked by a more narrow view.

What I Think

I was pulled into this picture from the first time I saw it, and it challenges me enough that I needed to look at it again after more than ten years. While I respect the opinions of the people who responded, there are some things they are not seeing.

The shadow in the picture is in the photo, not in the scene itself. Even it was in the scene, if the sun was in a position to make that figure, my friend would be squinting instead of looking straight ahead.

With all of that being said, I do not think this is a camera strap. Most cameras have the strap on the right side of the camera because it would be logical to wrap the camera around your right hand when you were not using it. If you were to turn the camera to take a picture, it would be more natural to move your left hand to the top. During the late stages of writing this book, my daughter was born and my parents travelled to Florida to visit us. There were hundreds of pictures taken by almost two dozen people. I asked each, with no explanation of why, to take a vertical picture. With a confused look all 20 turned the camera this way and had their strap hanging down below the camera.

Some Math to Confuse You

You must often think of evaluating evidence as a series of probabilities, and if the odds that it is a ghost outweighs the odd of it not, then you must see it as paranormal, or at least remain open to the possibility. Unfortunately many people feel there are no odds of anything being paranormal, and even if there are, it is abstract to use as a comparison. For the strap, use this math. If the odds of the strap being caught on camera is 1 in 10, which may be a bit conservative, and the odds of the strap being bent in the middle is 1 in 20, than the odds of both of those things happening together is 1 in 200.

Those odds lean towards a natural occurrence. For every 200 pictures you take, you will get 1 strap that shows like a shadow in the picture and that strap will have a twist that makes it look like it disappears in the middle. Now you need to factor the other aspects of the picture. Say the odds of getting a strap on your camera that does not appear in the middle of the picture and has no slant is 1 in 100. We are now looking at 1 in 20,000. Just when you have a handle on that math, factor in one more variable. What are the odds of getting a picture of a shadow in the same location of a grave? If those odds are 1 in 1,000, and that is very liberal to anyone who does not believe in ghosts, we are now taking about a 1 in 20,000,000. In other words, for every 20 million picture you take, all of these elements will be there naturally.

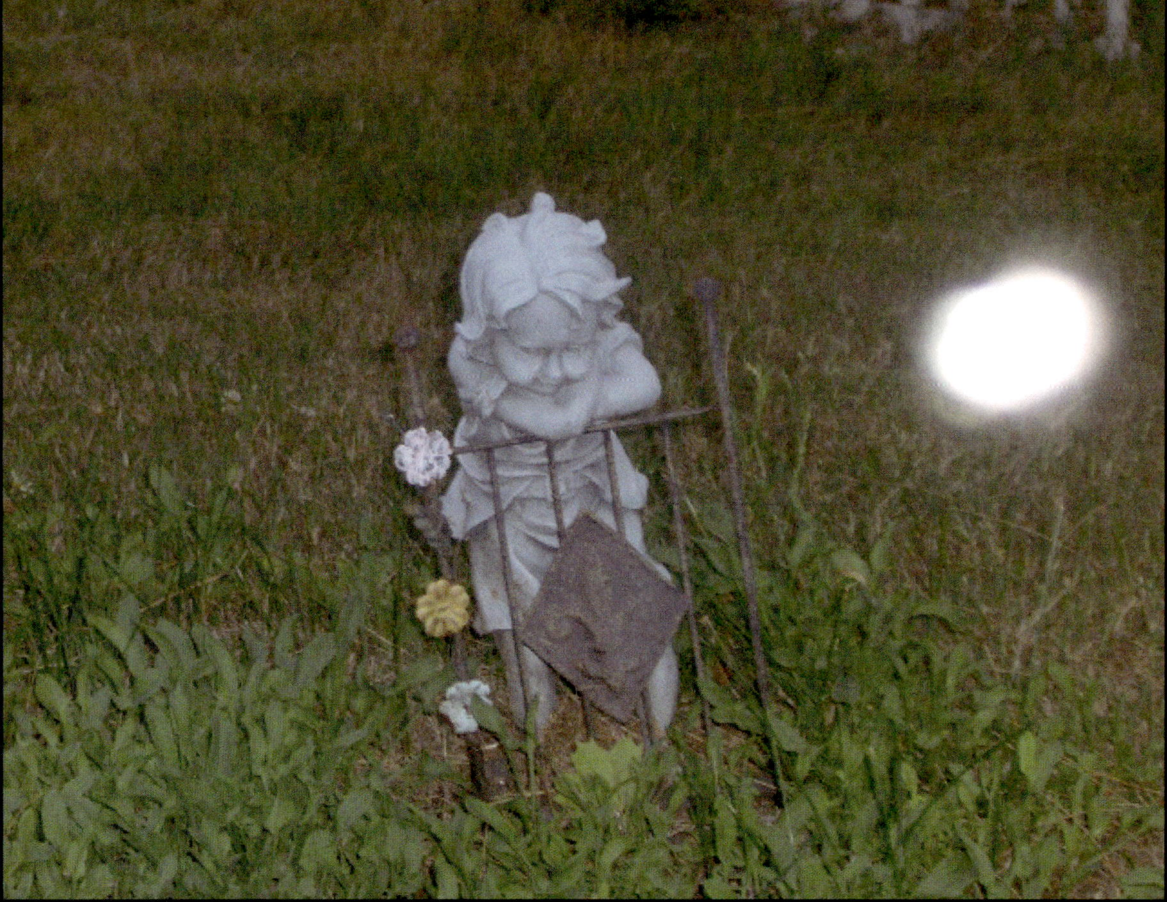

A cemetery orb.
Picture courtesy of Clarissa Vazquez.

9

The Great Orb Debate

TWO PARANORMAL INVESTIGATORS come to your door and ask if you need anyone to look for ghosts in your house. You want the more experienced person, as well as the one who has the best head on his shoulders, but how can you find out which one might be better for the job? You pull out a picture of a cemetery taken at night with bright balls of lights cascading down. The first investigator looks at the picture and asks where it was taken. It is an area of high paranormal activity. You turn to the second investigator to ask his opinion but he is already on his computer publishing the picture to his blog. "You should be ashamed," he says to you. "Anyone can see these are dust and moisture. The world needs to see these non-ghost ghost pictures. Now, do you have any pictures of real ghosts?" If you have a ghost, go with the second guy. He's been doing this longer.

Anyone who has been investigating long enough has been seduced by the lore of the orb, and usually if you have been in the business that long you have become cynical towards any circular light source. Sometimes you find old ghost hunters walking around in a daze, yelling at car headlights and light bulbs about how the flash of a camera can reflect off of small bits of dust and water. It is the kind of temperament that comes from crouching over pictures for hours on end and being to countless meetings or conferences that preach the evil of the orb photo.

To many who take looking for ghosts seriously, disregarding any and all pictures of orbs is part of being a "real" ghost hunter, and there are many that can be explained away. However, there is no badge for pooh-poohing a picture with a burst of light, and regardless of the people who will try to sell you a certification in paranormal investigating, there is no advanced degree in just shooting down everything you see. At times we are too programmed that orb photos are bad and we refuse to leave ourselves open to the possibility of good evidence. Like I said before, the best investigator is one who is open to the possibility of everything, so deleting a picture of an orb and knowing it is most likely not anything paranormal is not enough. You have to be ready to look closely at it and not evaluate on cruise control.

And it would be impossible to have a book about ghost pictures without a whole chapter on them.

The History of the Orb

DIGITAL CAMERAS HAVE moved the orb to the forefront of the paranormal debate. This gives the impression that they are something new, but people have seen these balls of light for centuries and reported them as if there was something supernatural about them. They were often seen and documented, even making appearances in art throughout recorded history. These orbs were deemed as important to the cultures that saw them, and even in cases of natural occurrences, people did not know enough of what they were seeing to think them just a part of the world around them. Instead, they offered supernatural and paranormal reasons for their existence, and at times molded sacred areas based on where they were observed.

Some Famous Orbs

There are some who claim the star that led the Magi to Baby Jesus was a UFO or a ghost orb. It may not make total sense, but it shows how people have often seen these balls of fire and thought they were signs from the other side. Here are some other names for orbs, many of which are still used around the world.

Tei Pai Wankas—A term from the Native Americans in New England. Other tribes have other names they use, but often they are thought to be the souls of warriors who have died.

St. Elmo's Fire—Famous in the boating world, sailors often saw a burst of light high in the masts of their ship and took them as signs of bad things to come. Named after St. Erasmus of Formiae, the patron saint of sailors, the explosion is caused by a sparking of the ions around an object.

Will-o-the-Wisp—This may be the unscientific term used for years, especially in Europe and by European immigrants, for orbs. In different stories, the lights have been explained as anything from the soul of people trapped on this plane for some reason to the lanterns of dead rail workers. They are often used to lead people astray and try to kidnap them. They are also related to the original folklore about the Jack-O-Lantern.

Boi-tatá—The Brazilians see the balls of light as an all-seeing snake that hunts people at night. This is a reflection of their culture, as they have some of the largest snakes, including the anaconda.

Ghost Light—This is more a terminology issue rather than a conceptual difference. Ghost lights seem to be a catchall for many of the different forms of light seen by the human eye and used in folklore.

How Are You Viewing It?

There is a saying in the paranormal world that one man's ghost is another man's UFO. In other words, depending on the witness', or even the investigator's, perspective, an event may be seen in any number of ways. There is a very haunted location I have investigated near a waterhole that is famous for large glowing orbs, sometimes seen submerged under the water. Many times someone has approached me with information about the same site, telling me they had seen an alien spaceship. Remember, as you hear stories of lights in the sky, some may have ghostly origins. If you get them when you photograph a location, you may want to run them by a ufologist (someone who investigates UFOs), just for their opinion. You will find the best of them are experts in photography.

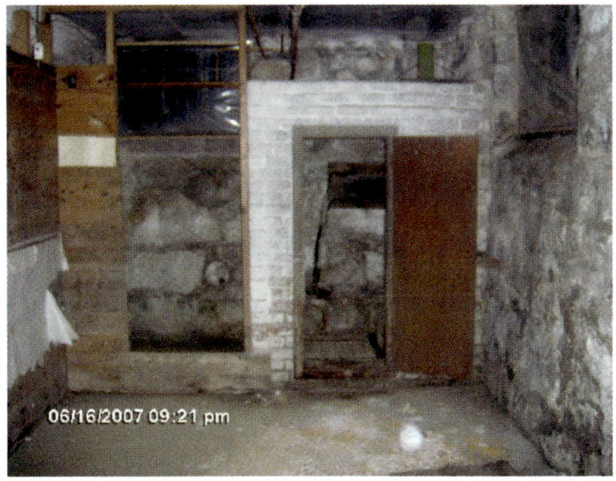

Figure 9.1
Orb captured in a haunted basement.
Picture courtesy of Jessica Stone.

Nothing New, Just a Different Lens

Orbs have been making their way onto film for some time now; we just never noticed. It's a bit like the VW Bug Syndrome, which says you will never see a VW Bug until someone points one out. Then they seem to be everywhere. While many attribute the high level of orb photographs to new technology in digital cameras, some paranormal investigators will bring up that intention idea again. But some of it might be due to noticing what has always been there.

They may not rain down the way they do in some of the pictures I've seen, but look through some of your old pictures. You will find an orb in that picture of you riding your first horse or at the school dance. I often find orbs on people's shoulder and over their stomachs. They can be evaluated as paranormal evidence, but because they do not show up often enough to be noticed on a regular basis, they become examples of conditions that can produce bad evidence. I have not found them to show in one particular place or at one particular time during the day, so just about any picture has the potential to have them in it.

The Paranormal Webster's on Orbs

IT IS MUCH EASIER TO GET a picture of an orb than it is to create a definition of one that is usable for a discussion.

A Working Definition

It is probably best to start with the physical side of things before we slip into what they are and their metaphysical standing. An orb is a roundish anomaly that appears to be lit or have its own light source. In a picture, think of them as those balls of light that appear whenever you use a flash. They may be caused by any number of things, which we will get into, but they may appear to the naked eye or only in photographs and are different colors, including blue, red, green, black, purple, and the most popular, white.

In a Paranormal Sense

There are several different theories as to what an orb might be from a paranormal investigator's eyes. Let's assume for a moment that what has been seen by the human eye or the lens of a camera is not something natural. That is a huge leap, as many people will tell you there are no such things as orbs. They will generally quote a percentage, but so much of evaluating evidence, and building a reputation as an investigator in some people's eyes, is weeding through pictures. Instead, for now, let us look at what an orb may be.

The Soul

One theory on orbs is that they are the light that is generated by the soul; we just never see it because of all of the flesh and bones and organs in the way. Think of every human as ET with his heart light. There is an energy within our soul and that energy survives us after we die. In rare moments it becomes visible to the human eye or may be photographed. No one who puts this forth this idea can really define those moments for us, but they believe in times of emotional strain or with the right energy conditions, seeing the soul is possible. It has even been theorized that the orb is a soul in its travelling form.

It may even be possible to see the soul light of someone who is living. Ancient wisdom talks of energy spots on the body, like the chakras, that become basins for the soul. These can sometimes be seen with a camera, or even a trained eye. This accounts for so many pictures with orbs near people's heads and midsections, traditionally two power points for soul energy.

Manifested Energy

There are some who do not like the idea of a soul because it becomes too entangled with religion and spirituality. This may be because they are not religious in their own lives or because they feel investigating the paranormal means putting a higher power aside for the sake of science. There can be no mixing of the two if you are to approach looking for ghosts and evidence that needs to be held up to science's standards.

These people will tell you the same basic premise, but add the bioelectrical aspect in place of the soul. In other words, an orb is the physical manifestation of the energy that exists in you when you are alive and does not immediately convert to another form of energy after you die. It says something about where people are coming from when they investigate.

Energy Drain

There may be a reverse exchange of power working in the spirit world. While some believe an orb to be a revealing of energy, or even a burst of that energy, others subscribe to the school of thought that the balls of light are actually a spirit taking in the energy around it and pooling it together to use it for something. Imagine a ghost as having a small reserve of energy but needing more power to make something happen, like move your keys or even appear in full form. They may even bring the energy in to survive in their current form, using extra sparks in the air as ghost food. Where that pooling and transfer happens you get bubbles that take the form of orbs. This may also account for why there is often a drop in temperature when there is a ghost around. They would be taking in that heat from those small pockets.

Entry Points

One of the paranormal ideas that has enjoyed a rebirth in the past few years is dimensional hauntings. The basic premise is that spirits exist in another dimension, or even that ghosts are people who exist in another dimension and have the ability to cross into ours, and that they have entry points. Some even go so far as to claim built up energy in an area, say when something tragic happens, can unlock these entry points. Where the spirit or dimensional traveler breaks through can be seen or photographed. While many believe these to look more like the vortexes we discussed in Chapter 3, some also associate orbs with these check points.

> **Snapshot**
>
> **You will often hear paranormal investigators quote, even those who are directed by what they feel is the science of ghost hunting, 1% or 2% of something. They say 2% of orbs may be something paranormal or 1% of cases may have demonic activity connected to them. Be careful of this figure. Almost always this is a number used to communicate there is a slim number that might be paranormal and not an actual percentage calculated mathematically. Well, at least 2% of the time it isn't.**

Kind of Natural but More Paranormal

Too often skeptics explain something away by offering something equally as odd. The best example may be that a person using a spirit talking board can move the planchette with their mind and there are no ghosts controlling it. Almost as conflicting is their opinion on orbs. The little balls of light are explosions of telekinetic energy in a room because of the energy of the people in the area. The more energy present, say with a child present or when there are strong emotions with no outlet, the more likely there is to be a burst. This may account for the presence of these lights where emotional events occur, like old hospitals or asylums. This telekinetic energy can be new, from abuse for example, or old, like a murder from 20 years ago. The electricity builds and builds and then sparks.

In the "Natural" Sense

Let's turn the coin over. Orbs are mistakes of the eye or the camera and there are no such things as ghost orbs. At the very least, most ghost lights are the result of some very natural circumstances. This does not mean that ghosts do not exist; it just means those pictures that have them, or even instances where you see them, cannot be held up as evidence. The difficult thing about the natural explanations is that they cannot offer reason to all instances of seeing an orb with your eyes.

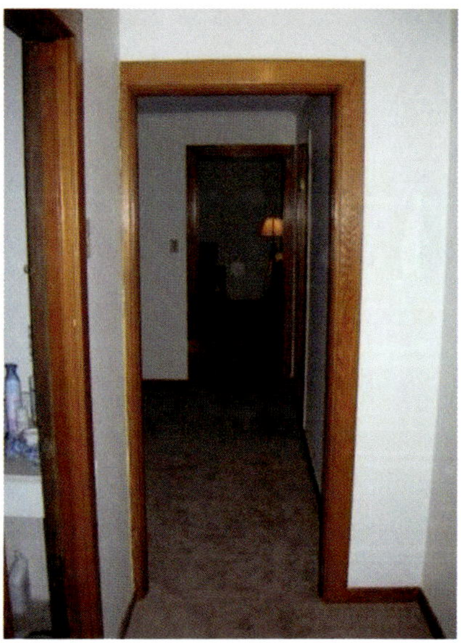

Figure 9.2
An orb seen down the hall.

The person living here would hear laughing from where he sat on the couch watching television. He eventually began snapping pictures when he heard it. I investigated a house where the owners saw little balls of light in the house. They would appear in the kitchen, the living room, and the bedrooms. They would move with what they described as personality. They would be either a foot or three feet above the ground, although there were times when they rose to the ceiling, and would shift direction quickly or hover. According to the family, they had several different sizes and colors, and they could correspond the personality of the balls of light with other activity that was going on throughout the house. For example, the smaller orb that would dart through the hallway was the spirit of the small child they heard giggling and running up the stairs. The larger, slow moving one was the shadowy figure that would hover in the corner of their bedroom.

Even with these exceptions, it is important to know the natural causes so you can see them in those spirit photos you might want to hail as proof of life after death.

Dust

Dust is easily the most popular suspect whenever you find a picture or a video with orbs. The term is a catchall for many of the undesirable specks that float in the air, including pollen, dirt, tiny bug remains, and pollution and smoke. When my mother-in-law comes over she often comments on the obvious dust on the bookcase, but she has no idea how dirty all air is. Even when you cannot see it with your eyes, it floats in and out of the rooms of your house, never mind the amount outside. Think of your house on a sunny day when you admire the rays of light washing into your den. What you are actually seeing is the light reflecting off of dust.

According to Gene Lafferty of the Buckeye State Paranormal and Haunting Investigators:

UV light from your camera's flash illuminates the dust and is then recorded by the camera's CCD. The same phenomena can occur in Night Shot video, except this time it is light from the IR emitter bouncing off the airborne particles.

The images below show how dust approaching the inverted focal point of the lens look more like orb phenomena. The camera lens' inverted focal point is the point that an object must be past to be in-focus. The closer they get to the lens the more they blur and become less distinct while dust particles near the focal point appear to be in focus and show apparent details such as a nucleus and rings. Dust past the focal point may or may not be recorded and if it is they simply look like white specks of light in your photograph. The crucial factor in the equation is the UV light source from your camera's flash. Digital cameras are sensitive to the UV and IR spectrums of light and this is why digital cameras are more likely to capture "orbs" than 35mm cameras. Snow, rain, and pollen are also subject to this type of photographic effect.

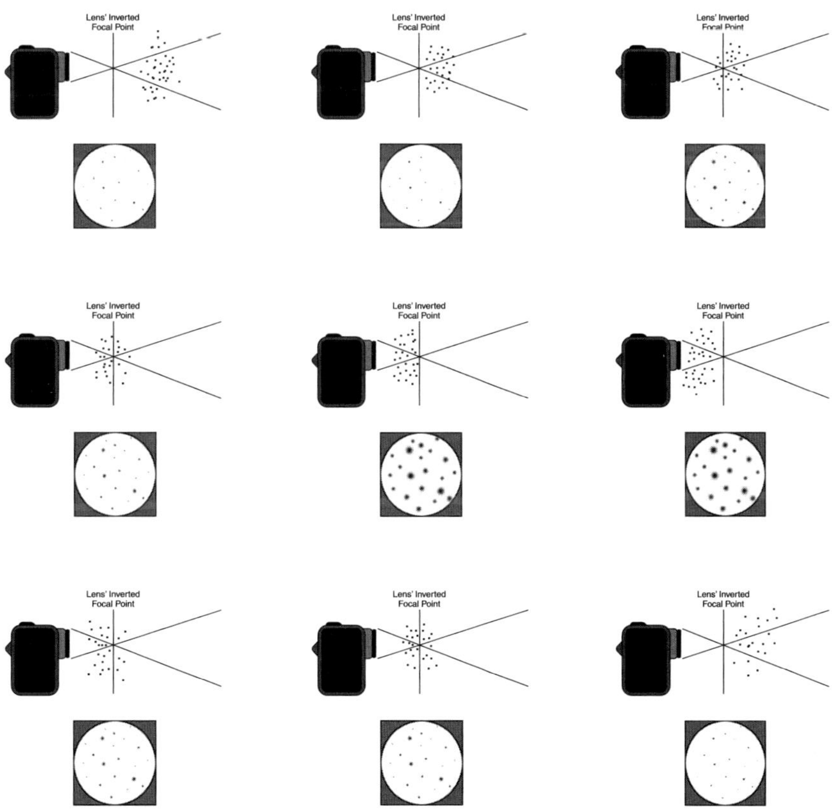

Figures 9.3-9.11
The different ways dust and particles in the air can be picked up by the camera.

Pictures courtesy of Gene Lafferty of the Buckeye State Paranormal and Haunting Investigators

Gene Lafferty has created the best explanation for orb photos I have ever read, and his group, Buckeye State Paranormal and Haunting Investigators, makes a real science out of their identification. The following section can get a bit technical, but it is worth reading and understanding.

It might not be as sexy as some of the paranormal ideas out there, but Lafferty's explanation will give you a better idea of orbs and how light can impact your investigations in general.

If you need to read through it twice to get it, don't worry, I did too.

Some of the Science of Dust Orbs from Gene Lafferty of the Buckeye State Paranormal and Haunting Investigators:

Diffraction is the spreading of light around the edges of a barrier. These form patterns called diffraction rings. In diffraction, the intensity of the bright lines, or fringes, is greatest for the central bright spot and decreases for the higher orders. Except for the central bright spot, the position of the fringe depends upon the wavelength of light. The central bright spot appears as the original, un-diffracted light.

The higher-order fringes contain a spectrum of the light colors comprising the original light. Their position depends upon their wavelength. One color of light is distinguished from another color by wavelength.

Dust orbs have certain characteristics, such as possessing some sort of nucleus, and elongation around the central axis towards the edges of the photos. These are the diffraction rings.

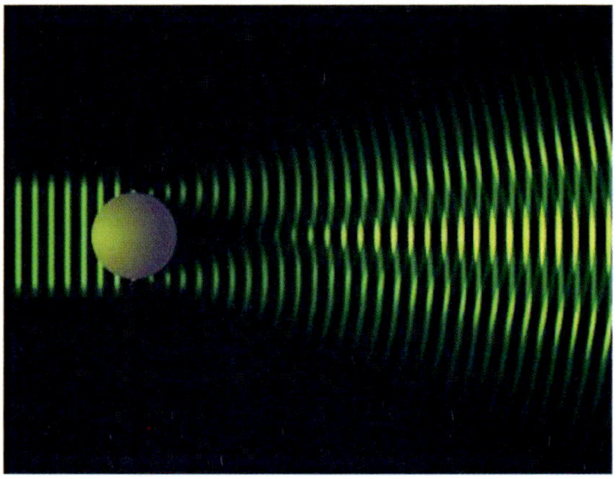

Figure 9.12
An example of diffraction.
Pictures courtesy of Gene Lafferty of the Buckeye State Paranormal and Haunting Investigators.

A simple way of thinking about it is to consider a drop of water hitting a pond. Ripples are produced as the drop strikes the pond's surface. Light behaves in a similar fashion. The problem with identifying dust "orbs" is that the ability to see the diffraction rings is dependent on the resolution of the photograph and if the "orb" is in focus (not too close to the lens). Figure 9.13 shows a typical diffraction ring pattern that is found in dust particles.

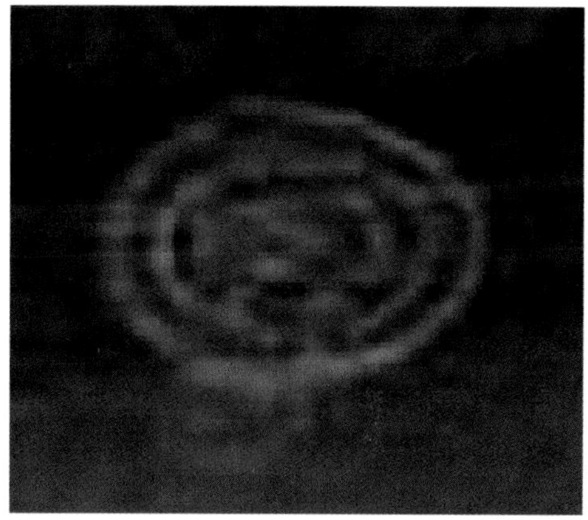

Figure 9.13
Diffraction ring pattern.
Pictures courtesy of Gene Lafferty of the Buckeye State Paranormal and Haunting Investigators.

When light interferes, the light waves produce alternating bright and dark bands of colors (interference fringes); nodal lines appear as dark bands and antinodal lines appear as bright bands. Violet light (with the shortest wavelength) is the least diffracted, and red light (with the longest wavelength) is the most diffracted.

Generally speaking, if you see diffraction rings in an orb, it is definitely dust as this phenomena occurs, in a photographic sense, only in very small and microscopic objects.

There are other signs to look for as well.

A corona is produced by diffraction of light by small particles. Every point on the illuminated surface is a source of scattered outgoing spherical waves. Along the central axis, the incident light direction, the crests of the two scattered waves always coincide to form a region where the light is strong. Moving away from the axis, there is a direction where the crests again coincide to give beams of enhanced brightness at an angle to the incident light. In between there is a region where crests of one wave coincide with those of opposite amplitude of the other. The two waves cancel and there is darkness in those directions.

There is another coincidence of wave crests at a larger angle and the light intensity is again enhanced. With increasing angular distance from the axis there are alternating bright and dark regions—a diffraction pattern. In reality, light is scattered from all around the particle periphery and other low-intensity waves arise from reflection and transmission through the particle. The net wave amplitude at any point is the sum of the amplitude vectors, not intensities, of all the individual waves. The result is a very bright central region surrounded by less bright rings, a corona.

Corona formation, to a good approximation, needs no knowledge of the particle's interior because the surface scattered waves predominate. It could be water, ink, or coal—the pattern is almost the same. It depends primarily on the particle's size, shape, and the wavelength of the light.

There is no need for the particle to be either transparent or even spherical; small ice crystals, pollen grains, and large dust particles all form corona. A white light corona is the sum of all the corona contributions from each spectral color.

Usually there will be more than one dust orb in the photos, and you get them most of the time at the location. Note that dust orbs are more likely to show up in a large number when you disturb the environment, such as when you just step into an empty room. You can analyze this effect in an image editing program by simply increasing the brightness of the photo. Some photographs show geometric shapes, such as diamonds and octagons. This is caused by a lens curvature error known as "coma." Cameras with very small lenses and short focal lengths (such as digital cameras) are more prone to coma than other cameras with longer focal length lenses, such as SLR cameras. When an object with a similar shape as the aperture of the camera lens is brought out of focus, the object will begin to take the shape of the aperture. In other words, if the aperture of the camera is an octagon, an out of focus dust orb will begin to take the shape of an octagon, particularly towards the center of the image.

Water

While some might include this with their dust explanation, there are some important differences. Although we usually measure moisture by precipitation like rain and snow, there is always a certain amount in the air, which can be measured by the humidity in an area. It is the reason why Arizona can be hotter than Florida, but you are less comfortable in the Sunshine State. There may have been no rain in the area you are investigating, but you need to understand the moisture you may pick up is present. The other important thing to remember is that water hides. Think of waking up on a seemingly dry morning and your shoes getting wet walking through the grass.

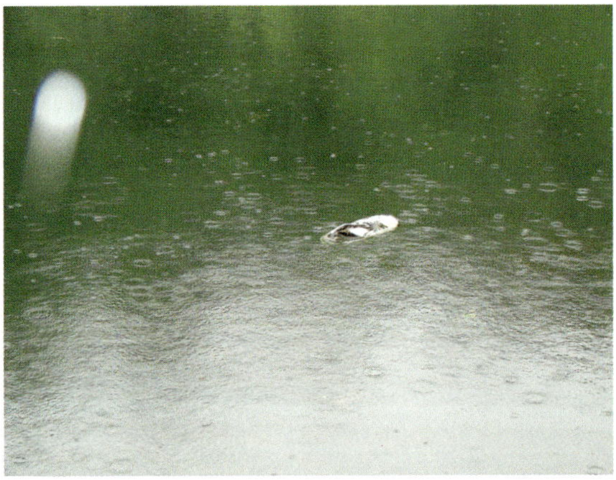

Figure 9.14
Although this picture was taken at a haunted site, it is an orb caused by water.

It may be easy to distinguish water orbs from other orbs. Turn on the lights in your aquarium late some night and watch the pattern that appears on the wall. Water keeps its form whether it is one drop or a gallon, it just becomes harder to have a source of light make it through. In your aquarium, just as a drop of water with a flash from a camera, the image will have a solid middle and then a less solid, semi-transparent halo around it. Oftentimes there will also be a tail, especially if the camera is catching a moving source of water like rain.

Bugs

I once received a picture, which I'll address in more detail in Chapter 12, where there were many things going on that could be considered paranormal. One image seemed to be a winged creature, which the person who took the photo thought to be an angel, given some other situations surrounding the picture. With a little research on the Internet, I was able to discover a common form of moth hatched around that time of year. While it is in no way conclusive, the active nature of new moths make the likelihood of a ghost in the picture less likely.

Bugs creep and crawl into every part of our lives, regardless of whether we see them or not. Leave a door open in some parts of the country, and even if you see nothing crawl in, you will be itching for hours. Airborne bugs are what concern ghost photographers, and there have been many a ghost hunter who has had to suffer through bugs even after the investigation is over. While their bodies are not round in most cases, the light reflected off of them often comes back somewhat sphere-like, which accounts for many of the blobby circle orbs that appear.

Remember when viewing pictures that may have insects, as with all bad ghost pictures, that size is a relative thing. For example, in Figure 9.14, the object seems to have some size to it, but that is only due to the proximity of it, not its actual size. As we have talked about throughout the book, in a two-dimensional image, size is established by the distance to the lens, so something very large in the foreground will seem small unless it has something next to it the viewer can relate it to.

They can cause more disruption when you are dealing with video evidence. We think of insects as having a place to go and a flight path, which may not always be the case. The sensitive nature of their navigation instincts, which are designed to sense things very quickly and make split-second decisions, make them dart and change directions very quickly. A bee flies with urgency, but mosquitoes, moths, and flies have less discipline. Those quick moving orbs may very well be insects trying to make a quick getaway.

Swamp Gas

The classic explanation of the paranormal is actually a real, exploding thing. The ground contains explosive gas like methane, and often these gases exist in the air in trace amounts due to anything from animals nearby to decomposing material. In the right condition, like an excess of static electricity in the environment, these gases can ignite and cause a small burst of fire. Because of the nature of the gas, it explodes in a ball.

The traditional thinking that this only occurs in an actual swamp is false. Different areas can have varying levels of gas in the air and can start the chemical reaction. It is not a coincidence that investigators get computer hard drives full of orb pictures at cemeteries. The boneyard is full of decomposing material, and in addition to the other influences that cause orbs, some of the images they get could be from this ignition.

The Human Touch

Orbs could be the souls of people who have passed on, but they could also have a living, breathing foundation as well. Human error, whether it be during the investigation or during the processing of the information, accounts for many of the false pictures investigators get. While a few are staged to promote a group or get attention, most are just mistakes. Some are avoidable in the field while others are mistakes you just need to know about during the evaluation process.

Think of any source of light as a potential orb, whether it be directly from a source or in the form of a reflection of that source. Even during investigations, ghost hunters have mistaken headlights and rear lights for spirits. They believe they are far from the road, but trees only make for obstructers if you are close up. You would be surprised how they can sneak into your line of sight, and when the road is off in the distance and at an upward angle, they appear to be manifesting and higher than they are. The same can be said for flashlights and other handheld lights, especially headlights that do a great job of creating a glow while hiding the hunter wearing them.

The best way to avoid these during the evaluation is to account for everybody and everything. Where are your fellow investigators and what are they using in the field? Does their equipment have little red lights that signal when they are on or flash when something happens?

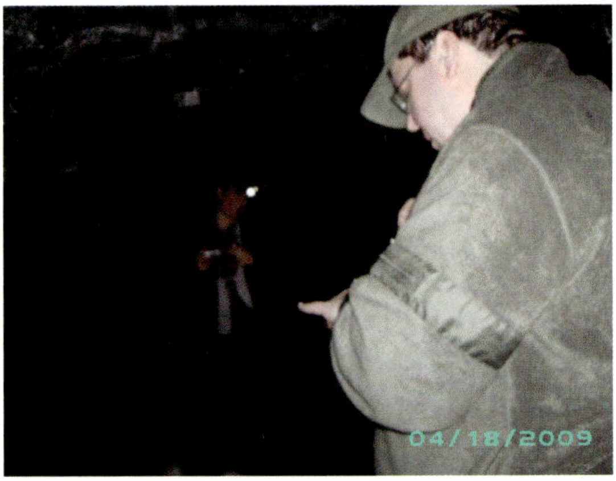

Figure 9.15
An example of how easily a light source or a reflective surface can be made to look like an orb.

Identifying a True Ghost Orb by Gene Lafferty

There are roughly 2%-5% of "orb" photos that cannot be explained. These photos either have an orb obscured by another object (showing that it is in focus) or show a definite change of movement. However a lack of data does not necessarily prove that unidentifiable orbs are ghosts.

Once you have eliminated possibilities, it is time to take a good, long, close look at the orb itself. What you are looking for in "orb" activity is a solid object that emits its own light. It will usually show up on film looking like someone just threw a golf ball across the screen. If the orb has signs of movement, such as a blurred trail behind it, you may have caught a real orb.

The other characteristic of orb activity that we consider is the coloration of the orb.

True orbs are colored in the "cool" end of the spectrum, such as white, blue, or green.

Any orb activity that shows up as red, orange, or yellow, is typical of dust or light refraction. Another way of telling a true orb is if it is partially hidden behind an object. A dust orb will show up as a complete circle and not obstructed by another object.

But remember, an orb is just a collection of energy, not the manifestation of a ghost. While orbs are usually present during paranormal activity, you can have orbs show up without paranormal activity.

Reducing Orb Photographs by Gene Lafferty

- Don't take photographs in dusty locations.
- After entering a cemetery, allow about 30 minutes for the dust that you generated by entering to settle.
- Avoid high winds.
- Don't photograph in rain, snow, fog, or any other adverse weather conditions.
- Use a lens hood to reduce lens flare.
- Be conscious of the number of bugs in the area.
- Be aware of bright lights in the area; some examples would be headlights, security lights, moon, etc.
- Don't use a flash.
- Don't use a cheaper 35mm digital camera. They are known to produce orbs more so than any other model I have ever seen.
- If you are using a digital camera, use the highest resolution setting on your camera.
- If you are using a digital camera, use the highest megapixel camera that you can afford. Why you ask? Take a look at Figures 9.16 and 9.17 taken at almost the same time with two different cameras: 3-megapixel camera vs. 6-megapixel camera. Notice the orbs in the room and then notice the lack of orbs in the room

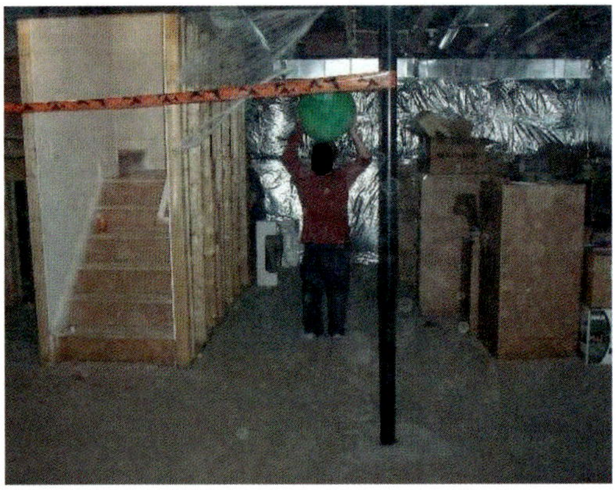

Figure 9.16
A 3-megapixel picture. Courtesy of Gene Lafferty of the Buckeye State Paranormal and Haunting Investigators.

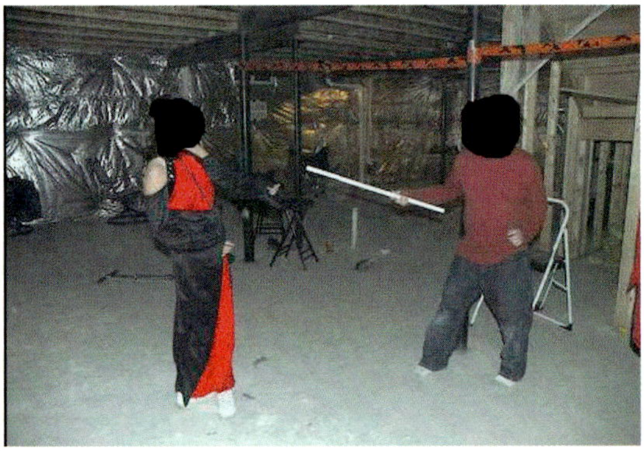

Figure 9.17
A 6-megapixel picture. Courtesy of Gene Lafferty of the Buckeye State Paranormal and Haunting Investigators.

A Little Bit of Practice Distinguishing Between Potentially Paranormal Orbs and Simple Balls of Light

Gene Lafferty and the Buckeye State Paranormal and Haunting Investigators team put together a pamphlet for investigators with some great information, some of which has been quoted in this chapter. They have included these pictures as practice to see if you can apply what you've learned in this chapter. Try to eliminate as many as possible as you look. All pictures courtesy of Gene Lafferty of the Buckeye State Paranormal and Haunting Investigators.

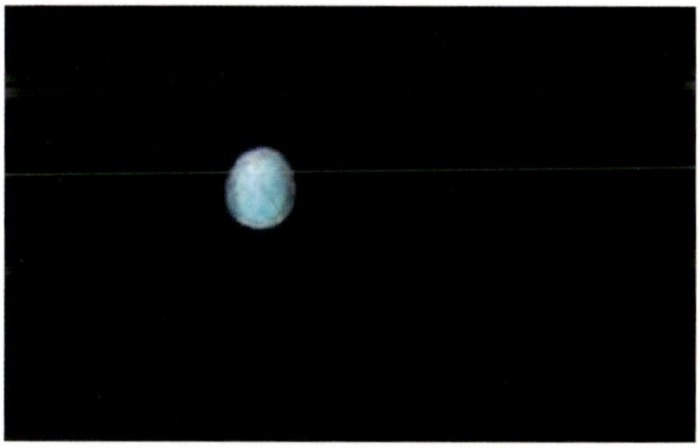

Figure 9.18

Figure 9.19

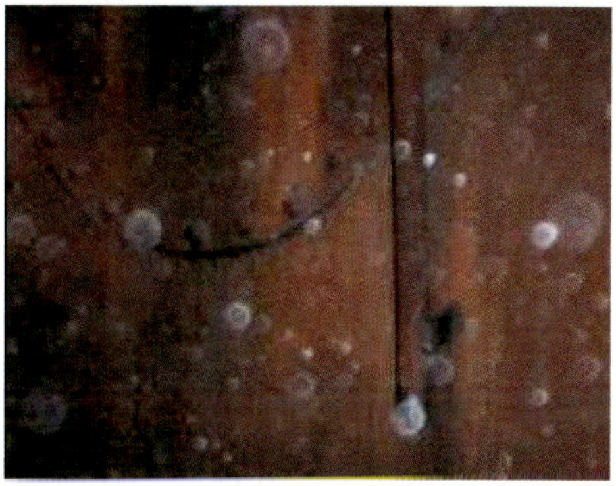

Figure 9.20

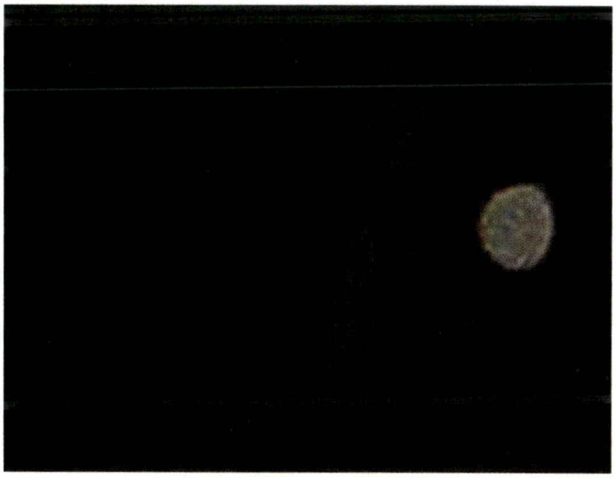

Figure 9.21

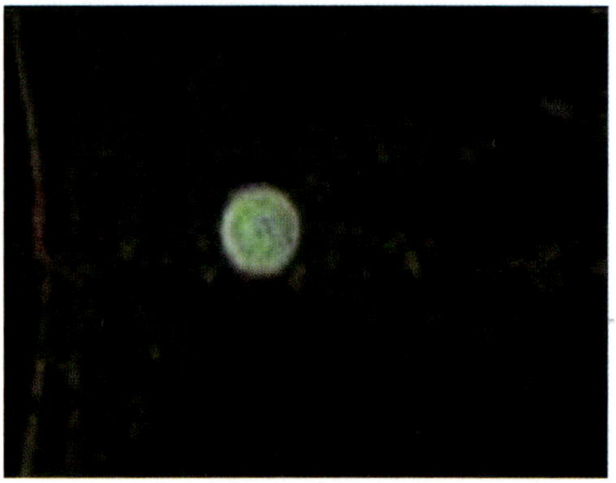

Figure 9.22

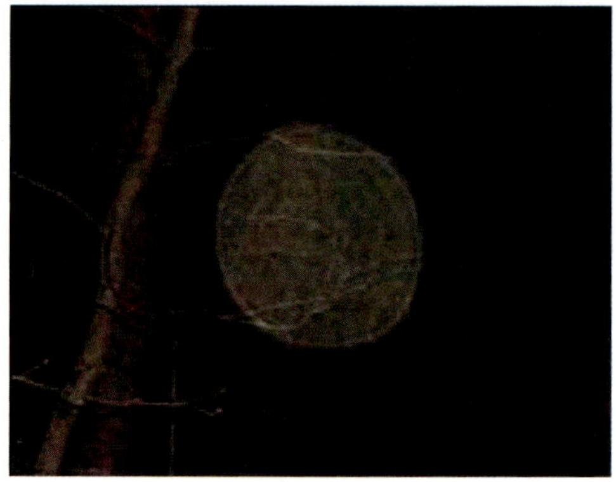

Figure 9.25

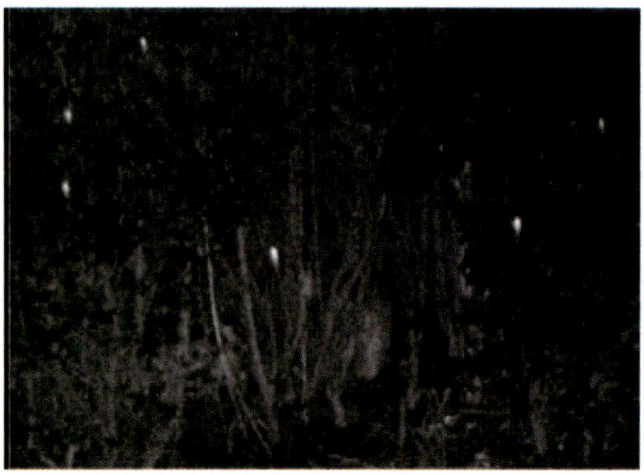

Figure 9.23

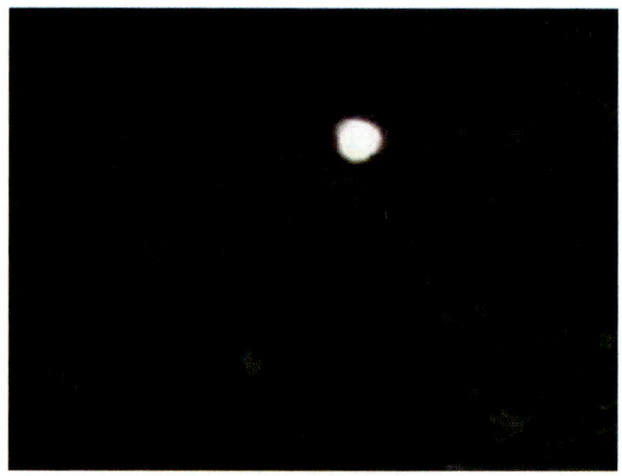

Figure 9.26

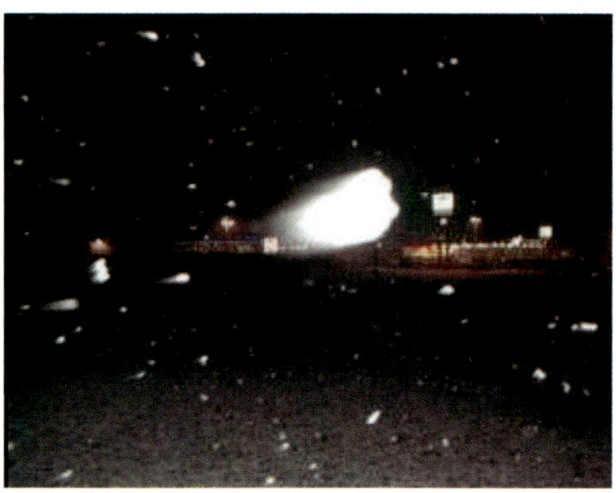

Figure 9.24

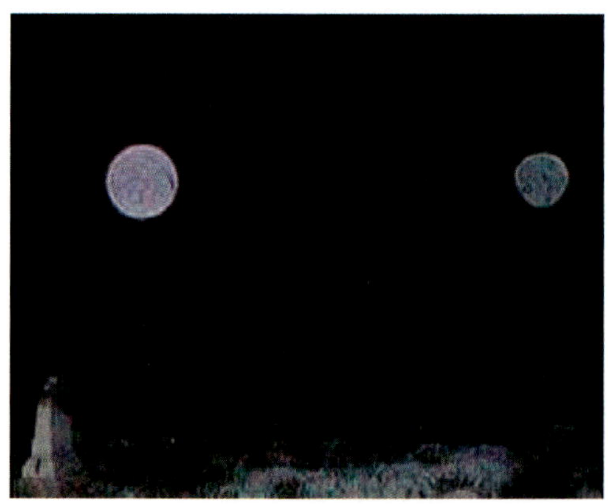

Figure 9.27

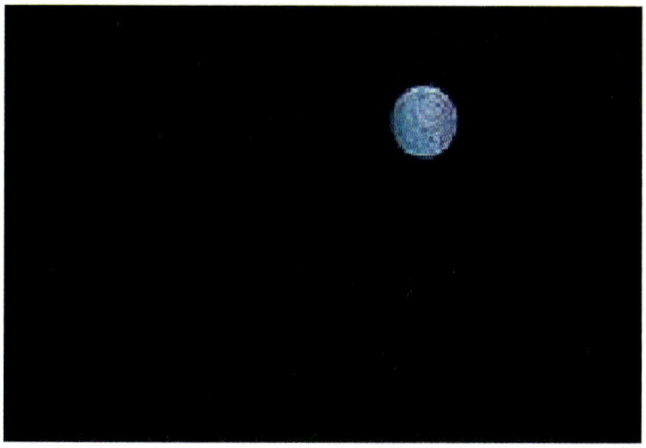

Figure 9.28

Answers

Picture 1 (Figure 9.18): True~ Energy Orb

Picture 2 (Figure 9.19): False~ Dust

Picture 3 (Figure 9.20): False~ Dust

Picture 4 (Figure 9.21): False~ Humidity

Picture 5 (Figure 9.21): False~ Dust

Picture 6 (Figure 9.23): False~ Rain shown in night shot

Picture 7 (Figure 9.24): False~ Snow

Picture 8 (Figure 9.25): False~ Pollen

Picture 9 (Figure 9.26): Positive~ Energy Orb

Picture 10 (Figure 9.27): Positive and False~ Energy Orb on Left/Dust on Right

Picture 11 (Figure 9.28): Positive~ Energy Orb

The Last Well-Rounded Opinion on Orbs

THERE IS A SUBJECTIVE ASPECT to looking at orbs. There might be some who cannot see the detail one investigator notices and classifies an orb differently because of it. This makes looking at these kinds of pictures frustrating, which is why so many people will not do it. While Lafferty's explanation makes sense based on science, he is still thinking of light as it exists in a perfect world. A picture lacks this kind of controlled environment, so you are unsure how the light creates the orbs people get on their cameras. This makes most of this section as close to perfect as we can get it right now, which may never get any clearer.

Let's instead think back to the two paranormal investigators at the beginning of the chapter. The second had it right when he reacted to the orbs and asked if there was anything else to see. Orbs are like tight-lipped lawyers, they cannot confirm or deny. If all you have is an orb and you have worked through all of the ideas presented in this chapter and still think it might have a paranormal origin, go back and get other evidence. Keep in mind, an orb in the same spot on two different days under different conditions makes a much better argument.

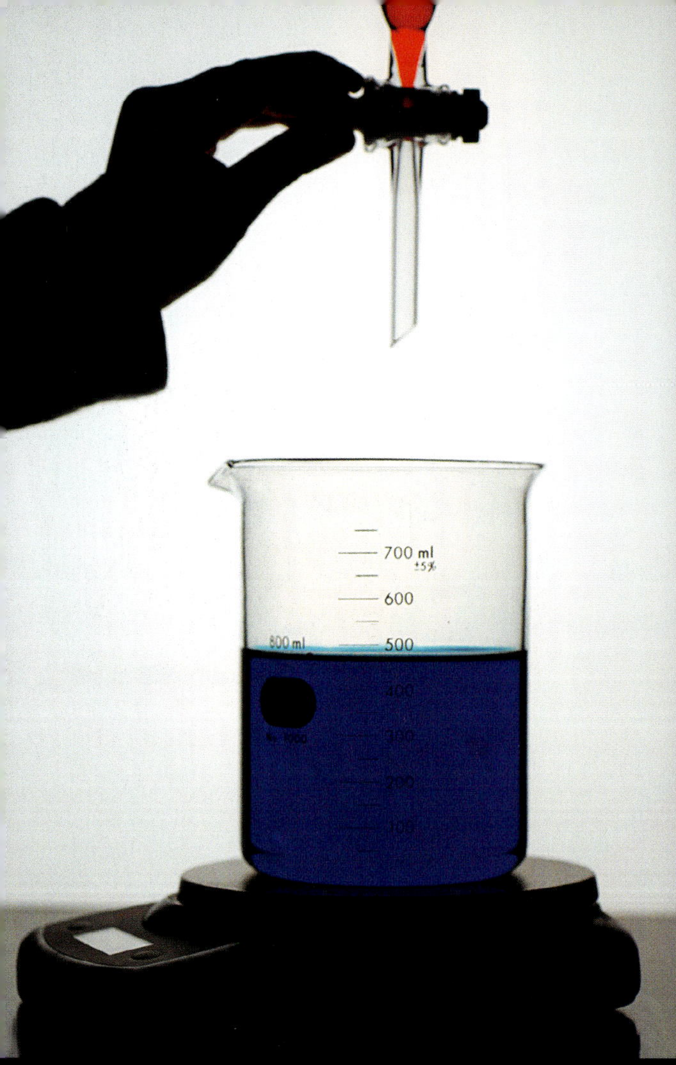

Picture courtesy ©istockphoto.com/Elemental Imaging

10

Looking Through a Different Lens:

Experimenting with the Paranormal

THERE IS A PART OF THE PARANORMAL WORLD, maybe the best part, that is all cobwebs and creaking floors. It is that raise of the hair on the back of our neck that gets us involved, and once that first step is taken, a whole new world opens up. It is not a world of howling winds and banshee calls but of EMF readings and thermal imaging. You do not need to pick a side and make a decision on what type of investigator you want to be, but there is a line. Some might call it the old school and the new school, but the two sides borrow from each other and influence each other. They just call it different things.

There are tried and true methods of calling spirits out and getting on their trail. These methods can produce results, but it is hard for them to produce evidence. For that, you need equipment and technology, and the paranormal world has a habit of avoiding plateaus. There are still people out there with divining rods and psychics, but there is also a whole new generation of investigators who are becoming inventors. The science may not always hold true, but the experiments sometimes produce results, and every day that goes by means another advance, or at least a stumble forward.

The questions remain the same, but the equation to get the answer changes. It's just important to remember that most of the new ways of seeing and getting ghosts on film refines a process but does not necessarily lead to enlightenment. Science has helped us get pictures of ghosts, but it has not helped us determine why there are ghosts just yet.

Let's Talk Science

PARANORMAL INVESTIGATING is a paradox. For centuries, the idea of ghosts has been the keepsake of religion, which is in direct conflict, most would say, with science. Science breeds technology, and technology helps us understand that the lightning is not coming from Zeus but from an electrical charge in the clouds and its attraction to the ground. Science peels away the mysteries religion uses to help generate faith, so many would feel to be able to explain a ghost, or to explain death, would turn religion on its head. Imagine the impact if we could discover a biomechanical change that results in the human personality and aspects of the physical parts of a human remaining after death.

That's heavy stuff, and it might come down the road. While some investigators like to think of themselves as scientists, saying that is much like saying you are an archeologist because you watched all of the *Indiana Jones* movies. It is more of pseudoscience in that experiments can often not be repeated and rely on interpretation rather than set standards. The variables make it outside of the realm of real science, but some of the ideas put forth by basic science are embraced by ghost hunters, so we need to see how some of these work to try to capture ghosts on film in new and inventive ways.

Evidence and the Scientific Method

If you read *Picture Yourself Ghost Hunting* you know I hate the word debunk, especially when it is used by people who claim to apply science to search for the paranormal. My trouble with the word comes from the idea that something is true in thc first place. If you assume something is a ghost, you can then debunk your own idea, but if you approach it from a mindset of discovery then you have no set judgment, and therefore no need to prove it wrong. That might be confusing, but so is using the word in the first place.

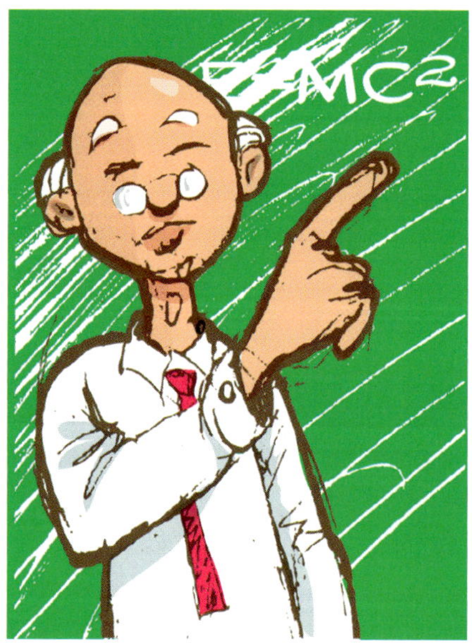

Figure 10.1
Picture courtesy ©istockphoto.com/Anton Brand

Finding a draft to explain a cold spot is not science. It is commendable to take away what is the natural but overlooked reason for something happening in a location, but that falls more into critical thinking and common sense. I am not aware of a scientist who claims he needs to debunk a treatment for cancer or disprove an aspect of thermodynamics to create a better airplane. When it does look to attack a previous idea, it does so to replace it with another, not just to say one thing is wrong. In other words, a ghost hunter should focus on what is unexplainable and not pat himself on the back for finding that something is not paranormal.

The science of the paranormal is flawed, but there is an element of scientific work that can be embraced by ghost hunters and used when trying to create experiments that might advance the study of the paranormal.

The scientific method is the basis of all observable and testable science. Here are the ABCs of the scientific method. You observe something and try to speculate on the truth of it, allowing for certain truths to already exist, like when you heat something, it gets hot. You then create a hypothesis, which is an educated guess as to why something is the way that it is. You then come up with an experiment that can test your truth while isolating all of the other elements and variables to create a controlled setting. You then experiment and observe. Based on your observation, you either embrace your hypothesis or revise it with the new information.

This process becomes almost impossible because you cannot isolate things in a paranormal setting. Ghosts are not like rats and do not appear at will to be experimented on. So the scientific method has to take a different form. If you are looking to capture ghosts on film, you need to rethink the method into something that can work in the field. It may not be the best science, but at least you will have an organized way to go through the process and a repeatable experiment to share with others.

Think of it like this then. You can take a picture of a ghost. For our purpose that is a truth. A ghost exists as energy vibrating as some type of wave that registers as a visual image with certain equipment. That's another truth. There are elements within a paranormal environment that may make it easier for a camera to pick up these ghosts, so if we manipulate those elements we may be able to increase the odds of getting a picture of a spirit. Okay, that may be a bit more of a stretch, but it makes sense. The only thing you need to work on now is understanding what elements you may be able to change.

Hypothesis

TO EXPERIMENT WITH THE paranormal you have to think about what has an impact on a camera and cross-reference that with theories on what a ghost is. There are several ideas you can play around with, and each has its own idea and use in the paranormal field. Unfortunately, we are somewhat limited in what we can do with the equipment we currently have. Perhaps we could expand these elements in the future, adding new ways to experiment with temperature or radiation for example, but for now, it might be better to stay with things we can control, even if we do not understand them.

It might be best to define what we have already established as commonly thought truths about ghosts and how a camera works. Imagine each of these as being a theory rather than anything set in stone. A ghost is something that has been left in an environment and may be able to release or absorb energy to make itself known. That energy exists, or at least travels, via waves from one place to another, and those waves need to follow rules. Now, if we can do something to interfere or record those waves we may be able to see ghosts in different ways. Both have to do with waves of energy.

Lighting

Light is perhaps the most relevant and basic idea for a paranormal investigator to manipulate. You do it every day. You want to see something in the dark so you turn the lights on and change the environment in the room. You want to take a better picture so you use a flash or turn lights on and get the image you want. You want a better picture of a ghost so you decide the best way to light that spirit and try to get the perfect evidence.

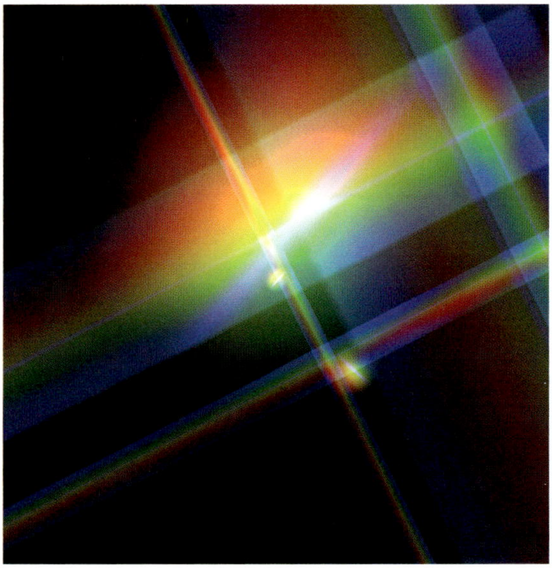

Figure 10.2
Picture courtesy ©istockphoto.com/Andrew Robinson

Light exists as waves, some of which we can see, say sunlight, and others that are outside what we can see. A camera increases the range we can see, and special cameras, like infrared or ultraviolet, stretch that even further. If a ghost is around you it may be possible to increase the odds of seeing that spirit by changing the lighting and influencing the register of waves in that environment. This is why many ghost hunters prefer to work in the dark. They feel too much light interferes with a ghost's ability to show through, because visible light comes through too strong. Imagine trying to tune in an AM station as you stand under a transmitter from an FM station. Depending on the radio, you may get nothing or a weak signal.

You may be able to get new results by throwing lighting on its head and increase your odds of capturing ghosts on film by influencing how the camera gets its light. I know investigators who use a strobe light to try to get results. Rather than changing the frequency of the waves around the ghost, they believe they can confuse the lens into seeing something. When you turn on the strobe light, a person walking towards you disappears and reappears closer to you. Your mind fills in the gap, but your eyes only see it like individual frames of movie film.

Some of the experiments in the next section look to mix up the lighting of an area or change how the camera picks it up. Some are based on science while others are based on nothing more than stories in the field that make sense but remain unexplained. Take them as a springboard for other avenues as you discover more about your equipment.

Frequency

Waves come in all sizes, and their strength, how they travel, and if we can see them is determined by this length. There is a very small spectrum we can see, and the increase from our equipment does only a little to make more of this spectrum available to us. Imagine if something is hiding in between these waves. Science has established these standards because they have been tested and proven to exist, but what if there are small cracks in them and a ghost is something that lies in the wave in this way. If we could do something to interfere with these waves, like add another element to them, we might be able to disturb them enough for something else to come through.

I was changing my newborn when I added too much powder to her diaper. We both coughed, and the sunlight came through the puff of powder. Another element was added, making the sunlight, which is there but not seen as individual rays, visible. The second group of experiments involves throwing a dissimilar wave into the mix to see if it makes investigators see better. Unlike the first group, this is a bit more active. Most of the things that can help with this are harmful to people. You can't hit a haunted room with microwaves or X-rays. Instead, an investigator may be able to get a better picture by adding other visible waves and sound waves.

Experimentation

THERE IS NO STANDARD in a field that looks to question the standards, and that questioning is based on looking at a situation and seeing how you can turn it on its head. While the reasons for being able to see ghosts may not be clearly defined, we can push the envelope of getting evidence by experimenting. As discussed, we may be able to see and record ghosts for different reasons, or see them better by manipulating those reasons, so it is time to get our hands dirty and think outside the box.

Don't think any of these experiments are going to work, but have a small part of your brain thinking there is no way they can't. None of these should be done in place of a full investigation, especially if someone has asked you to come into her house because she feels frightened by what she is experiencing. These should be supplemental moments, or even things you try to perfect in your own home, and not the primary means of getting evidence. Make sure to document all aspects of the experiment so anything you get as a result may be duplicated and scrutinized after the fact and by other investigators.

Looking at the World Through Rose-Colored Glasses

I was meeting with a now defunct paranormal group when the conversation began about looking at the paranormal in a new way. This is the kind of talk that comes up often when investigators are hanging out and not looking for anything in particular. Most of the time the talk is of new ways to get ghosts to talk or communicate, so this one stood out in my mind. It is based on light and the spectrum of colors and how the human eye processes something based on filters.

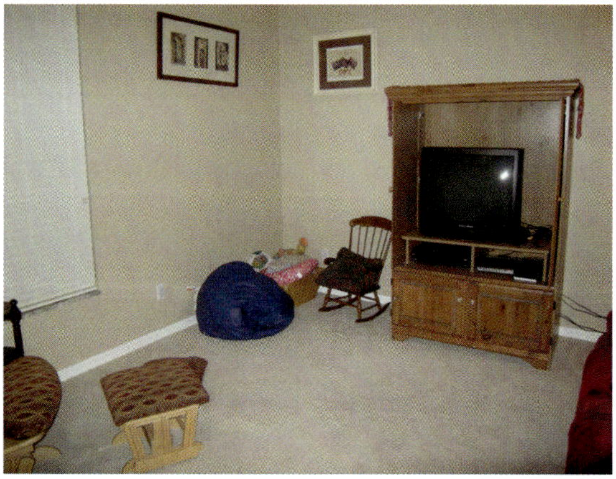

Figure 10.3
The control picture taken with a flash.

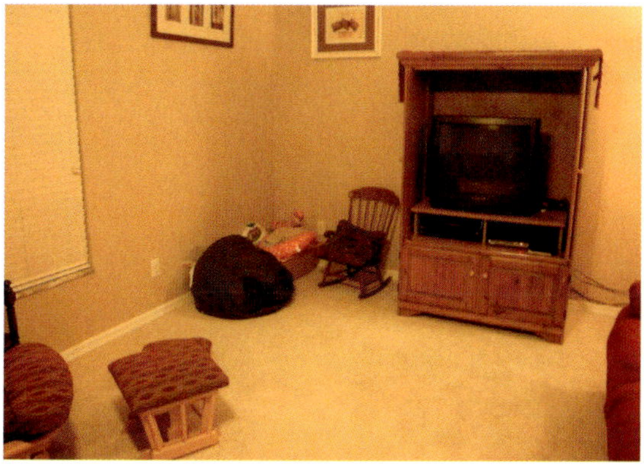

Figure 10.4
The control picture without the flash.

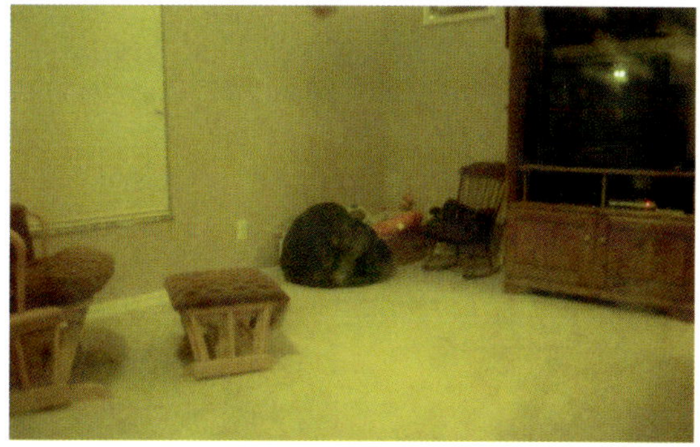

Figure 10.5
Taken with a green filter. The anomaly in the corner of the picture is an imperfection of the filter.

Imagine that when a camera takes a picture, it takes in the entire spectrum of light. Sunlight contains all the primary colors, and most lights allow your eyes to see the same rainbow. This is then what the camera records. Imagine for a moment ghosts can only exist, only fluctuate, at the same frequency as red. You, and the camera, cannot focus your eyes only on red because the other colors get in the way and make red so weak you only pick it up slightly. Every once in a great while you might see a ghost. What would happen if you flooded an environment with red? It might be enough to reveal something there that registers on that frequency. It's the same idea as turning up the red when you evaluate the image you get.

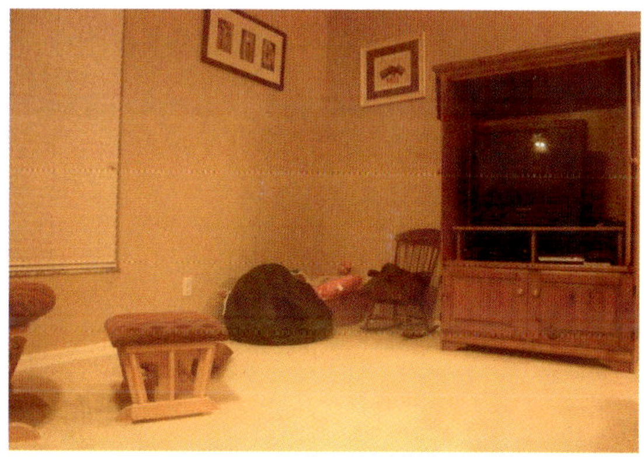

Figure 10.6
Here is an extension of the experiment. This picture was taken through sunglasses designed to block UV rays.

This can be done a number of ways. One way suggested to me is to flood the room with red LED light and take a picture. This might be expensive, especially because you would have to purchase enough to overwhelm the scene and you would need to repeat the same process with other colors. An alternative might be colored light bulbs or something like colored plastic wrap, making sure not to melt it with the light.

If you have the resources, I would suggest the theater gels they use to create mood during plays. This may be why ghosts are often seen in theaters in the first place. You may also be able to place the filter over the camera lens itself for the same effect.

Making Light Out of Nothing at All

When I was on *Ghost Chronicles*, an Internet radio show hosted by Ron Kolek, we began discussing the best way to get visual evidence, and this idea was thrown around. I know I have spoken out in this book about going dark, but this is an extreme example. You rely on complete darkness and let the camera do all of the work.

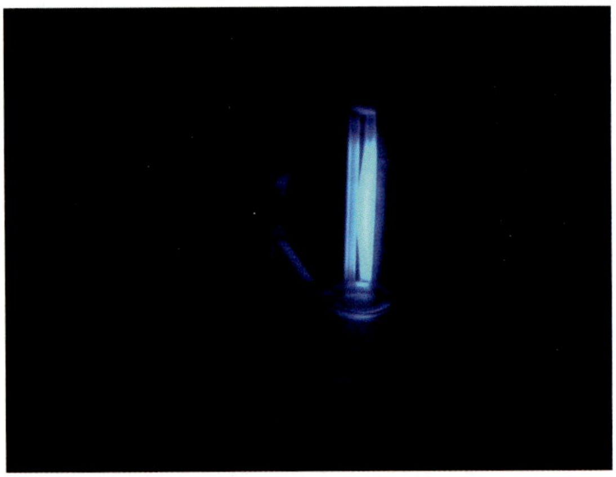

Figure 10.7
The setup of this experiment with only a black light conducted by the New England Ghost Project.
Picture courtesy of Ron Kolek.

Set up in a room where there has been paranormal activity reported. This would probably not work outside where you do not have control over the entire situation. Turn off all the lights, including turning down shades and even stuffing something under the door to guarantee no light is getting in. Using a tripod, turn your camera's shutter speed to its slowest possible setting and snap a picture. This works even better if you can set your camera to have a delay in order to make sure your hand is not even on it during the process.

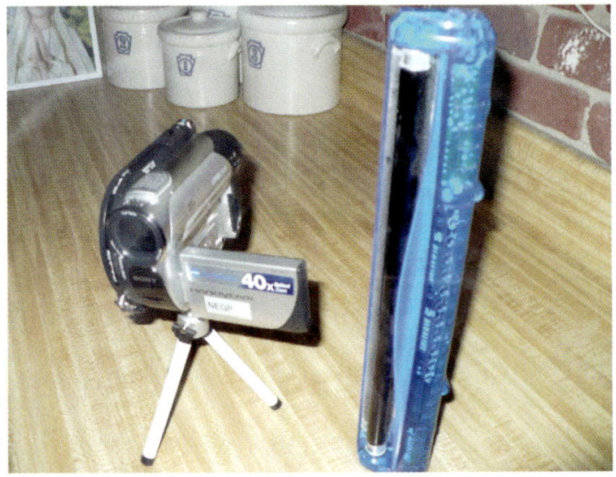

Figure 10.8
And the resulting photo with no ghost.
Picture courtesy of Ron Kolek.

Ask questions, the same way you would during an EVP session and make sure you are behind the camera. If you have a remote that allows you to snap a photo from a few feet away, use it; otherwise, touch the camera to reset it every few minutes and repeat the process.

The idea is the camera's shutter will be open so long it will capture the slightest bit of light. If a spirit creates any light, even for a brief moment, the camera will capture it without allowing any other light to disrupt the capture.

EVP Meets Visual Evidence

Movies have used the television for dramatic effect for years, and when the television shows nothing but static there seems to be an even higher level of drama. From *Poltergeist* to *White Noise*, a television showing no television has made the moment, but it might actually work in a paranormal investigation.

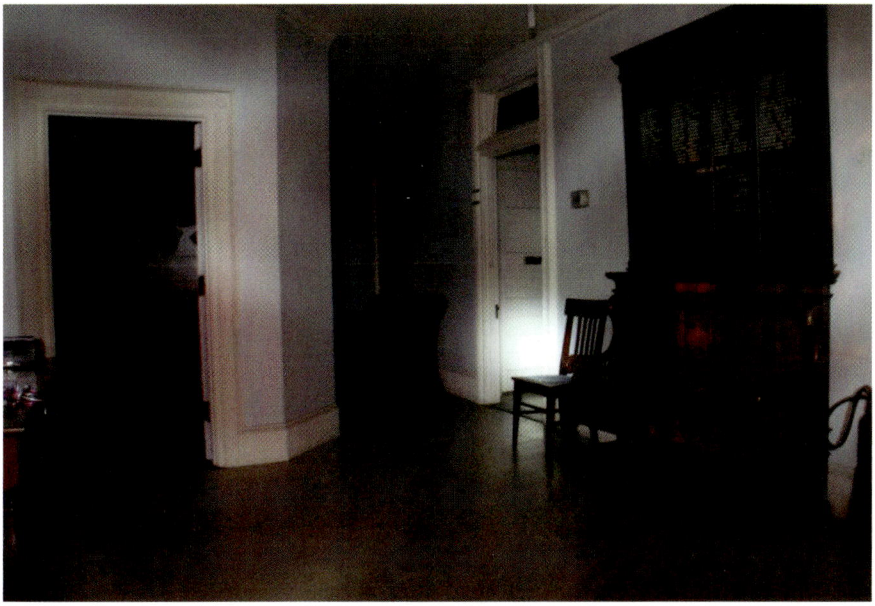

Figure 10.9
A similar experiment conducted using no light, although this environment was not secure.
Picture courtesy of Josh Mantello.

This has become harder in recent days because of the new digital requirements for televisions, but you can still experiment if you have an older television or if you disconnect it from your cable box. You might even be able to do it on an open channel with a DVR or with nothing connected to it.

Old-school television works on the idea that a channel is broadcast with a certain signal and your television is set to pick up that signal. If you turn to a channel set to pick up a signal that is not broadcasting, it leaves it open to receive any other signal, even from the other side. Again, make sure the setup is hooked into something that can record, turn to an open station, and start recording. You can let it just run or ask questions, but anything that can and is willing to communicate is open to.

This has been used to get EVPs for quite some time, but the same process can be used to try to get visual evidence as well. If it is then run though a computer (remember our discussion on chords and cables in Chapter 6?), you may be able to separate the audio and visual tracks.

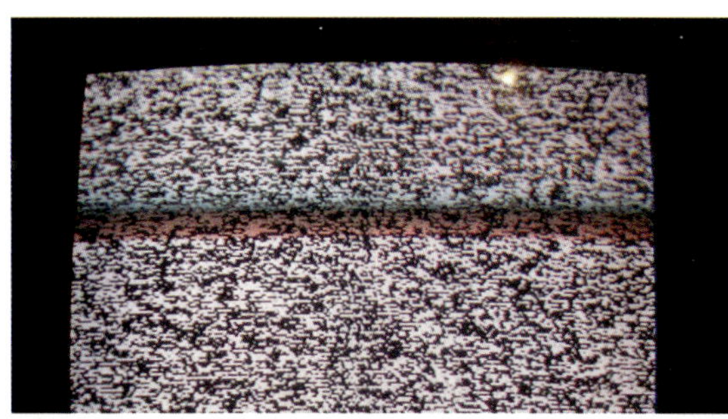

Figure 10.10
White noise where spirits might be looking to communicate.

Looping

Sometimes something works and science is at a complete loss to explain why. It can offer something in the way of explanation, but really, the "why" is based only on the fact it works, which is a bit of an alteration of the scientific method. One such experiment is known as "the loop," and while this method gained popularity about 20 years ago, there are not many people doing it anymore. With new equipment in the field and a new way to look at it afterwards, it may be time to reintroduce it into investigations.

Think of Jimi Hendricks. Take something that picks up sound waves, like a guitar pickup, and put it near something that amplifies and puts out sound waves, like a music amp, and the result is two sets of waves crashing into each other. Now, imagine you have a tape recorder to the feedback asking if anyone on the other side wants to talk. That disruption, or even the energy generated by that crash, may be enough to get results you normally would not. Try doing the same thing with visual evidence.

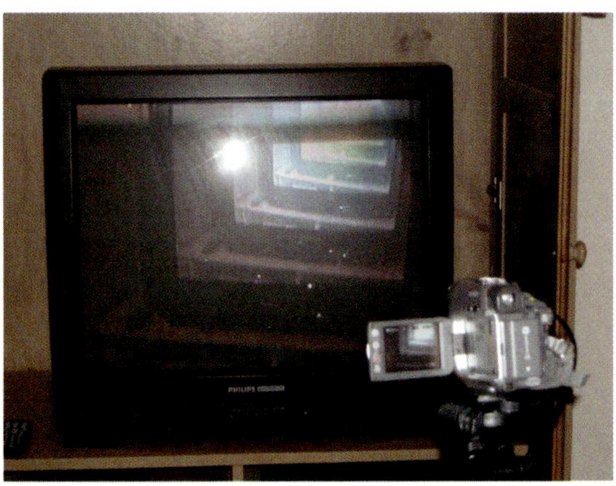

Figure 10.11
The setup of the looping experiment.

All you need is a television and a video camera to try this experiment. Connect the camera to the television using whatever method your camera requires, but it might be worth your time to run it through a VCR as well so you can record the results. Aim the camera directly at the television. What you should get is a seemingly infinite picture of the picture of the television. This is thought to disturb things, like creating visual feedback, and spirits have been known to use this loop to communicate. Begin taping on both the camera and the VCR and conduct a vigil of sorts, asking questions and requesting the spirit make contact. When you are finished, you can review both tapes and see if something was able to make contact. You may be able to speed both processes up by running the results on fast forward and watching closely for any disruption, but as always, running it at normal speed will make sure you don't miss anything.

Today this experiment can go one step further. You can use the same idea and point a webcam, or even a camera running through your computer, at the screen or a mobile DVR into its monitor. This will allow you to do the same trial in the field at a known haunted location.

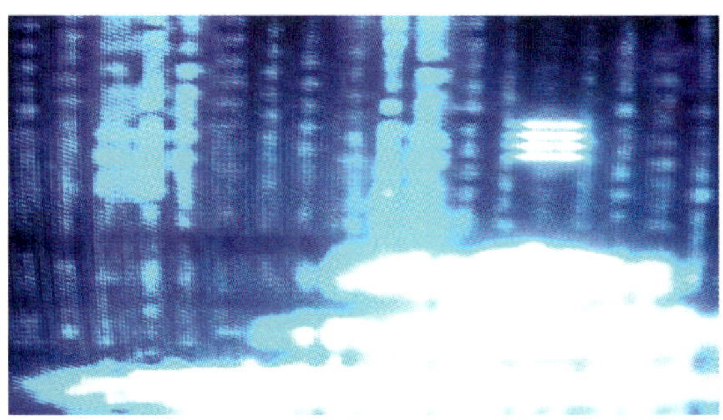

Figure 10.12
A picture of the image captured on the screen.
Picture courtesy of Jeff Belanger.

Are You Willing to Forget Science?

There may be no reason for this to work, or it may touch upon the very nature of ghosts existing as waves that may be recorded or imprinted by something set to serve that function. It may work only because of intention, and for this reason it hearkens back to the old days of spirit photography. This can only be done with a film camera, but if the truth be told, it does not require a camera at all.

Open up a fresh new roll of film and then pull all of the film out. That's right, unroll it and place it on a shelf or on the floor in a haunted environment. Ask the spirit to make itself known or conduct the investigation the way you normally would as if the film did not even exist. When the investigation is over, reroll it and send it on for processing or load it into one of the newer scanners that accepts negatives. You might be surprised by the results, although if you got something it would be hard to identify just why the image showed up.

Evaluation and Rethinking

THE GREAT JAMES RANDI has had his million-dollar challenge out there for a while, and since its inception, no one has ever been able to collect the money for being able to prove the paranormal in a lab setting. There is a reason for this that goes beyond the idea that ghosts do not exist. Trying to investigate the paranormal is like catching lightning in a bottle, and trying to record or capture that on film is like trying to then hold it in your hands. Just because you do not get evidence does not mean a place is not haunted, and if you get evidence, it does not mean the location is haunted. There are too many variables that we cannot control and too many questions that remain out of our reach. Sometimes looking is only for the purpose of saying something did happen.

Think of the evaluation in a different way than a traditional scientist would. Note what worked and what did not, and notice the way these experiments might influence other aspects of the investigation. For example, if you are conducting the shutter experiment in one room, note any rise in EMF or how the temperature changes in other parts of the house. The trial is not just for the trial's sake. See each investigation, and the results you get, as a way for you to try to understand how one aspect of the supernatural, such as energy and frequency, might influence the whole.

All of these experiments should be done several times and may even become part of your normal investigative process. Just because they do not work once does not mean the idea behind them is not solid or at least worth several tries. Failures are part of the process, but any movement in the field is exciting and keeps things fresh. Coming up with your own may even challenge your own ideas and produce something no one has thought of yet.

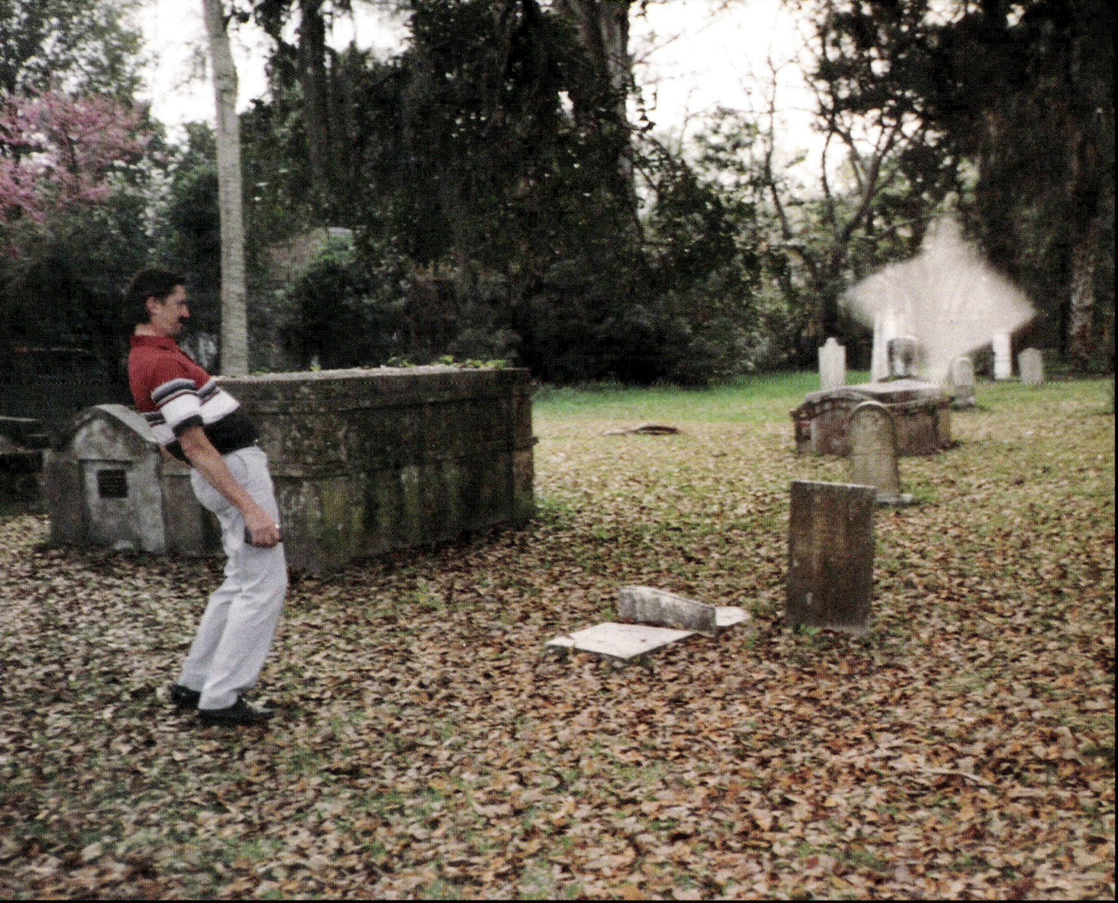

A paranormal scene caught and sent to me for evaluation.

11

That Uncomfortable Moment:

Getting the Word Out About Your Picture

A WOMAN IN MY WORKPLACE heard what I do with my spare time and approached me when no one was looking. Like most of the people who come and talk to me about ghosts, she whispered just in case someone should be paying attention to the conversation. After all, she was president of the Parent Teacher Association and a good Christian, and a belief in any of this was embarrassing. Yet there was a photo she had taken she could not get over, and she needed someone to tell her what it might be.

It had been taken with a traditional film camera and she had done me the favor of blowing it up. It was a cemetery with an angel-like figure floating near a headstone, and a few other unexplained orbs and rods faint in the background. The man in the picture was leaning back, although she stated he was standing straight up when the picture was taken. She was waiting, looking over my shoulder, and judging me judging the picture. Then my mouth opened, and I wasn't sure what to say.

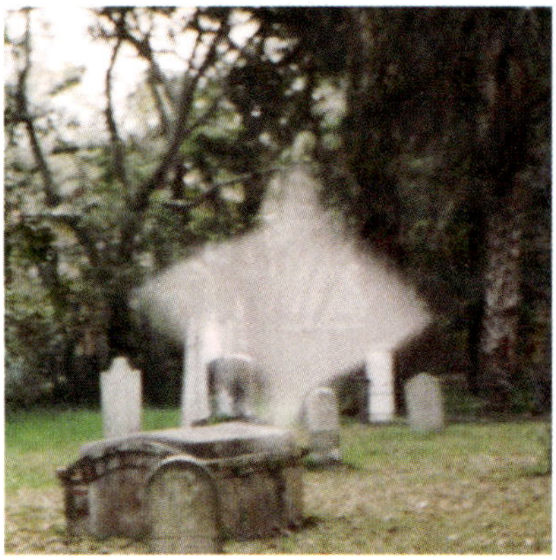

Figure 11.1
A close up of the bug the submitter thought was an angel or a ghost.

Whether you are looking at your own evidence or evaluating others, there is that moment when you have to react to what someone has taken. This becomes more uncomfortable if the picture has been e-mailed to you by someone you do not work with, usually someone outside the paranormal field, and you know they are just waiting to hear what you have to say. To them it is the key to life after death. To you there are some circles of light and a swirl of fog. They are asking for an experienced opinion, but what they are looking for is a gut reaction to match theirs.

Problems

I'VE HAD MANY CONVERSATIONS, especially ones with people who have not been investigating that long, and eventually I have the courage to ask the question I am fascinated by with all paranormal investigators: why do you do this? The majority of the time the answer will eventually come around to influencing the non-believer. Paranormal investigators are obsessed with convincing people outside the paranormal that ghosts are real. Oddly enough, when I ask the same person what they think will convert someone, they almost always say a personal experience is the only thing that will change peoples' minds.

The Real World Doesn't Really Care

If you investigate with the intention of capturing the perfect piece of evidence that will make the world take notice and shift public opinion, you will spend many a night disappointed. Surveys may declare people believe in ghosts, but most Americans do not believe you should or can get evidence. If you share with people who do not believe, be prepared to be ignored or ridiculed. There are worse things that could happen, but some ghost hunters get discouraged by this.

You could have the most compelling picture of something clear-cut, and there would still be someone who claims you faked it anyway. They might not even have the vocabulary or knowledge to understand what you have captured.

Instead, focus on people who might be on the fence, and put your evidence out there for people to see who will look for you. In other words, if you are focused on changing minds, create a place that will be searched for and found by the non-paranormal person who is just starting to indulge her curiosity. Start a website that features some of the pictures you get during investigations, assuming a group you may belong to does not want to dominate the evidence you have acquired, and keyword it with locations or other words related to where you are from. Someone in your town is searching the web right now because he has had an experience and doesn't know what to think about it. Your picture might give him the boost to come forward with his story.

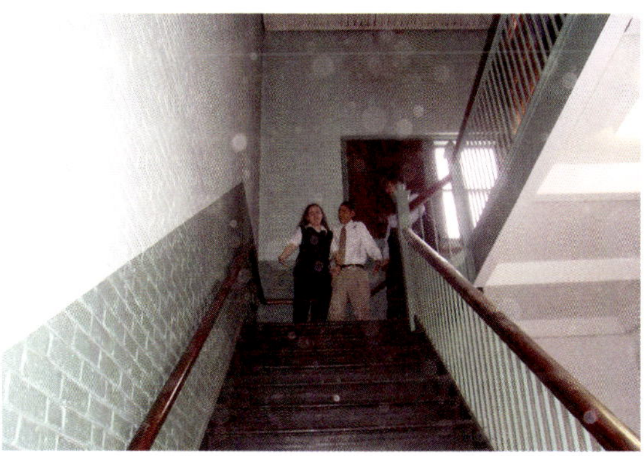

Figure 11.2
Most investigators refuse to look at orb pictures like this.

And Some in the Field Don't Either

One of my favorite sayings, and the one the people around me hate using as much as I do, is that no one cares about your record collection. It's a really mean thing to say, partly because people are very passionate about their albums and partly because they know it to be true. Have you ever seen the look on your friend's face when someone he knows eagerly passes him their iPod to show him a band they just discovered? It is uncomfortable for all involved.

Even though the picture may mean a lot to you and offer convincing evidence, you are probably too close to it and too passionate about it. When you show a fellow investigator, you expect him to jump up and down, maybe even shed a tear, and when it does not happen, you feel like the evidence is not good. It may not be, but do not take the reaction to mean that. Evidence is rarely as convincing to someone else. The most you can hope for is that the other investigators are open-minded about it.

There are several reasons why other investigators may be hesitant, all of which are more indicative of people being who they are as opposed to their worth as a source of your integrity as an investigator.

- **Approach**—Everybody looks at the paranormal through a different lens, so it is not unheard of for people to be a bit put off by the way you approach things. This trickles down to the evidence you produce. If you used a psychic, for example, during the investigation and the other group does not approve of the use of psi, they might look down on your image.
- **Narrow-mindedness**—Many people believe the paranormal exists in only one way. They may not buy into ecto, for example, and so any picture of ecto is to be ignored. If they do not believe in something and it is in one of your pictures, they might ignore all of your pictures, or even a picture that has the object in it. I know many investigators who will not evaluate any orb evidence, even though they preach that there is a chance a small percentage might be true. I have found the same thing with rod pictures.
- **Pride**—Don't think people can separate themselves as people and investigators. If anything, the exact opposite is true. Some people will just be jealous you got evidence and they did not.
- **Discrimination**—I recently received an e-mail from a young woman who said the group she joined, and paid dues to, will not look at the visual evidence she gets during an investigation because she is an investigator in training. She has not done her time in the field so there is no way she can produce evidence. This is, of course, ridiculous. Even people with no training who are not looking to take a picture of a ghost can get evidence.

You may think finding a like-minded group or individual to look at your proof is the ideal situation, and in the next section, we will review what to look for in an evidence yardstick, but someone who opposes you can be a benefit to you as an investigator. Having to defend yourself often helps to clarify what you feel and what you might be able to improve. Nothing is worse in the paranormal than yes-men.

The Boy Who Cried Ghost

With the number of pictures people can receive and the time it takes to review other people's evidence, it is important to run the picture through your own evaluation once more before you submit it for someone else to look at. I have received pictures from people over and over again and explained the same things to them. After getting 20 pictures of mist taken during parties or cookouts, how enthusiastic am I going to be about opening up the 21st? Many sites will not look at a picture of an orb because they are too easy to explain away. As you compile a list of trusted resources to use, ask yourself if you cannot use what you already know about ghost photography, especially what you have learned by reading this book, and find a natural cause for the smudge you see.

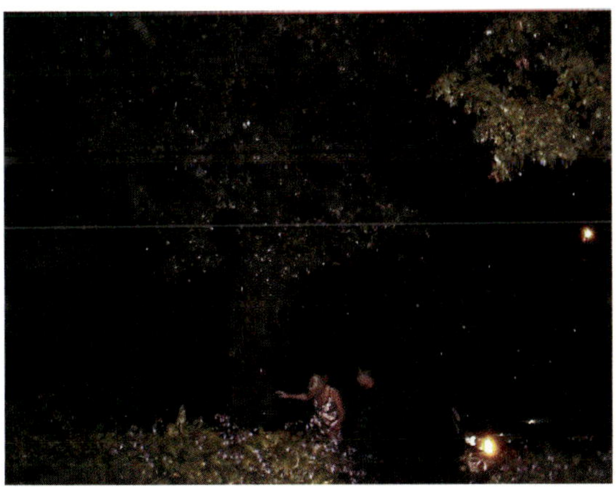

Figure 11.3
A picture received that had explainable lights in it. I told them the rain and the car headlight might be responsible for most of what they were seeing.

Do not publish every picture you find. Try to explain them yourself, hold on to them, and then revisit them when you have more experience. You may find the same ghost shows up time and time again in your pictures and may be explained away as a problem of your camera. Save your most unexplained for experts so you can maintain a relationship with them. You should also genuinely learn the lessons these people put forth to you. If they tell you that the shadow is actually caused by the flash of another camera in the room, watch out for that during investigations and think about that when you assess your pictures.

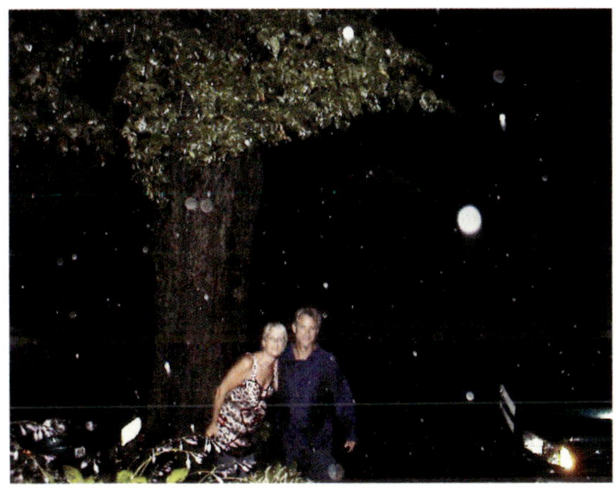

Figure 11.4
When I was sent a second, almost identical picture, I stopped trying to explain it to them.

Sources and Resources

PART OF THE PROCESS of being a paranormal investigator, for many people, is being part of a group, even if that group is just some people you can investigate with or bounce ideas off of. I enjoy, as a freelance investigator, meeting groups because I am entranced by the structure of some of them, but also because I like seeing how groups organize their meetings. Every meeting I have been to with a formal paranormal group involves an evaluation of the evidence from the last investigation they went on, and some of them look more like students forced to stand up and give an answer they don't know in ninth-grade chemistry than talking with friends and peers. The tension is so high, what should be a think-tank becomes a competition for who can come up with the best reason for your evidence being worthless.

There is nothing better than another set of eyes to look at what you have gotten. There is always someone who has a question that makes you look at it differently or brings up something you did not think of when you saw it. It is one thing for you to see something in the peace and tranquility of your home, but having it hold up to other people's eyes is quite another. When you find some good people, and when you can provide something that challenges them, you can raise your investigating to another level. The issue is finding people you are comfortable with.

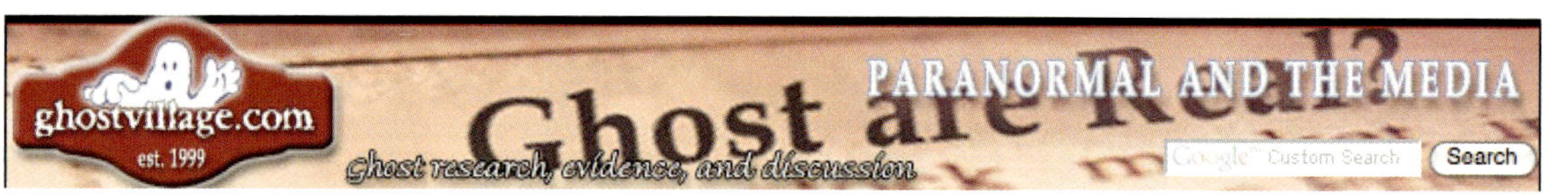

Figure 11.5
Ghostvillage.com, a place you can connect with people in your community who will evaluate your pictures.

A Ghost Photo: The Perfect Olive Branch

I get seven or eight e-mails a week from people looking to join my group. They take one of three approaches to me. They either claim to know nothing but have an interest or they have 20 years of experience in the field but have just recently left their group. The third gives a list of shows they watch and equipment they have and ask to just tag along and hope that something will come of it. Connecting to a group is the safest way to investigate, and also provides a valuable resource to look at your evidence. What I have found, especially recently, is that groups are becoming too tight and less willing to take on members. If they are willing, there are so many people out there investigating you can never be sure if a group you contact is right for you.

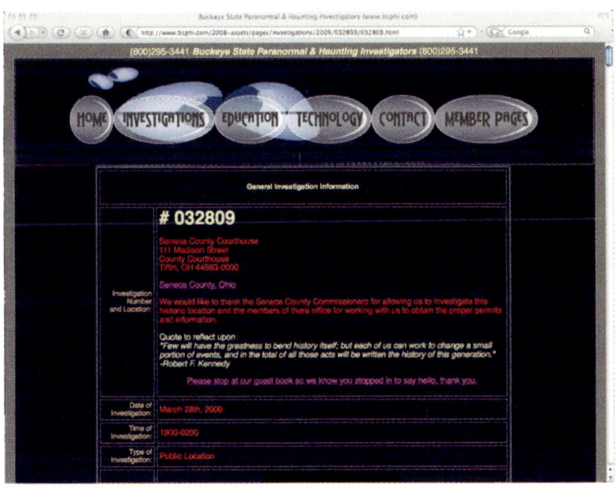

Figure 11.6
Buckeye State Paranormal and Haunting Investigators at www.bsphi.com is another group willing to look at your pictures.

Having evidence already may be the best way to approach them. You can always e-mail them and say you have heard about them and value their opinion. You just want them to look. The olive branch has been extended, and what they respond tells you more about them than sitting in on a meeting. Do they return your e-mail or ignore you? Do they give you the party line about not looking at anything that does not come from their investigators? Do they return your e-mail and ask follow-up questions before giving you an honest opinion on the picture?

These all define who they are and the kind of fit you may be for them. For example, Robyne Marie remote views through pictures, meaning she travels to the location in her mind and sees things others cannot, especially spiritual things. If you have a hardcore science approach to the paranormal and she e-mails you back about what her psychic side is telling her, she might not be the right person for you to connect to. This method also tells you whether they are willing to hear from other people and be more likely to invite you to join.

Snapshot

Want to know about the skills of a paranormal group before knowing whether to join them or ask their opinion on evidence? Send them a fake picture or one that clearly has something about it that can be explained. If the group claims it to be absolute proof and asks to post it on their site, think twice about them. Just make sure to play dumb and never tell them you were testing them. Paranormal egos are easily bruised.

What to Look For

If you are looking for a group, or even if you are just looking to have someone give her view on your picture, you need to approach it like computer dating. You may be able to approach someone at a conference or event, but chances are you will be e-mailing them looking for a moment of their time. There is much to be said by someone's online profile, be it from posts they have made on other sites or what they have on their own sites. Finding the right one becomes a series of "best matches" on what you are looking for from the paranormal, and speed dating may be the best way to find true picture love. Keep in mind, a good paranormal website does not make the best one to use for evidence. For example, one of my sites, Massachusetts Paranormal Crossroads, was designed to get paranormal ideas and haunted locations out there, but it does not offer much in the way of evidence.

The net can be used to tell a bit about an investigator aside from the site he is associated with. There was a local group that did an investigation and happened to get the attention of the local media. I had never heard of them, and they had only been together for a few weeks, but the newspaper article made them an overnight sensation, if there is such a thing in the ghost world. The web is loaded with references to paranormal, and evaluating what investigators say online gives you a hint of who they are. You should sift through radio interviews, newspaper clippings, and interviews on paranormal sites and message boards and forums.

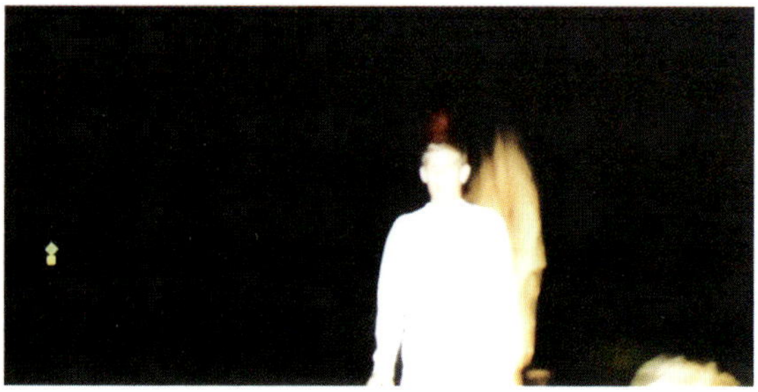

Figure 11.7
Another picture given to me for evaluation that I sent on to others for advice.

Some of these suggestions are generalizations, but they are a good guidelines to follow. For each of these suggestions I can name a group that I respect that goes against it.

Eight Elements of a Good Group to Review Your Evidence

1. They have a presence on the Internet and their site does not come from a free service. This might be a bit snobby, but anyone who is somewhat serious about the paranormal can afford a site, and having one defines their investment in what they do.

2. They have more than a handful of pictures on their site that come from investigations they have conducted on their own.

3. Their pictures are organized on their site so you can clearly see what they are claiming is there.

4. They provide reasons for pictures being paranormal and not natural. A good group can say why a picture is natural or why a picture is genuine, but a really effective group does both.

5. If there is a members section, the group should be more focused on who people are and not worried about their titles. I am leery of groups with more people who specialize in demonology and cryptozoology than tech specialists.

6. A good group to look at is one that defines what they look for in pictures. Some groups go overboard with the "article" sections on their sites, but it is always good to see what they think a good ghost picture is.

7. Years in the field does not always translate into having a good eye, but it helps. Look for people who have been doing it for a while.

8. It may be beneficial to have a local group look at your pictures. Not only does it help to connect with people in your area, but the people involved might have some idea of the context of the back-story behind the haunting or at least some information on other spirits nearby.

Groups to Avoid

- **They have too many orb pictures**
- **They spend too much time criticizing other groups**
- **They refer to things on television shows too often**
- **The group consists of teenagers**
- **There are no pictures except ones from graveyards and asylums**
- **There are more pictures of the group at parties or posing than evidence pictures**

Some Sites to Approach

I always suggest looking locally and establishing a relationship with several groups that can look at your material. Then branch out to others, especially those groups that have gained a reputation of being critical. Make your own list of people who are too harsh and some who are too willing to accept any pictures and then balance them with some who fall in the middle, like the old bell curve in school.

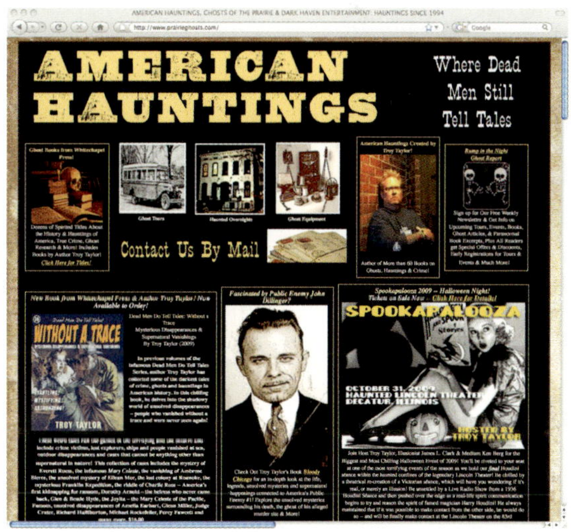

Figure 11.8
Troy Taylor, author and creator of American Hauntings at www.praireghosts.com, is an expert in ghost photography.

In no certain order, here are some groups I respect and that may be able to help you look at a picture.

Ghost Research Society
http://www.ghostresearch.org/ghostpics

Ghost pictures
http://www.ghost-pictures.org/Submitted-Ghost-Pictures.htm

Cape And Islands Paranormal Research Society
http://www.caiprs.com

Buckeye State Paranormal and Haunting Investigators
www.bsphi.com/

American Hauntings
http://www.prairieghosts.com

Ghost Study
http://www.ghoststudy.com

Massachusetts Paranormal Crossroads
http://www.masscrossroads.com

The Shadowlands
http://theshadowlands.net/ghost

Lessons to Learn Just By Looking

As a school teacher, I spend much of my day trying to figure out how to reach my students. The one thing every book on teaching will tell you, and one lesson every good teacher needs to learn on his own, is that students learn differently. Getting them to absorb and remember the lesson often becomes an exercise in multiple approach communication. You write it visually on the board and then talk about it. When that is done you let them try it for themselves and then ask questions so they feel invested.

One of the most effective ways to get something across is to present it visually. I learn by watching someone doing something and then getting my own hands dirty. When I mess up, I watch again or ask what I did wrong, and you can benefit from this approach to investigating, taking effective pictures, and then looking at the evidence. By looking at the images other respected groups are putting out there, you see how they have set up a shot and how they have distinguished between a ghost and a natural element. Many will even tell you why the picture falls on one side or the other.

Do I Dare Post It to a Message Board?

There is an episode of the television show *West Wing* where one of the president's main men goes online and finds out there is a message board dedicated to him. He is flattered, but a bit put off by one of the posters, and decides to chime in. Within minutes the whole thing goes bad, and no matter what he posts he cannot seem to save himself. I have come across the same thing in the paranormal. There is that temptation to defend or clarify something about yourself, and it is hard to have a positive outcome once you have stepped your big toes in cyberspace.

Posting to a message board is easy and requires very little commitment. You can even post to several, and all many will ask of you is that you register. It is the quickest way to put your picture in front of many people and get a whole rainbow of opinions from people who have some experience with the paranormal, and it is also a good way to become part of a community. In addition, they allow you some level of privacy, exploring anonymously, so you can always hide behind a nickname or screen name.

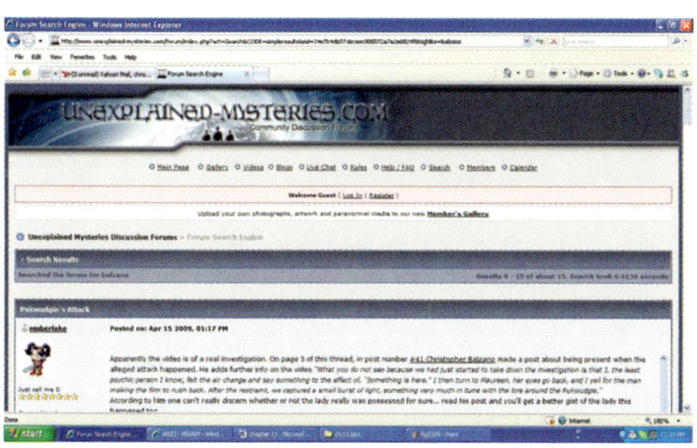

Figure 11.9
Unexplained Mysteries, where the DVD for Picture Yourself Ghost Hunting, and I, were attacked.

This anonymity allows others to hide as well, and one of the hardest things about evidence, especially when you have an emotional connection to it, is the reaction it may induce from others. Message boards can be vicious places to be avoided at times, and can get very nasty and personal. I have seen rational discussions turn quickly and then gain momentum. They get sidetracked and spend too much time debating a small point. You may want to know what might have caused a streak in your picture and they spend a dozen posts discussing why streaks are not demons. That may be useful, but it is not on point. At times there may be many posts telling someone they made a good point and then posts telling those posters that their post about the post was also good. Are you confused yet? This is then further muddled by posts about televisions shows, good bands to listen to, and flat-out flirting.

There are some good ones out there, or at least threads that may be worth dropping in on. Do your research. When you see sites where opinions are respected, and if you feel comfortable, post your evidence. Just make sure you have a tough skin and do not take anything they say personally. Most importantly, do not respond to anything other than intelligent questions and never meet an insult with an insult or a clarification. Redemption will never come.

You also need to make sure you are ready for what might be appropriate feedback, even if it is not phrased in a way designed to make you feel good. You are putting yourself out there, so make sure you can handle it. If someone does not like what you have offered, it is an opinion. If they explain why and it makes sense, you have to take it to heart.

Posting to Your Own Site

If you investigate the paranormal, especially if you are part of a team, chances are you have your own website. The question becomes whether to post pictures you have a question about on it. The face that you present is the way the world sees you, so it is a difficult balance to deal with. On one hand, you do not want to put forth bad evidence and be seen as promoting the negative image of the paranormal. On the other hand, I am all about saying I care enough about what I am doing to say I need someone else's opinion.

If you decide to put your borderline pictures up on your site for others to look at and comment on, make sure you clearly announce that is what they are for. You should go even further by making a different page to not muddle the line between the two. You might even want to start a whole new site just for questionable images.

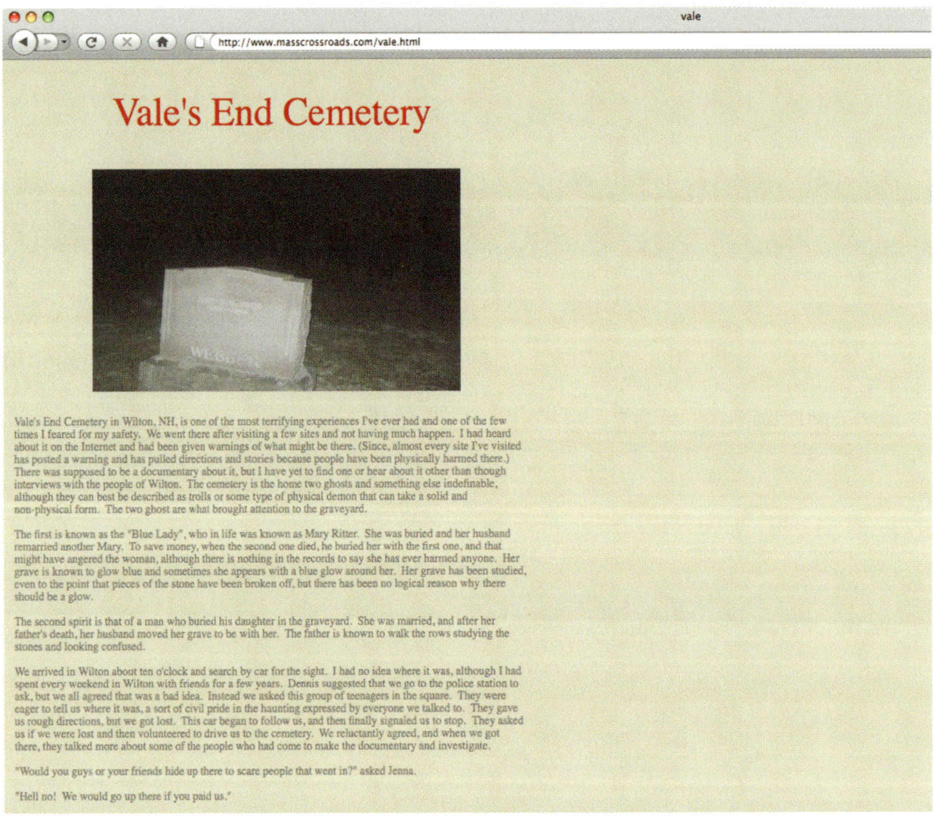

Figure 11.10
Massachusetts Paranormal Crossroads, where I post my evidence for people to comment on.

Getting the Picture Ready

THE PARANORMAL WORLD is just like the professional world, but without anyone making money. The better you look, or the more professional you are in your approach, the more likely you are to get a positive response. Many paranormal investigators have very little time to devote to a stranger, and the more reputable or well known the person or group, the more they have to sift through e-mail asking for advice or presenting evidence. For example, larger sites such as Ghostvillage or Haunted America Tours receive hundreds of e-mails in a month, and that number goes up to thousands around Halloween.

Many of the paranormal pictures established paranormal investigators get feel like just random shots with no work from your end to get any real opinion on them. When you get in touch with them, let them know why you are looking to them and how much you would really appreciate their help. Most will take time out if the picture and background are there and you go beyond just asking them if they see a ghost in the photo.

Snapshot

It is not just the teacher in me. Grammar equals time and effort and caring. If you want to be taken seriously, take time to write well when you communicate with people you are asking to evaluate your pictures.

Here my pic what do u think.

This is the body of an actual e-mail I received. If the sender could not take the time to write clearly, why should I take the time to look at the image? You do not need to be Shakespeare, or even write like you are looking for a job, just avoid bad grammar, abbreviations, and unclear language.

What They Need to Know and How to Format the Picture

The Picture

Most people who look at your picture online will want it in the best, most accessible format. While many have software on their computers like the kind we discussed in Chapter 8, the picture should arrive to them as a JPEG. There are other, more powerful ways to save it, and the new advances in computers will always have new interactive formats, but JPEG is universal enough to be downloaded by everyone. The picture should be saved with the best resolution you have and not compressed. Almost all e-mail servers will send a picture of any size you can make, so don't worry about sending a file over 5 megabytes.

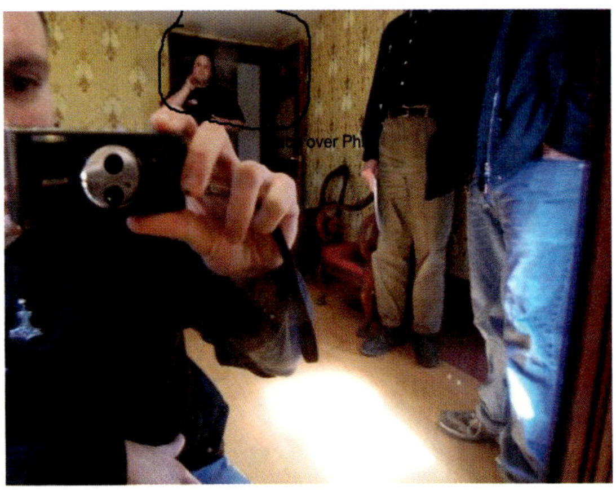

Figure 11.11

Try to avoid pointing out where the person needs to look and let it come naturally.

Picture courtesy of Gary Manley.

> ### Snapshot
>
> **There is an easy way to find the accurate camera information on your image or one you get from someone else to evaluate. In most image editing software you can find the source by looking at the characteristics. Here is another clue. Open up the picture in MS Notepad. It will be turned to code. The first line will tell you the source. For example:**
>
> SONY DSC-H2 H H 2007:04:18 16:25:26 PrintIM 0300 (from a camera)
>
> DSC00267 Hewlett-Packard Company HP PhotoSmart C20 Camera (from a scanner)
>
> JFIF d d ÿì Ducky 7 ÿî Adobe dÀ (from Photoshop, and possibly a doctored picture)

The picture should be the raw information with no editing or cutting on your end. This allows them to get the purest form of the picture and takes away any funny business on your end, although there is no way for them to know if you have altered it in any way. There will always be the potential that the picture was tampered with, but all you can do is have clean hands on your end. Do not outline or zoom in on what you think the paranormal element of the picture is, even if it exists in only a small portion of the shot. You can tell them where it is and give them the option to read it or not, but a red circle over a vortex will put what it is and where it is in their mind. If the evidence is compelling enough, and the investigator knows what they are doing, the image should stand alone.

It may also be useful to include other pictures of the same scene so the investigator can see the environment without the suspected ghost. They were not involved in the ghost hunt, so they do not understand an image out of context. Sending a few establishing shots will give them the chance to weight the variables and develop a more educated opinion.

Useful Information to Pass On

You do not want to make a part time job out of submitting pictures, so come up with a template you can use over and over again. This can then be used during your evaluation process, making it serve two purposes.

It is important to include the following information

- Type of camera used
- Any settings you used on the camera, including if a flash was used or your autofocus was on
- Time of day
- Location, either in a general way (the basement of a home) or specific (at the Boarhead Inn in Toledo)
- Weather conditions, including a pollen index if you have it and barometric conditions
- Any back-story or details of the haunting if you know them

Picture Review

Name of image:
Investigator:
Location:
Date:
Other Investigators:

Location back story:

Camera used:
Flash:
Other settings:
Weather conditions:

Other information:

My assessment:

Figure 11.12
A template I created to give the appropriate information to other investigators.

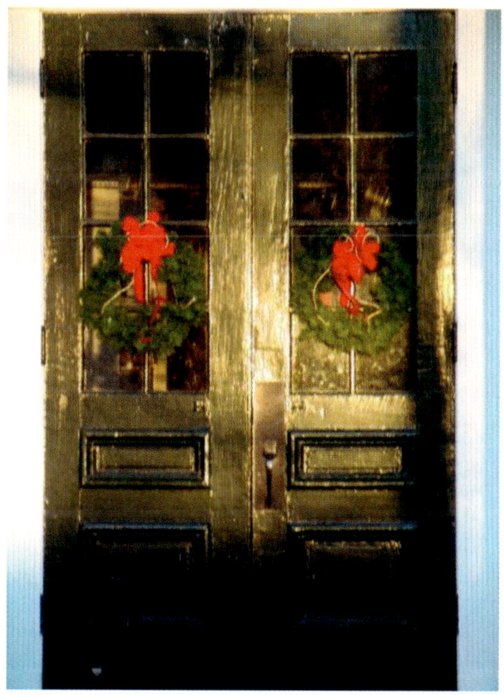

Figure 11.13
A good example of a picture contribution. It began with a picture. Picture courtesy of Pat Martin.

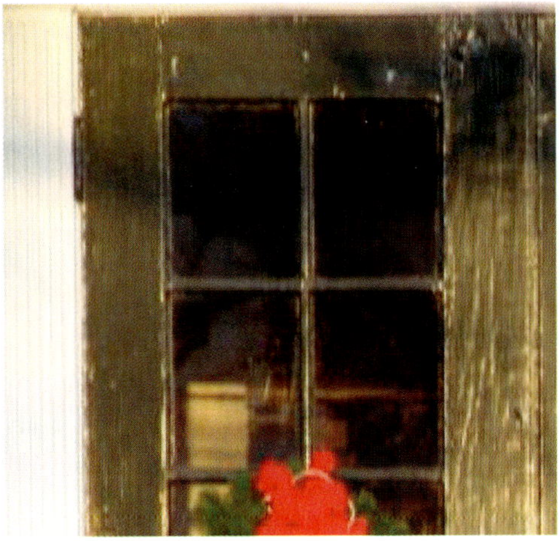

Figure 11.14

Then a close-up of the figure in the picture, a spoiler of sorts.

Picture courtesy of Pat Martin.

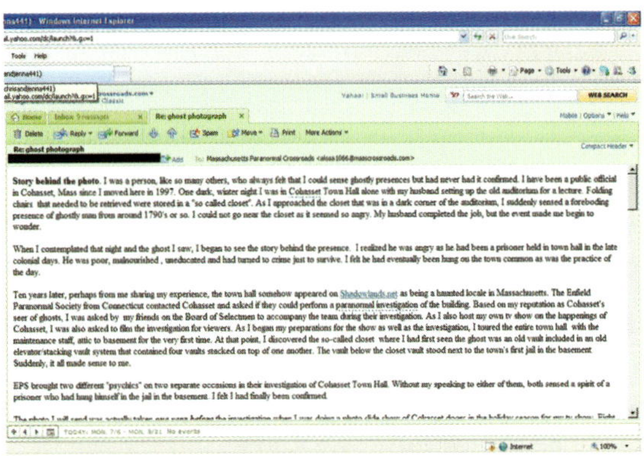

Re: ghost photograph

To: Massachusetts Paranormal Crossroads

Story behind the photo. I was a person, like so many others, who always felt that I could sense ghostly presences but had never had it confirmed. I have been a public official in Cohasset, Mass since I moved here in 1997. One dark, winter night I was in Cohasset Town Hall alone with my husband setting up the old auditorium for a lecture. Folding chairs that needed to be retrieved were stored in a "so called closet". As I approached the closet that was in a dark corner of the auditorium, I suddenly sensed a foreboding presence of ghostly man from around 1790's or so. I could not go near the closet as it seemed so angry. My husband completed the job, but the event made me begin to wonder.

When I contemplated that night and the ghost I saw, I began to see the story behind the presence. I realized he was angry as he had been a prisoner held in town hall in the late colonial days. He was poor, malnourished , uneducated and had turned to crime just to survive. I felt he had eventually been hung on the town common as was the practice of the day.

Ten years later, perhaps from me sharing my experience, the town hall somehow appeared on Shadowlands.net as being a haunted locale in Massachusetts. The Enfield Paranormal Society from Connecticut contacted Cohasset and asked if they could perform a paranormal investigation of the building. Based on my reputation as Cohasset's seer of ghosts, I was asked by my friends on the Board of Selectmen to accompany the team during their investigation. As I also host my own tv show on the happenings of Cohasset, I was also asked to film the investigation for viewers. As I began my preparations for the show as well as the investigation, I toured the entire town hall with the maintenance staff, attic to basement for the very first time. At that point, I discovered the so-called closet where I had first seen the ghost was an old vault included in an old elevator/stacking vault system that contained four vaults stacked on top of one another. The vault below the closet vault stood next to the town's first jail in the basement. Suddenly, it all made sense to me.

EPS brought two different "psychics" on two separate occasions in their investigation of Cohasset Town Hall. Without my speaking to either of them, both sensed a spirit of a prisoner who had hung himself in the jail in the basement. I felt I had finally been confirmed.

Figure 11.15

And then a description of the picture, conditions, and the background of the case. In this situation, she e-mailed me her own personal experience and then something that happened when a group was asked to come in and investigate.

I also suggest a second document, like a spoiler, that the evaluator should look at only after he has examined the picture. This includes what you think is in the picture and where it might be in the image. This is the kind of information that can taint the evaluation but bring another level of examination after they have looked at it and formed their own opinion.

Snapshot

Here is a good approach letter, or at least one that would encourage me to download the picture and take a look:

Dear Mr. Balzano,

I have seen the work you have done in the paranormal for the past few years and wanted to approach you about a picture I recently took. I was investigating a private residence, and when I evaluated the pictures afterwards, this one really left me with no explanation. I was hoping you could look at the picture and tell me what you think.

I have also attached some information about the picture that might help you come to a conclusion.

Thank you for your time, and I look forward to hearing from you.

Evaluation Outside the Lines

Contests

If there is a way for the paranormal to promote something or bring in money, people will find it. One of the old standbys is the paranormal picture contest. This is where investigators submit what they think their best picture of a ghost is and people vote on it. There is really no review of the material to know whether the picture is accurate or not; you either win or lose, but it does get your picture out there and your name in front of people as well. I personally do not recommend it because it changes your perspective from a person who is looking for the paranormal to someone trying to win something. It reduces you to trying to win the science fair as opposed to making advances in the field.

The best friend of the paranormal picture contest is the one who asks you to submit your best fake picture of a ghost. Usually this means one you manufacture, not one that you think is a spirit but isn't. I actually take more stock in this type of contest because it keeps the different ways you can fake a picture out there for all the public, and investigators, to see. We all become better at looking at images and deciding their credibility by looking at good and bad photos.

This may seem hypocritical, but I highly suggest looking online for these contests. Looking at them, and seeing what people are holding up as the strongest pieces of evidence, will make you a tighter looker yourself.

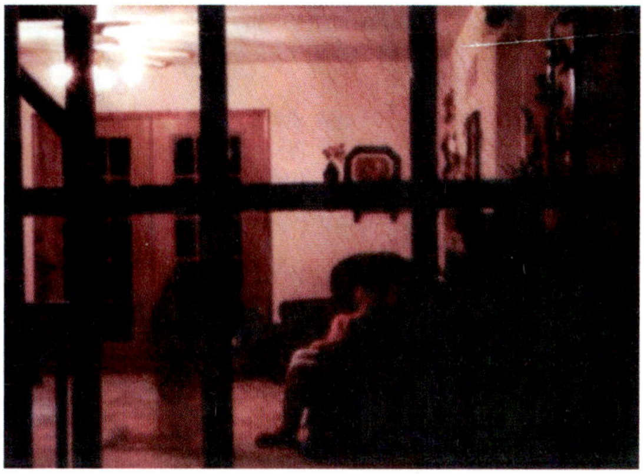

Figure 11.16
A picture submitted by author and investigator Rob Conover that won a photo contest hands down.

At times the contests can move the field forward. In the spring of 2009, Psychologist Prof Wiseman, from the University of Hertfordshire, sponsored a contest designed to bring out people's ideas of the paranormal. Of the more than 250 pictures submitted in under a month's time, the best were analyzed by experts who then picked the best one. The most convincing ones were posted on the website, www.scienceofhaunting.com, and the winner was a shot by Christopher Aitchison at the haunted Tantallon Castle in North Berwick on the East coast of Scotland. The image shows a person in fifteenth century clothes peering out a window high above the courtyard.

What is interesting about the contest is not that people found ghosts in their pictures. That is a common occurrence, especially by those who are out there looking for them. Instead, the odd thing is the motivation by Wiseman. He claims the contest was more to see how people thought of ghosts, or in other words, what do people see in their mind's eye when someone mentions ghosts. They then found those objects in their pictures and submitted them. The results tell us more about our vision of the paranormal than whether or not ghosts really exist. This psychological and sociological slant tells us more about ourselves than about those who have passed, but the publicity put ghosts on the minds of both the public and scientific community.

Video Sharing

It seems like a very fashionable thing to do today to get something on video and then shoot it up to YouTube or a social networking site like Facebook or MySpace and let the world know what you are doing. It is also very fashionable to criticize people for doing it, which I am not going to do. Connecting with others is an important aspect of the paranormal, and these sites allow you to talk and share with people faster than any other method. It also works well when you invite others to download what you have and see if they can run it through software to see if they can get anything.

Remember to stress that this is evidence you want people to look at and give their opinion on. When doing some promotional material for *Picture Yourself Ghost Hunting*, I added some scenes from the DVD to help sell the book. One involved a scene where a woman suffered a psychic attack from an unseen force. People began personally attacking me for posting it, even though it was offered up as a commercial, not evidence. Allowing people to look at your work invites a whole new wave of criticism, but do everything you can to separate what you are presenting as solid, well combed evidence and material you want others to tear apart. Then make sure you have a thick skin because most won't.

Approach the endeavor with a pure motive and you will do fine. If you start posting because you want to become famous for having the best ghost video on the web, people will automatically discredit what you are trying to do.

The Live Investigation

Inspired by television shows that are now featuring special live episodes, investigators with knowledge of the technology are taking to the Internet to invite others to hunt alongside them. They are mostly done to promote those doing the investigating, and you can imagine how hard it is to actually see anything during those webcasts, but they are worth stopping by. The cream of them rises to the top, so you may have to view a few really bad ones before you connect with the ones who are using the technology in the right way, but witnessing the investigation will help you form good habits for your own ghost hunts. At the least, they will expose you to what other people are doing in the field.

It Will Never Be Enough

ASKING PEOPLE TO LOOK at your pictures is a lot like putting your hand in a bear trap. You may be able to slip it in and out without anything happening, but every time you do you risk losing your hand. There will always be something wrong with the picture, and even when nine out of ten people you approach are baffled, there will always be whispers of a fraud or an unseen natural cause.

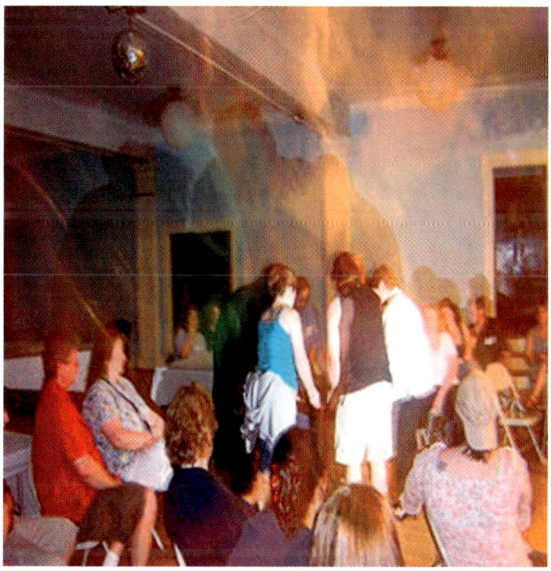

Figure 11.17
A fake picture I recently passed around to get opinions on. Picture courtesy of Josh Mantello.

...and then they ask you

Like a bad mafia movie, the favor will come back to you some day. If you ask others, you must be willing to give when the time comes, it does not matter if it is sugar, or picking someone up at the airport, or looking at a ghost picture. Think of it as a compliment and give your honest opinion. It might determine how you are viewed by others, so just run the picture through the same tests you do for your own pictures.

At some point, you have to allow the picture to stand. None of the people you talk to were on the investigation or can fully appreciate the nuances of the photo, so you have to step back from it, label it as something unexplained, and file it away. One of the reasons I try to avoid paranormal television shows is that they strive to prove something as haunted or not haunted, and after keeping the audience's attention for a certain amount of time they feel obligated to do that. The audience also feels obligated to know that, so they contribute to the issue. It has to be enough for you, on some level, that you took a picture of a ghost and that picture may take you a step closer into categorizing the location you got it at as haunted.

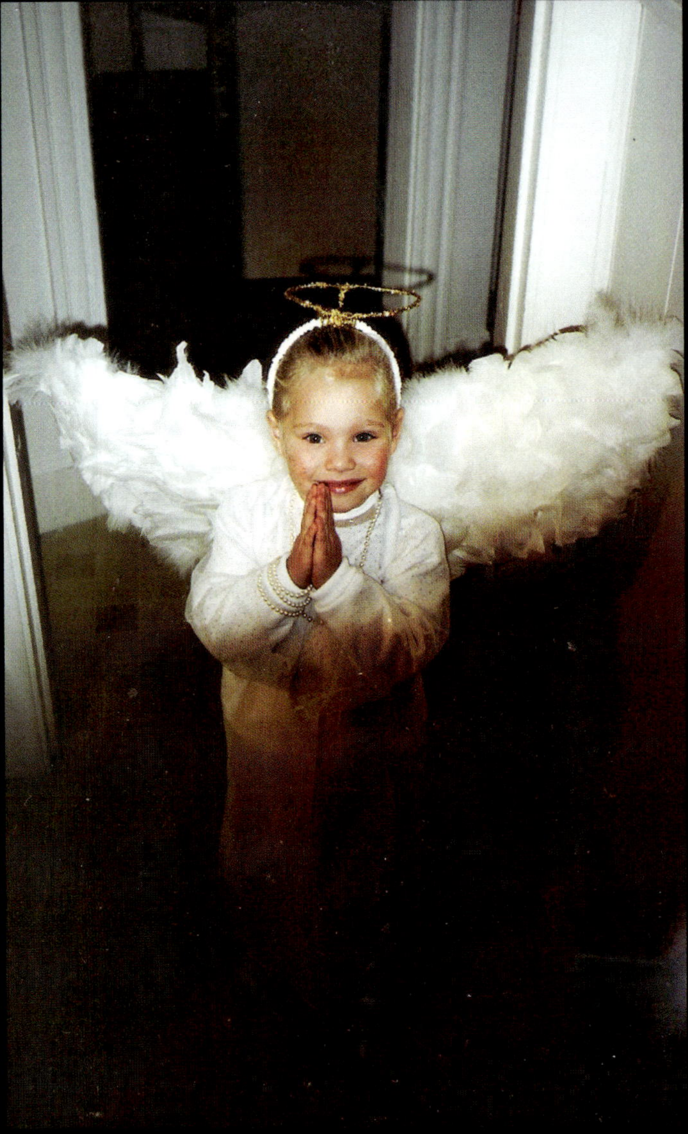

after this picture was taken, this little girl began to experience unusual paranormal events.

12

Some Final Thoughts on Ghost Photos

THERE IS SOMETHING EVERY PARANORMAL investigator has to look at as he continues to engage in ghost hunts and do paranormal research. At some point the science will fail you. Whether it is because it no longer explains something going on or because it only brings you to a certain point, following only the science of ghost hunting will eventually leave a small part of you empty. It usually happens after the excitement of an investigation is long behind you and you have captured something. You have shown it around and people can find no reason behind it and you sit and look at it once again. A question will come up and science is helpless to truly answer it. So what does it mean?

The Science May Fail You

THERE ARE SPIRITUAL AVENUES you can go down, and rather than address those we will just talk about how it shifts your focus. Paranormal science, which we must remember is based on scientific ideas but not actual science, can explain why it may be possible to capture a ghost on film and why a certain type of ghost looks a certain way or has certain properties. Although some people are inventing tools designed to trap or contain ghosts, the very idea of which should make the investigator scared and not excited, it has helped little with getting rid of ghosts or solving the problem of how to deal with a haunting. This is part of the reason paranormal television shows began to stray from showing investigations at private homes.

More importantly, it has yet to answer what this means for us as humans living through a potential afterlife. What does a ghost say about life? Can we help people on the other side and can we guarantee our own transition? At what point does a spirit need an ear instead of thermal imaging?

I would hate to get heavy so close to the end of the book, so let me deal with the issue, which more paranormal investigators are coming to me with, by letting you in on a secret. Most of paranormal investigating has nothing to do with the science of energy or movement or even physics and theoretical physics like parallel universes and the relationship between space and time. Paranormal investigating has more to do with the living. Remember, psychology, sociology, and anthropology are sciences too. Throw in a little spirituality and you get a bit closer to the complete picture of the paranormal world.

A fellow teacher of mine dabbles in photography in his spare time. While visiting his wife's family in Central America, he hired a scout to bring him into a jungle area to take some pictures of wild animals. During the trip, he was lying in wait in some tall grass thinking about what he was doing. He was overwhelmed by the moment and was thinking about everything in his life that had led him to that moment. He started to tear up when he spotted a jaguar 50 feet away staring at him. The animal cocked his head as he raised his camera and focused through his tears at the animal that was locked on him. The moment was intense, a mixture of emotion and fear, and after he took the shot, the beast stretched and walked away. The picture is the most beautiful one I have ever seen of an animal.

There is a science behind what we do. There are things you need to know about your equipment and how to take a good picture and how to see and capture ghosts. These are the foundations of investigation, but they are not where it begins or where it ends. The best photos you take may have very little to do with the science of the paranormal. Many, perhaps even the best, have to do with heart.

Learning from Your Mistakes

YOU NEED TO CRAWL before you can run. One of the exciting things about spirit photography is that you are probably able to start it today. You have a camera and now a little knowledge, and the rest of it is a series of challenges for you to stumble through and make mistakes on. Take comfort. Each investigation gets better, and each picture you think is perfect that someone else is able to explain is a lesson of some kind. A real paranormal investigator loves the journey, not just the results. It is just as important to find bad evidence as it is to get the perfect shot.

So I'll let you in on one of my paranormal mishaps. I had taken my son out on his first trip through the neighborhood for Halloween. My whole family was there, so there were flashes going off all over the place as he slept in his chicken suit and woke up long enough to drool.

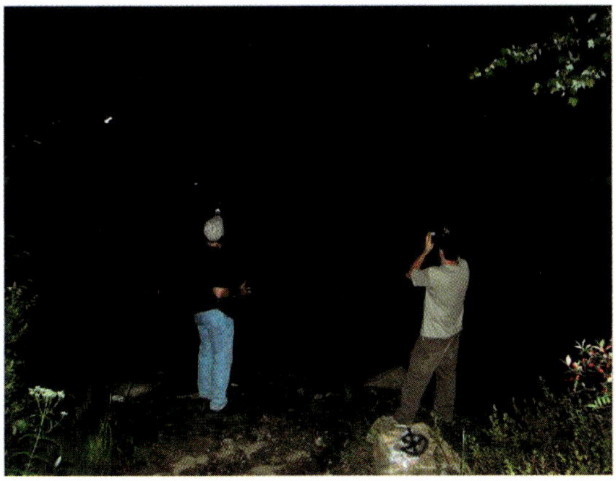

Figure 12.1
The common mistake, orbs in the field.

Living near an extremely haunted location I had not investigated yet, a few of us decided to go out and look for ghosts when the children went to bed. I picked up my camera and we left for an unscheduled and unscouted hunt.

The location was on the banks of a lake, and as I told the back-story, my friend snapped away with her camera. When I paused, I did as well. The night was pretty well lit, but we used our flashlights and I kept having to manually program my flash to go off. Knowing equipment often malfunctioned in the field, I took this as proof something was trying to prevent us from investigating. Some of the pictures I got that night show bright yellow vortexes, which fit in with the story of the location being a gateway between two worlds; I had captured something ancient and evil.

Then I noticed the same vortexes were over my sister. Surely, she was not ancient and evil, although I shrugged it off because she was living in a house where we had recorded paranormal activity. Proud of myself, I showed the pictures to someone I respected and they laughed. I had never taken the Nightvision off the camera. In the first models to have it, the camera would not allow the flash to be used with the feature, and if you did, the filter took in too much light and made it look like light was exploding all around you.

Some Stories from Others

Think of these stories as being worth the read for their entertainment value. These may seem like common sense mistakes, and hopefully after reading this book you will avoid them, but they were very real to the people who experienced them. They are lessons in what not to do, but in a larger sense they are a single lesson you still need to learn. No matter how long you investigate, there is always something to learn.

Clarissa Vazquez: Co-Founder, Colorado Coalition of Paranormal Investigators

Most new and inexperienced investigators go through their "Orb Phase" where every drop of water, every dust particle, every bug is considered evidence and paranormal in nature. CCPI was no exception.

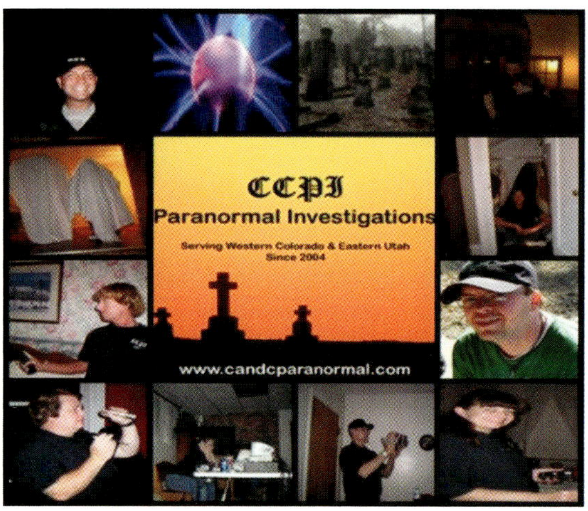

Figure 12.2
Clarissa's group, Colorado Coalition of Paranormal Investigators.

When CCPI was still in its infancy, and it was still just the two of us, we investigated a building that was constructed in the nineteenth century and used as a dance hall, brothel, and other interesting things. It was the first time we used a video camera, one without night shot, and recorded two consecutive hours of an empty room with all of the lights on.

We were amazed to discover the orbs that would miraculously appear every time one of us entered the room to check on the video camera or audio recorder we had going. We sat up all night, eyes wide open, and screaming in disbelief at the ghosts that were buzzing our heads unbeknownst to us at the time we took the video. By dawn, we had watched the same two hours of video footage three times. We were in tears—we were so happy about our amazing success on that investigation. We later learned that it was dust buzzing our heads.

On a happy note, it was, and remains to this day, the most fun I have ever had doing evidence review.

Alan Dunski: Equipment Manager/Lead Investigator, Wisconsin Paranormal Investigators

Ashley, Katie, and I were walking down the stairs to the basement. I was leading us down. Just as I reached the basement floor, I looked up to have this very fast object fly right at my face. Now keep in mind that we investigate with lights out and I only had a red headlamp on at the time. I stopped instantly and said aloud, "What was that?"

I am a very calm investigator and not much spooks me at all, which had Katie and Ashley even more worried. I paused, trying to gather my thoughts as to what in the world I had just seen. I was silent for a bit when Katie asked, "What's wrong? Were you pushed?" I answered, "No, do you have your DVR on?" She told me yes so I started asking questions.

My first question was a simple, "hello?," and as soon as I asked that, we all heard a bunch of rustling around in the boiler room. I started walking that way, not knowing what in the world was going on. I asked another question, "Hello, is anyone down here?" and got more rustling right after my question. Nothing happened in between my questions, only right after each question. I started walking closer to where the sound was coming from.

While I was doing this, Ashley and Katie were still at the bottom of the stairs, huddled together, breathing hard and scared stiff. I asked one last question and just as I did this, I heard the noise again, cranked my head to the left, and saw a bat flying right at my head.

I decided it would be a good idea for me to leave the basement to find something to catch the bat and release it outside. Just as I reached the top of the stairs, the bat went right at the girls' heads and the screams were even louder. That was their cue to run up the stairs out of the basement. I honestly had thought that this was my first true 100% paranormal experience, but no.

We have come across different light formations on our DVR system when reviewing evidence. If you were to just look at the screen without knowing what was going on you would think that there were true orbs dancing around, but upon further review, we have found that when an IR illuminator is aimed at another one, it tends to form balls of light. Also, when someone is in front of one of the DVR cameras and they take a still picture with the digital camera, it appears as if their head explodes on the DVR camera.

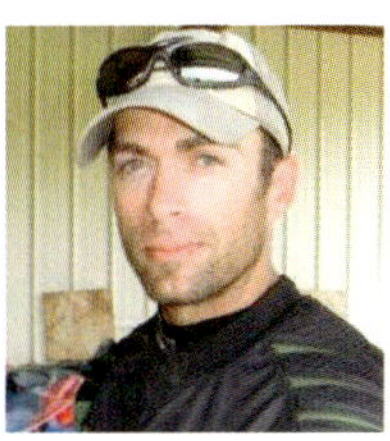

Figure 12.3
Alan Dunski.

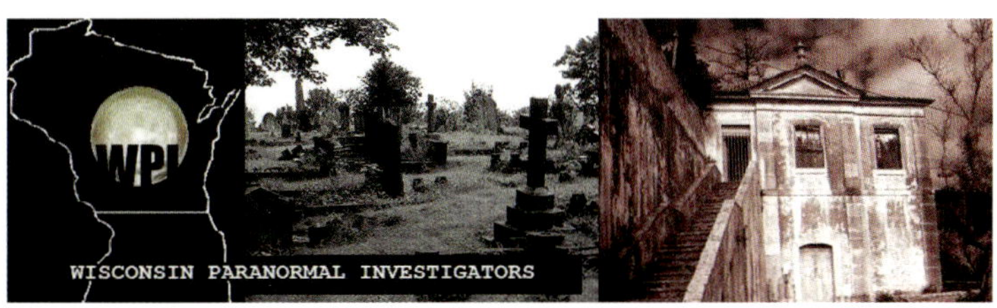

Figure 12.4
And his group, Wisconsin Paranormal Investigators.

Ericka and Rick Benson: Co-founders, Blue Spirits Paranormal Investigators

We use to find a lot of shadows in our investigation pictures until we got uniforms for our investigators. If you put navy blue silk screen letters on a black shirt, you get letters that have a neon effect on an IR camera. No more shadows that can't be identified.

Jessica Stone: Investigator

I was at the Houghton Mansion and I took a picture in the basement. I didn't look over any pictures until later that night when I was alone in my hotel room. When I zoomed in on a picture, I scared myself because there appeared to be a little creature sitting there. Later my common sense prevailed and I realized it was just matrixing.

Robyne Marie: Investigator/Host of Lights Out Paranormal Radio

As a medium who does remote viewing, it's comical to me when groups from all across the globe send me photos to analyze "clairvoyantly." They do so because they have seen something within the photo they have questioned or feel is of mystical nature. I am also a psychologist, so I know that the human mind tends to see faces in everything. I have hundreds of photos where the sender suggests they see something demonic, faces in leaves, skeletons, witches. It's always something scary to them. I wind up debating my debunking with the groups, as they really want to find evidence so badly. They imagine they see something. Every shadow becomes a shadow person. Red eyes in the night when I can see a car driving by with its brake lights on right next to a cemetery. I have to laugh, but sometimes it becomes a heated discussion with some of these people.

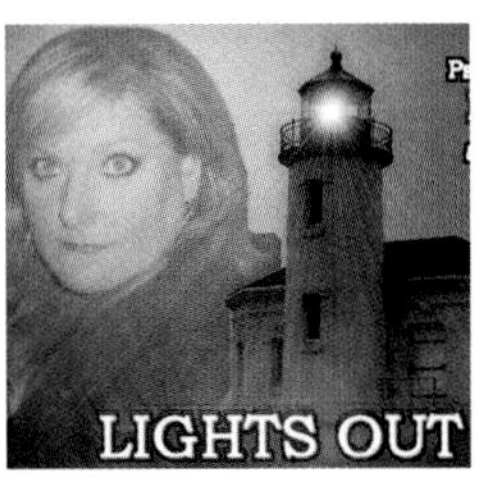

Figure 12.5
Robyne Marie's radio show, Lights Out Paranormal Radio.

Pat Martin: Investigator

When I arrived at the General Stanton Inn for the initial photography run through before the EPS team arrived for the formal investigation, one of the General Stanton office staff asked me to evaluate a photograph a guest had taken in the bar. I immediately saw the face of a man with a strange hat in an orb on a wall between two people who were starring into each other's eyes. She then affirmed that I had seen what she had seen.

Later, I came across an oil painting in the attic that spoke to me (I have psychic abilities as well) and I brought it downstairs to see if it was for sale as the inn housed an antique shop below. When I inquired about the painting, the staff explained that the painting was taken to the attic several years before because it gave some of the patrons "the willies." Turns out, it had hung in the bar in the exact spot where the orb in the photo between the two people was captured by my camera. Upon closer examination, the strange hat seen in the orb photo was the same as the historical helmet worn by the solider in the painting. All the facial features were the same as well.

It was quite a confirming experience.

In the News

ONE OF THE BEST WAYS to stay in touch with what people are seeing with their ghost cameras is to watch the news. Whether you search the news yourself or subscribe to a paranormal news service like the one offered by Ghostvillage or some other sites, the non-paranormal media will often latch upon a good ghost story if there is a picture to go along with it. Just about every week there are stories about someone who captured a picture or gets something unusual that defies explanation. Oftentimes the story is more compelling than the actual picture.

One of the most interesting recent news stories came out of the *Charlotte Observer* from Charlotte, NC, a town that has made the news several times for ghostly images. This one revolved around a young girl who had just been given word she would not live to the end of the week. As nurses watched the security cameras later that night, they saw a ghostly figured bathed in yellow walk down the hall and into her room. This kind of thing has been reported by nurses and doctors before, but the story usually ends with them discovering the person has died. Instead, the girl had a miraculous recovery and left the hospital within a few days. The picture was preserved on the camera.

Most stories are not as uplifting but come out more frequently. They often are found as video on legitimate newscasts from across the country or in papers not known for being supporters of the paranormal. The problem with the images is that they contribute to the "boy who cried ghost" factor we discussed in Chapter 10, but they do make things interesting. They also are often presented by people who have something to gain from people thinking the place is haunted, like a haunted pub capturing evidence of something you can come down and maybe see for yourself while you have dinner. If nothing else, their popularity tells us the public is still clamoring for ghost pictures. If you get a really good picture, even try sending it to a newspaper or newsletter, especially if there is a good location attached to it.

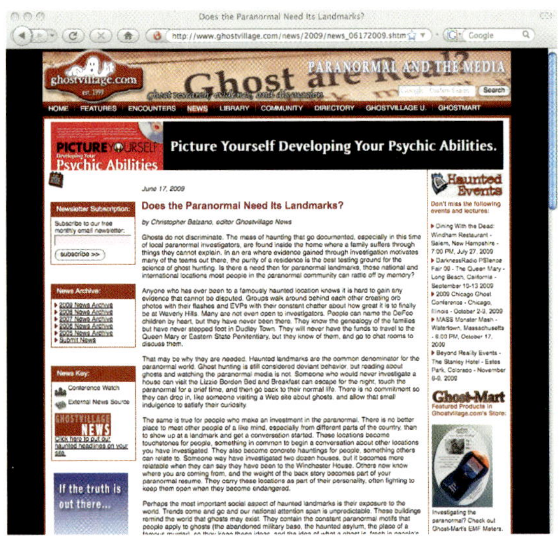

Figure 12.6
Ghostvillage's news section, one of several paranormal newsfeeds out there.

Have Fun

WHEN INVESTIGATING STORIES of haunted asylums in Massachusetts, I was surprised to find people often saw ghosts outside of the building. Some were seen in the attached cemeteries, but most were observed walking on the grounds, far from the echoes of suffering associated with the hospitals. When I asked what witnesses saw them doing, they always responded they walked the grounds without a care in the world, and one report even said the man was running his hands across the uncut lawn. This was in direct conflict with the assumed ghost in this kind of location, and it forced me to ask why. Then it came to me. In a sea of confusion and mental health disorder, these times outside, which were part of their therapy, might have been the best moments in their lives. If their spirits were trapped there, perhaps the happiness they experienced was just as strong as the sadness.

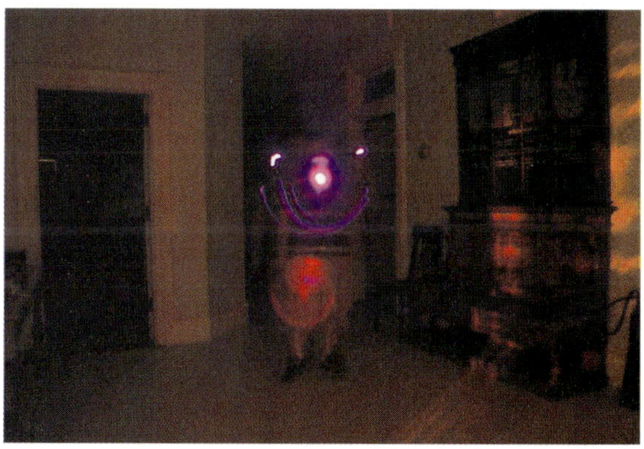

Figure 12.7
Smile while you try to separate genuine pictures from fakes like this. Picture courtesy of Josh Mantello.

We assume all ghosts are tortured spirits, but the stories I hear do not back this up. Even though it may be sad to think of a child wandering alone in the afterlife, they have a habit of playing with toys and being mischievous. That sounds like fun to me. Maybe the paranormal does not need to be so intense all the time. Find a search engine and look at some paranormal groups in your area, focusing especially on the member pages. You will find pictures of investigators, usually men, looking straight at the camera with their arms crossed and scowls on their faces. There are not many smiles. The message is that you need to be serious, and at times physically intimidating, to be able to investigate effectively.

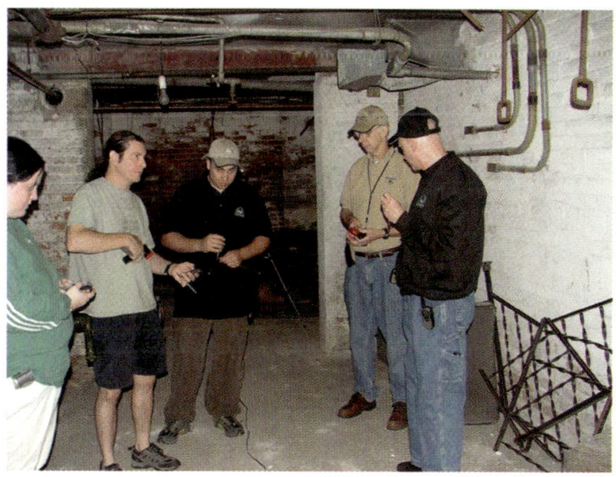

Figure 12.8
A perfect picture of cooperation. Three groups are working together.
Picture courtesy of Josh Mantello.

Nothing is further from the truth. There are times during an investigation that call for seriousness. You may be dealing with a family who has suffered from their experiences or who are genuinely frightened by what has happened to them. You may be in a situation where something frightening is happening to you that wipes the smile off of your face. You may have experienced something yourself that taints the way you see the paranormal and now ghost hunt trying to find some peace of mind because of what happened to you. This does not mean there are not times where levity shouldn't break through. Do not take yourself so seriously. Conducting straightforward work that needs to be taken seriously does not mean it needs to be grim.

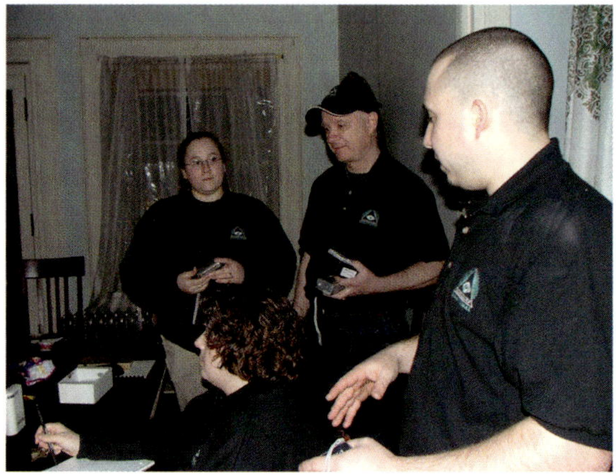

Figure 12.9
There are moments during an investigation to talk about other things.
Picture courtesy of Josh Mantello.

Embrace the social aspects of looking for ghosts and capturing them on film. Joke around as you set up and close up shop. Let getting together to look at evidence or your group's meeting time be fun. Use humor when interviewing someone about their experiences to get them to open up.

Most people will get involved in paranormal investigating as a hobby, but you do not need to neglect your family because of it. Do not allow others to say you are not worthy to look because it is not your obsession, and do not allow anyone to say that because you smile you are not to be trusted. Some of the best investigators I work with can balance those moments that call for intensity and those that are casual enough to crack a joke. There should be respect. You should not be doing limbo on someone's grave or throwing out one-liners while interviewing someone who has had an experience, but that is where that balance needs to be created. A good investigator learns where that line is.

One of the events I spoke at was taped by the person running it and it was then posted on the Internet. I was asked to speak for an hour, and being who I am, I mixed the stories and ideas I was talking about with jokes and moments of humor. The comments people were making alarmed me. *How can he joke,* they wondered, *while talking about such serious things*? I argue a talk like what I was giving was for entertainment, and unless you are collecting some kind of payment for your services, which is frowned upon in the paranormal world, you are looking for ghosts as some form of entertainment. Allow yourself to be entertained.

You may just find those funny moments are what you remember when you are not out in the field and that camaraderie is the reason you keep going out. Who knows, maybe that human side of you will be what makes a ghost want to make itself known.

Your Future in the Paranormal Scene

IF YOU ARE READING THIS LINE and have not gone out and tried to get a picture of a ghost, I have not done my job. There are moments where you need to follow informal rules put forth by investigators because they are good and straight ideas to follow, but there also comes a time you have to put your hands over your ears and just go for it. There is a great essay written by George Orwell called "Politics and the English Language." He lays down some rules for effective writing and communication and the final rule is to ignore everything he has just said if you can think of a reason to do it or if you feel it makes what you are trying to say more original. I give you the same little jewel of advice.

The world of capturing ghosts on film is the closest thing we have to actually holding the paranormal in our hands. You are starting something only a small percentage of people around the world understand and are willing to try. Embrace that. Sometimes forget what the paranormal community will say about what you do. Go with an experiment that makes no sense and try to explain why it worked or failed after the fact. Trust your stomach and put science in your back pocket for a night. Break every idea I have put forth in this book over the course of the next year just to see what has happened.

You perfect field work by falling and getting up and seeing what you tripped on.

So if you haven't already, grab your camera and go capture something.

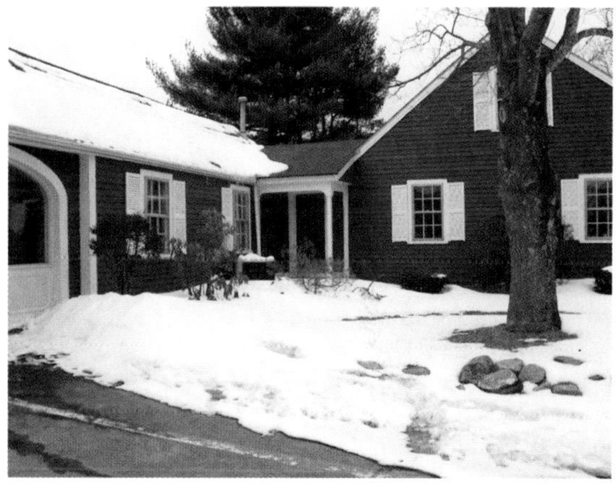

Figure 12.10
The benefit of investigating haunted restaurants like the Country Tavern in New Hampshire is that they may feed you.
Picture courtesy of Josh Mantello.

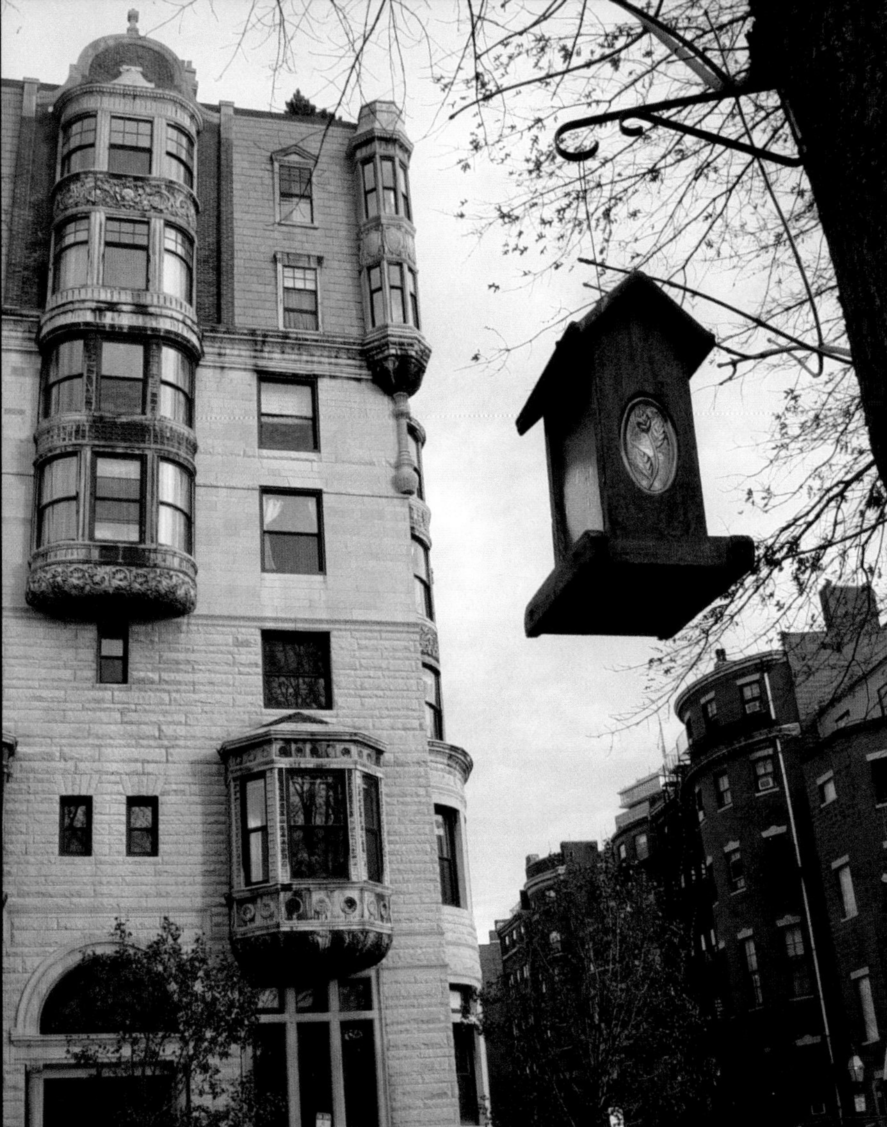

Index

D

H

I

K–L

M

N

O

Z

License Agreement/Notice of Limited Warranty

By opening the sealed disc container in this book, you agree to the following terms and conditions. If, upon reading the following license agreement and notice of limited warranty, you cannot agree to the terms and conditions set forth, return the unused book with unopened disc to the place where you purchased it for a refund.

License:

The enclosed software is copyrighted by the copyright holder(s) indicated on the software disc. You are licensed to copy the software onto a single computer for use by a single user and to a backup disc. You may not reproduce, make copies, or distribute copies or rent or lease the software in whole or in part, except with written permission of the copyright holder(s). You may transfer the enclosed disc only together with this license, and only if you destroy all other copies of the software and the transferee agrees to the terms of the license. You may not decompile, reverse assemble, or reverse engineer the software.

Notice of Limited Warranty:

The enclosed disc is warranted by Course Technology to be free of physical defects in materials and workmanship for a period of sixty (60) days from end user's purchase of the book/disc combination. During the sixty-day term of the limited warranty, Course Technology will provide a replacement disc upon the return of a defective disc.

Limited Liability:

THE SOLE REMEDY FOR BREACH OF THIS LIMITED WARRANTY SHALL CONSIST ENTIRELY OF REPLACEMENT OF THE DEFECTIVE DISC. IN NO EVENT SHALL COURSE TECHNOLOGY OR THE AUTHOR BE LIABLE FOR ANY OTHER DAMAGES, INCLUDING LOSS OR CORRUPTION OF DATA, CHANGES IN THE FUNCTIONAL CHARACTERISTICS OF THE HARDWARE OR OPERATING SYSTEM, DELETERIOUS INTERACTION WITH OTHER SOFTWARE, OR ANY OTHER SPECIAL, INCIDENTAL, OR CONSEQUENTIAL DAMAGES THAT MAY ARISE, EVEN IF COURSE TECHNOLOGY AND/OR THE AUTHOR HAS PREVIOUSLY BEEN NOTIFIED THAT THE POSSIBILITY OF SUCH DAMAGES EXISTS.

Disclaimer of Warranties:

COURSE TECHNOLOGY AND THE AUTHOR SPECIFICALLY DISCLAIM ANY AND ALL OTHER WARRANTIES, EITHER EXPRESS OR IMPLIED, INCLUDING WARRANTIES OF MERCHANTABILITY, SUITABILITY TO A PARTICULAR TASK OR PURPOSE, OR FREEDOM FROM ERRORS. SOME STATES DO NOT ALLOW FOR EXCLUSION OF IMPLIED WARRANTIES OR LIMITATION OF INCIDENTAL OR CONSEQUENTIAL DAMAGES, SO THESE LIMITATIONS MIGHT NOT APPLY TO YOU.

Other:

This Agreement is governed by the laws of the State of Massachusetts without regard to choice of law principles. The United Convention of Contracts for the International Sale of Goods is specifically disclaimed. This Agreement constitutes the entire agreement between you and Course Technology regarding use of the software.